Law, Governance and Technology Series

Volume 65

The *Law, Governance and Technology Series* is intended to attract manuscripts arising from an interdisciplinary approach in law, artificial intelligence and information technologies. The idea is to bridge the gap between research in IT law and IT-applications for lawyers developing a unifying techno-legal perspective. The series will welcome proposals that have a fairly specific focus on problems or projects that will lead to innovative research charting the course for new interdisciplinary developments in law, legal theory, and law and society research as well as in computer technologies, artificial intelligence and cognitive sciences. In broad strokes, manuscripts for this series may be mainly located in the fields of the Internet law (data protection, intellectual property, Internet rights, etc.), Computational models of the legal contents and legal reasoning, Legal Information Retrieval, Electronic Data Discovery, Collaborative Tools (e.g. Online Dispute Resolution platforms), Metadata and XML Technologies (for Semantic Web Services), Technologies in Courtrooms and Judicial Offices (E-Court), Technologies for Governments and Administrations (E-Government), Legal Multimedia, and Legal Electronic Institutions (Multi-Agent Systems and Artificial Societies).

Mariavittoria Catanzariti

Disconnecting Sovereignty

How Data Fragmentation Reshapes the Law

Springer

Mariavittoria Catanzariti
University of Padua
Padua, Italy

European University Institute
Florence, Italy

ISSN 2352-1902 ISSN 2352-1910 (electronic)
Law, Governance and Technology Series
ISBN 978-3-031-60733-2 ISBN 978-3-031-60734-9 (eBook)
https://doi.org/10.1007/978-3-031-60734-9

This Springer imprint is published by the registered company Springer Nature Switzerland AG
The registered company address is: Gewerbestrasse 11, 6330 Cham, Switzerland

To my beloved uncle Francesco,
my hungry heart

Preface

This book has been written during my years at the European University Institute that have been an invaluable experience for research exchange, cross-sectoral studies and intellectual growth. To all brilliant scholars and to the wonderful mankind met on my path go in different ways all my deepest thanks.

On a personal note, I think that a book may ultimately reflect an intimate part of ourselves that we return to the others for memory and hopefully for some utility. Of course, what a book means to its author does not entirely reflect all that shows up to the reader, and it does not need to necessarily. What is related to the moment in which a book is written is not entirely visible or at all emerging. For reasons that have to do with the meaning of our life stories, I decided to dedicate this book to my beloved uncle. In fact, this thought has been the lifeblood of this book. The last three years fed this desire, condensing all that my uncle and I shared until now and before. The drafting process has been accompanied by a life event, from which all together felt apart and reshaped new dimensions and possibilities day by day. This feeling has been internalized into the awareness of fragmentation under both forms of fear and hope, as well as into the need to pave new paths, many times, collecting bits and pieces and managing them all together. Then, the idea of data fragmentation has been something that grew up with personal fragments. The lesson learned is this in a nutshell: when all gets fragmented and this is the starting point, the *datum*—the "given" of life, what remains on balance and what in a way or another represents reality—the sovereign instinct to self-preservation needs to reconnect itself to new ways of survival in order to face fragmentation. Likewise, institutions must change to survive digital transformation. As human beings, we are fortunately more than what is *datum,* and our duty as humans is to preserve this surplus. Even when fear disconnects from hope—for example, when the body disconnects from the brain and soul—the task of preserving the human surplus represents the life instinct of self-preservation, in its very sense. The disconnection from any kind of contingency—body or space, territory as the case of this book—must be reconnected to something else. To pursue this objective, the ability to stay within a given status and within a porous space that no longer corresponds to any possible existing space is the new contingency. This, on the one hand, represents the opposite feature to the fluctuating and fleeing nature of interconnected data that needs to transform itself and the context to survive; on the other hand, the aspiration to stay within a spatial dimension (i.e., data stored in a physical space) is what data pretends to do to comply with the principle of territoriality.

Such a personal inspiration made me convinced over the time that every legal phenomenon is inherently based upon the need to keep the needed power for accomplishing its task, or at least, to loose as little as possible power in order not to be ineffective (or to save it as much as possible, depending on the perspectives). Keeping power also means persevering without necessary much ado. As a precept, such a personal theoretical assumption has driven the rationale of this book: sovereign power never dissolves even when it is hampered by some threats and even if it disconnects from physicality to keep forward. Reconnection does not mean the transformation of physical space into digital space (e.g., by the use of localization requirements). As a paradigmatic example, data governance is accelerating the disconnection of sovereignty from territory. Digital phenomena do not have one single space, as they happen everywhere once at all. This only apparently has threatened state sovereignty considered an absolute power vis-à-vis other sovereigns. In fact, the only nonvisible factor that can be replaced to activate the reflexive capacity of the law is territoriality, e.g., the relation of the law with territory. In the meantime, data fragmentation has reshaped new forms of power and sovereignty. However, the lack of territorial contingency—the necessity of territorial triggers to achieve government objectives—and the fragmentation produced by data at various levels have not much to share; they are only incidentally overlapping phenomena. This takeaway is interesting if applied to the law of data as a mechanism of social change because the law should be able to enact sovereign mechanisms to perform its duties in any event, should be a territory or not. If it does not, then it fails. As long as law production is modelled on data fragmentation—meaning on what the impossibility to anchor data to overall phenomena and tangible spaces implies—the impact of data and advanced technologies, as a result, is also subject to a legal counteraction that naturally recouples together subjection and emancipation, embeddedness and distance, freedom and responsibility, never the one without the other. This is not much different from daily struggles against various types of threats. It is nothing other than an application of the philosophical precept elaborated by Baruch Spinoza, *perseverare in esse suo*: "Each thing, as far as it can by its own power, strives to persevere in its being" (Proposition VI, *Ethica Ordine Geometrico Demonstrata. De origine, et natura affectuum*, Part III), which coincides with the natural right of every living form of experience—including that generated by data. This ethical principle can be explained for Spinoza by the fact that there is not anything that has in it something by which it can be destroyed or that takes away its existence; in contrast, everything opposes any force that can take away its existence; and therefore, as far as it can and is in it, it strives to persevere in its being.

The effort by which each thing strives to persevere in its being is the very institutional essence of the thing itself according to Spinoza (Esposito 2023, p. 66).

Things can only do what follows from their definite nature.[1] We assume this is a principle to be applied even to data and reality that is data driven.

A possible objection to this assumption is that ethical principles cannot be consistent with issues related to data regulation.

However, this is an ethical principle that corresponds to political and legal reflections.

As observed by Spinoza in the *Tractatus theologicus-politicus*, the natural right of every man is determined not by the right reason but by desire and power. Nature is not enclosed within the laws of human nature, which are concerned only with the true usefulness and preservation of mankind but extend to infinite other laws that pertain to the eternal order of all nature, in the context of which man is only a very small part among other things in the framework of a more general order: by the mere necessity of this order, all things are determined in a certain way to exist and operate.

At the same time, data—legally defined now in many recent pieces of EU legislation as "any digital representation of acts, facts or information and any compilation of such acts, facts or information, including in the form of sound, visual, or audiovisual recording"—is the metaphor of life in its numerous dimensions that should freely flourish according to its own nature, which is *borderless* indeed. Even data continue to escape territory by its very nature, whereas territory continues to appropriate power shares.

Spinoza theorizes that the ultimate goal of the State, then, is freedom. The freedom of each individual to remain in his or her own state is not only the highest form of natural law but also the civil private right *par excellence* (Chapter XVI, § 4 *Tractatus theologicus-politicus*).

This principle can be applied to new entities such as interconnected data and AI systems as well as to individuals scattered over the world and localized or delocalized forms of power. All conflicting forces strive to pursue their own purposes over a territory that becomes the geographical representation of liberty because it cannot be hidden or deleted. However, it encompasses the tension between the geographical aspiration of a group to appropriate a territory and the legal geography of the state to rule over a territory.[2]

This is also true for coping with the physical boundaries of a human being—body and brain—when they are rarefying. Rationality, on the one hand, and rationalization of practices, on the other hand, are not enough to defend liberty.

The impact of data flows on the law opens different paths depending on the ability of the law to resist them and to co-work its coexistence. Only the law can reshape itself from its internal mechanism toward social change. As pointed out by Teubner, "*the law's own terminology allows itself to be challenged, in accordance with the conditions of its inner development logic, by social theory constructs, and thereupon to be inspired to create quite differently structured new formations*" (Teubner

[1] *res aliud possunt, quam id, quod ex determinata earum natura necessario sequitur (Propositio VII, Ethices. Pars III).*

[2] Spinoza refers to the Jewish state for which he states that it is not possible to transfer the whole natural right from individuals to authority.

2014, p. 210). The way by which data seem to reshape the law is nothing but the result of how the law can respond to it, depending on the strength of its reflexive capacity. The more the law is rooted in social structures and institutions, the less data fragmentation reshapes the law. This means as a strategy that grounding the law on territoriality in the digital context will result in the long run in an inevitable surrender of the law to its servant function toward any technique including technologies in the first place. Quite often giving a new shape to something is only a way for the law to pursue self-preservation, e.g., being able to produce order.

What this book aims to highlight is that physical disconnection preserves sovereignty in a natural way, e.g., by reconnecting data to various paradigms of authority regardless of physical trajectories. The territorial basis for authority is not always sufficiently legitimate to justify jurisdictional claims over data. The continuity between data and power is represented at various levels—legal, technical, functional, logical—by the rules of data sharing that link together public and private as well as different dimensions that are not necessarily spatial but can be normative as well. They conceptually do not need a territorial space but rather rules on access and usage to make data more interconnected. Sovereignty spreads out into new granular dimensions that attach to different factors, not necessarily territoriality. Territoriality has historically played the role of making jurisdiction certain or making sovereign powers qualitatively equal. If looked in these terms, the architecture of territoriality looks like a construction that has been historically conceived to perform specific functions in the broadest generalized possible way.

Looking at the enormous and pervasive phenomenon of massive data flows gives the account of new actors, new forms of power, and new creative responses.

This idea does not underpin a defensive approach toward digital flows but rather a dynamic way to look at the law's performance from the perspective of the materiality and from the perspective of the localization, which are not overlapping and too often confused as the result of operational solutions. When physical boundaries—such as those of a territory or a body, everything that requires being located within a visible frame—are no longer capable of pursuing traditional tasks to which they have been allegedly addressed—for example, enabling sovereign powers to perform within material limits—then it is time not to overuse them and to let them go. The law is always necessary and never superfluous in its ordinary functioning, as it serves contingent purposes. If contingency shows up in one way or another, it does not mean that sovereignty rarefies nor dissolves. It only needs to look for new ways to survive and be described.

I will be forever grateful to the person who inspired my reflections with his brilliant life and his hungry heart. With the one and the other, he has been always able to encompass fragmentation. His infinite love for his work, his family, his friends, and life's beauty has transformed fragmentation into a universal way of being and sharing. He respected himself and the others because of their right to self-preservation and their opportunity over this earth to share life as the only way to face fragmentation.

In his stormy weather, he tried to resist the flow as he could, like an angel dressed as a warrior, respecting the rules of his own being. This book is for him and for all those hungry hearts who face inevitable flows, finding their way to disconnect from materiality and reconnect into the flow of freedom.

Rome, Italy
June 2023

Mariavittoria Catanzariti

References

Esposito R (2023) Vitam Instituere. Geneaologia dell'istituzione, Einaudi, p 66
Teubner G. 2014. Law and Social Thoery: Three Problems, ANCILLA IURIS (anci.ch) 2014: 183 – Synopsis

Contents

Chapter 1
Introduction

1.1 The Lexicon of the Book

While designing this book project, I had in mind a set of possible starting points. To approach the topical but traditional issue of the transformation of sovereignty produced by data, I faced two main theoretical options: a top-down and a bottom-up approach, depending on whether starting from the monolithic vision of state sovereignty and ending up on data regulation, or beginning from data's disruptive capacity to impact sovereignty. Each of these options implies the assumption that the starting premises completely affect the consequences for their significance: in the first case, this means that sovereignty most likely survives to data that needs to adapt to it; in the second case, data can be considered a threat to sovereignty that therefore needs other theoretical notions, as well as governmental tools. Current doctrines present shortcomings in grasping reality and often limit themselves to accommodate the facts. I thus tried to approach the relation between the concept of state territoriality and data from interior lenses. As much as I dug into this, at times I thought that everything had already been discussed albeit in different branches of knowledge, such as international law, cyberlaw, political science, history, legal theory, and geography, and that the effort of a new book was not worth even the effort of connecting the dots of the existing debates (Andreucci and Pescarolo 1989; Bathelt et al. 2011; Benda-Beckmann et al. 2009). However, there was an underlying dissatisfaction emerging from the fact that digital law and digital rights continued to be approached from the internal perspective of the law without a deeper consideration of their reciprocal transformation. My loadstar was then to explore issues related to the long-run coexistence of data and state law that have not yet received a single answer and that have been dealt with based on this shortcoming—indeed, that they cannot be addressed with a one-size-fits-all solution. They are therefore scattered through sectoral disciplines and multi-operational systems across legal areas to be coherently presented. Yet I did not find all the answers I was looking for, but I tried

M. Catanzariti, *Disconnecting Sovereignty*, Law, Governance and Technology Series 65, https://doi.org/10.1007/978-3-031-60734-9_1

to decouple mechanisms that trigger certain debates and the theoretical, conceptual, and methodological gaps of them. After all, digital transformation presents such a disruptive strength that all the analysis involving its impact on the law cannot be exhaustive, but not useless. I then opted to offer some insights into the gist of legal constructions in relation to data-driven technologies that, in my opinion, may produce data fragmentation.

1.2 Data Fragmentation

The operation of this book is ambitious because it brings together heterogeneous terrains even methodologically, sovereignty on the one hand and data on the other, without any pretence of bending one to the logic of the other.

With data fragmentation, I refer to the ways by which the use of data presents the ability to carve-out reality, offering only bits and pieces of it quite programmatically. The descriptive power of data is able to create contexts, relations, facts, and results that may be relevant to the law in different ways, depending on their quantity, the manner in which they are aggregated, the logic in their use. This is shifted into sectoral regulatory fragments that are related to the subject-matters identified by data flows. Only apparently the phenomenon of data fragmentation can be mistaken with legal fragmentation. Digital law silos are the result of the legal reworking of the "multi-situationalism" brought about by data fragmentation. This refers to the domains covered by different legal regimes related to digital law. Nor should this phenomenon be confused with the fragmentation of the concept of sovereignty in relation to an object that is not unitary and distinguishes internal and external power (Cannizzaro 2020, p. 65).

The examples are many, from tailored services offered by platforms to specific individual behaviors, from functionalities of public administration enhanced by the use of AI to the simple way of describing facts with data. However, they also include broader mechanisms of sovereign deference or comity-limited remedies through which compliance with the law depends on how state powers control the functioning of technological infrastructures, e.g., the way by which technical solutions can be compliant with state sovereignty (Woods 2018, pp. 384 and 399). This fragmentation of course affects the law and its mechanisms of understanding social complexity. Nonetheless, given this fact, does data also fragment the law and its sovereign character? Or does sovereignty disconnect itself from traditional spaces to find new spaces?

I will focus on how the conceptualization of territory and sovereignty as well as the related legal constructions are affected by data flows and whether and how it is still relevant for digital law.

The hypothesis of this book is that it is not true that one logic, the logic of the earth, prevails over the other, the logic of the digital world, but that they are rather non-relevant to each other; therefore, they can resist one another. This sort of disconnection of sovereignty from territory appears to be the only possible way by which sovereignty and data flows may coexist. This is a book that somehow tries to contend against those positions according to which data and territorial sovereignty need to be integrated. This is not a book on the global reach of jurisdictional claims over data. It is a reflection on the multifaceted concept of sovereignty and its capacity to resist powerful shortcomings such as digital data flows. It is a book on the institutional geopolitical order and how it is affected by data that moves across states' lines.

I do not object to this position, but I only maintain that the problem is not the possibility of the coexistence but the way by which it is put in place. However, does a legal order conceived as such reflect reality? Or is this fiction creating tensions of different kinds in the long run?

This is a question that has been posed partially in different ways and from different perspectives. In this research, I felt that it would be worth going to change slightly the terms of the reasoning by trying to draw the lines of how and why some crucial doctrinal debates have been architected along regulatory paths, political choices, and disciplinary boundaries. The reasons are of course multiple, but this book mainly focuses on the epistemics of legal constructions in relation to information technologies and their primary source, which is data.

I not only aim to acknowledge the emerging takes on the challenges presented to sovereignty by digital flows—which have been largely related to their borderless nature—but my ambition is to shed further light on a positive coexistence between territory and data that still deserves research and focus and that cannot be solved by pretending to apply the logic of data to the logic of territories or, more often, vice versa.

Data presents a challenge to sovereignty because of its fragmented character, which cannot be simplistically overlapped with its borderless, immaterial, and non-territorial character (Daskal 2015, p. 326) nor with the solution of extraterritoriality prompted by many states in cross-border data regulation (Eichensehr 2017, p. 145). This apparently simple statement has not yet received the attention it deserves. The traditional idea of forms of control over things and persons is completely dismantled by data that, in relation to goods, institutions and individuals, represents fragments of reality assuming a different meaning across its multiple representative capacities of reality. Data has the ability not only to cross the borders of the territorial state but above all to be completely permeable to any contents. The shape of data and its constant interdependence from contents define the relationship with the surrounding space in a manner that is different from what can be measured or appropriated throughout material and divisible trajectories paved over territories. We can summarize in short that data—although they can generate calculability and measurement of reality—is non-countable upon measurable routes, and this creates the most relevant friction with the human way to be physical and real-effective—with the Heideggerian *dasein*, the being within the world (Heidegger 1927).

1.3 A Natural Camouflage Between Law and Data

Data can camouflage and challenge the boundaries they approximate and become increasingly porous to its transfer. The point of this book is the following: are we sure that what has been presented as the fundamental legal construction of territoriality principle, a legitimate power limited by and exerted over a limited territory, needs to resist the fragmentation that is produced by data? Is there a real conflict of laws between territories that contend their power over data fictitiously crossing their physical trajectories and data itself? Or is the relationship between sovereignty and data something more structured beyond the space that is occupied by different powers?

The issue at stake of this book is deeper and more complex than the possible conflict of laws produced by the mismatch of territorial jurisdiction and the cross-border character of data flows, whether the idea of sovereignty is somehow still relevant for the digital transformation. If this is the case, we should think of the reasons that make sovereignty, even in most of the immaterial and intangible realms such as the digital one, still an inevitable concept. Although one can intuitively agree that the physical control of territories by authorities and the immaterial governance of data run on parallel and non-convergent routes, there is still no answer on why physical control over a territory and data governance do not clash, although they are incompatible concepts. They do not clash as far as they give rise to mimetic forms of retaliation between different established orders.

In particular, we should consider whether the most relevant concept of sovereignty in the digital domain can still be territoriality. This central role is not only because sovereignty has regard to a certain object that has a material connection to the territorial state—basically data that must pass through physical cables under the sea or underground—but also with respect to other powers that are not sovereign at the same time because one instead exerts sovereign powers over data while the other does not. On the one hand, over time, the misuse of territory creates frictions that result in forms of retaliation by states and undermine the geopolitical order and balance. On the other hand, reciprocal reactions depend on a bad use of the legal notion of territory. Conflicts of law strongly depend on the rules affecting control over territories. However, data itself—its routes, the meaning and purpose of its circulation—follow logics that are completely unbound from the control of territory. This book refutes the most common objection that infrastructures are physical, and that data can be understood along determined physical trajectories because this approach is a consequence of the centrality of a territorial logic rather than its reason.

This book moves from the observation that sovereignty paves mimetic paths while ruling on its objects and, by doing this, it defines its space of action. This book does not have cyberlaw as its focus but rather the underlying phenomena emerging from data flowing on data infrastructures that causally affect the applicable legal framework. In other words, it asks what a possible effect of an alternative model of sovereign powers would be. Arguably the disconnection of sovereignty preannounced in the book's title is not from online dimension to exert physical traction over data physically, rather it is a disconnection from territory to possibly reconcile sovereignty with data.

It maintains that the link between cause and effect in applying territoriality to data has been too rarefied, and instead, it should be respected to frame it theoretically and offer operative solutions. Sovereignty over data does not need the primacy of territorial connection to be justified. Territorial connection can be one of various criteria by which data can be covered by jurisdictional claims.

Treating data fictitiously as goods or appendixes of persons—as every object that is relevant for the law—is symptomizing of a trend that draws the emerging reality, or the social production with Benkler's words, towards traditional categories (Benkler 2007). Would it be sovereignty compatible with new phenomena? Is it a sufficiently generalized pattern to be applied even in digital fleeing environments? However, if these traditional categories are placed on premises that are valid only under certain conditions, it is then obvious that the results can be inadequate to understand reality. We argue that once sovereignty is constructed, although upon its link to territoriality, it stands alone even if this connection comes less. This is due to the ability of the law to elaborate new mimetic artificial forms that substitute artifacts constructed on the physicality of land and labor (Mezzadra et al. 2024).

1.4 Sovereignty and Territory: Un Unbreakable Hendiadys?

Data flows do not necessarily follow physical trajectories in the sense that one traditionally could expect, and when they follow them, the reason has nothing to do with the exercise of sovereignty, rather with the logic by which infrastructures are built across space. However, the ownership and management of digital infrastructures cannot be based on the physical location where they are located. If it is undeniable that there is a physical component of data related to infrastructures, this cannot necessarily justify an exclusive power of states to regulate all cases related to data that pass over data infrastructures located within states' premises. This conceptual limit implies assuming a different approach with respect to issues related to sovereignty. If data remains territorial in fact—meaning that it is treated as a physical entity—sovereignty needs to perform by exceeding territory and constantly forcing its physical boundaries. For this reason, extraterritorial claims over data have not to be seen as an exception to the territoriality principle but rather as confirmation. The attitude of sovereigns to act extraterritorially is a practical way to exert control over data wherever it is only based on a justification that the legal notion of territory can be expanded upon legitimate justification. However, because of the lack of a logical linkage between data and territory, extraterritorial claims over data are not always justified. The challenge is to create a most suitable theoretical framework that reconciles the nature of data with the requirements of legitimate powers as well as with prerogatives of actors legitimated to regulate over data.

Sovereignty operates by differentiation from all that is not sovereign and draws lines of demarcation from equally sovereign powers. In contrast, data fragmentation reshapes the rationales of the law not only in relation to a changing object of regulation—which is data—but also in relation to their granular nature, which permeates its boundaries with all that are different from what is included in them. Second, if a state acts in a way that exceeds the scope of its power, it will certainly incorporate data that flow outside its territory. In this way, data completely lose any linkage with established and legitimate power and may represent forms of reality in various circumstances.

What is interesting is not the space of action occupied by data when they flow and then perform certain acts but rather their capacity to create their own space depending on the use that is done of them. This empirical take has been grasped by the European Commission, which has started to set up a set of specific actions dividing them into data spaces that depend on the specific function to which data are devoted.

Boundaries have the function of limiting space (Boaz and Burak 2017), and sovereignty needs its own space to perform its action, but not necessarily on a physical space. This book moves from this assumption to explore how the physical character of legal rationality has informed the relationship between law and technology.

The idea behind this book is that sovereignty needs to be disconnected from territory to resist fragmentation. The pervasive capacity of data to blend boundaries as a valid normative mechanism does not substantively affect other sovereign powers. The schmittian idea of law originally means measure (nomos), whereas data relates to an idea of a countable world. The legal and digital rationality means, to a different extent, measuring, which is why confusion is easy.

Disconnection does not necessarily mean abstraction from a physical location where sovereignty can be exerted. The idea of disconnection replicates in fact the character of absolute sovereignty that rendered the sovereign *ab solutus* from its own power. Disconnection also relates to contingency of facts with respect to which data is able to modulate distance in a way that is not the ordinary way of the law. Although the law and its architecture of sovereignty defines its distance from the object it rules out in a predetermined way, data does not. This involves a specific picture of distances from objects and from the place where these objects lie or operate. As much as sovereignty gains traction over territories and independence from data flows, it achieves a functional disconnection that enables it to preserve itself. The way by which this problem has been addressed thus far has resulted in an increasing number of sectoral regulatory regimes related to data that potentially clash each other and are at least not coherent.

Digitalization also offers sovereignty chances to be disconnected from fictitious factors. The assumption of this book is that territoriality is the ordinary way by which legal fictions have been tailored on measurable routes such as physical ones to regulate some phenomena. Are there other successful ways that ensure an equivalent regulation of data flows? This question opens various possibilities, the main of which are opposite: either rejecting the model of territoriality, which is not feasible with respect to entities that have a corporeal character, or completely replacing the territorial logic with artificial territorial coordinates created by technology.

1.5 The Hypothesis of the Book

The hypothesis of this book is that data has thus far been considered according to territoriality-bound legal rules. This naturally creates frictions as states act and react to each other to exert as much power as possible to expand their territorial and material legal scope. As far as data is considered according to territoriality rules, this may create conflicts of law. Data can instead be unleashed from the fictions of space normativity to understand its own logic. This does not imply that jurisdiction ends to exist; rather, it becomes a mechanism to comprise data from a relational perspective. In fact, data is aimed at reaching out other data, confirming them, denying them, complementing each other, neutralizing power. Contemporarily, sovereignty paves its own paths registering what factual reality shaped by data offers.

New types of legal forms have mushroomed around the edges of existing schemes, blurring their borders and extending their reach: data processing, data anonymization, data mining, data profiling, data interoperability, data re-use, data sharing, data altruism. The pervasive logic of extraction from data makes data flows un-relevant to the space they occupy but make their effects potentially spread over all ambits of life.

Nonetheless, data fragmentation urges legal interpreters to reconfigure the relationship between law and space. Data regulation in fact cannot be modelled on forms of digital exceptionalism that are tailored to old structures (Clopton 2016). Territoriality has only been the contingent form of state authority. In relation to data, it might set up new modalities of functioning and use.

This implies that sovereignty can metaphorically be disconnected by a traditional concept of the space which is physical but can also be reassembled through different coordinates that are always normative but functional, meaning that they fulfil and perform a precise function. The hypothesis of the book is in fact to disconnect sovereignty from recognizable and material trajectories as a way to "switch off" useless functionalities and saving "energy". The activation of a "stand-by mode" of sovereignty in relation to traditional sites of power generates new possibilities for interaction between the fragmentation of reality represented by data and the law. The concept of space can change together with the concept of time. So far power has territorialized data because it mimetically sought to anchor its action to paved paths of power. However, reaching out data regardless of their quantitative amount, only as regulatory objects irrespective of the substantive differences between the objects that they represent and the information they vehiculate, is an operation that reveals to be inaccurate in the measure of power exerted (Costabile and Coco 2018, p. 13). Territoriality must therefore be stripped of the scapegoat character of power in relation to the regulation of data flows. It must be defused when it cannot be justified by a concrete function.

This theory has its roots in the thought of Spinoza, who also identified a principle of ethics as a political maxim. In the Ethica Spinoza argues that "Each thing, as far as it can by its own power, strives to persevere in its being" (Proposition VI, *Ethica Ordine Geometrico Demonstrata. De origine, et natura affectuum*, Part III , Spinoza 2007) whereas in the Tractatus he recalls this principle by theorizing that the ultimate goal of the State, then, is freedom. The freedom of each individual to remain in his or her own state is not only the highest form of natural law but also the civil private right *par excellence* (Chapter XVI, § 4 *Tractatus theologicus-politicus, Spinoza,* 2021).

Inspired by this theory, the book argues that there is an ineliminable tension between sovereign power and data in their ontological representative and therefore potentially neutral essence. Both these forces remain in place as a result of their internal compulsion to persist in pursuing their own logic.

In fact, it is the law itself that reappropriates data by posing the problem of their representative function and freeing itself from the unifying and monologist trap of the territory that prevents or limits data flows under certain conditions. The function of sovereignty is to exercise legitimate power, not to territorially limit action. Instead, the function of data is to represent and reconfigure reality. In this relationship it is quite intuitive that territoriality has little to do with it. Sovereignty needs not fear the renunciation of territory, it does not necessarily need territory if it does not serve a specific purpose. Of course, this precise purpose can no longer be a *fictio iuris* because the capacity of data is far closer to reality than any *fictio iuris*. By *fictio iuris*, we refer to a legal phenomenon, whereby a rule is applied to a case other than the one for which it was intended, by pretending that the factual conditions of the latter have been fulfilled (Todescan, 1979). In the case of data the factual condition is completely disregarded for their neutrality with respect to the place where they are located or scattered or transferred.

This book ultimately contends that the principle of territoriality cannot act as *fictio iuris* for data and that a reconfiguration of a new jurisdictional order is needed.

1.6 Plan of the Book

The book crosses two different layers. The first layer, including chapters two and three, shows how the logic of territoriality has informed the conceptualization of online regulation. The second layer—covering chapters four, five, and six—delves into the attempt to disattend the territorial drift of online regulation, showing the tension between mimetic forms of power that can disconnect sovereignty from territoriality, one of the core legal categories.

Chapter 1 is the introduction of the book, which lays the foundations for reflection on the relationship between data and territory. This relationship evokes the inherent capacities of these terms, on the one hand the ability of data to parcel reality, and on the linkage between sovereignty and territorial space. The interaction between data and territory shows how the apparent territorial limitation to the circulation of data is irrelevant compared to the capacity of data to fragment phenomena. The introduction sets out the rationales for the critique of territoriality in data governance.

Chapter 2 explores the issue of spatiality with respect to data. It addresses the reasons why the state's sovereignty needs territoriality to appropriate fictitious or physical shares of power. By introducing the notion of territoriality and the implications of its applicability to data, it attempts to answer the question of whether territory is a formal container or instead an inherent legal mechanism to exert sovereignty over data flows.

Chapter 3 shows how doctrinal legal debates and solutions have sought to reconcile the regulation of digital transformation throughout physical coordinates. The chapter focuses on the contrasting theories related to Kelsenian normativism and Schmittian decisionism, offering two models of dealing with territoriality. Moving from the dichotomy decisionism/normativism as applied to digital space, the chapter theorizes that territory has been only one way to conceptualize space in a contingent manner but relation between sovereignty and space is normative, not necessarily physical. It addresses the issue of the juridification of online realm, addressing the relationship between data governance and infrastructures but also conceptualizes the idea of data space as a functional modality of data sharing whose function replaces space.

Chapter 4 waves the thread of the use and overuse of extraterritorial claims as a way to apply the territorial logic of data regulation, offering critical reflections on territorial drift and its consequences in various areas of the law, such as cyberspace and data protection. In particular, it focuses on one of the ways by which the clash between territoriality and data has been addressed in digital regulation through the rise of extraterritorial claims.

Chapter 5 reconfigures the boundaries between any idea of digital jurisdiction and the increasing quest for data sovereignty, focusing on the example of data localization requirements. Two apparently conflicting concepts emerge: digital jurisdiction, which potentially opens its remit beyond borders of any kind, and data sovereignty, which basically overlaps with the idea that physical borders overlap with digital borders. It examines the consequences of technology's ability to replicate territory through digital borders and questions the risk that the overuse of territoriality can circumvent technological neutrality and undermine geo-political order.

Chapter 6 finally offers an account of alternatives to territoriality, trying to dig into a new reconceptualization of the relationship between sovereignty and data. It aims to demonstrate that the future of data governance depends on the ability of sovereignty to disconnect from territory and envisages a possible pathway by exploring under what conditions it could be feasible.

Chapter 7 draws conclusions for an attempt of coexistence between territorial jurisdiction and non-territorial jurisdictional forms for data regulation.

References

Andreucci F, Pescarolo A (1989) Gli spazi del potere. Aree, regioni, Stati: coordinate territoriali della storia contemporanea. La Casa Usher

Bathelt H, Feldman MP, Kogler DF (2011) Beyond territory. Dynamic geographies of knowledge creation, diffusion, and innovation. Routledge

Benda-Beckmann F, Benda-Beckmann K, Griffiths AMO (2009) Spatializing law: an anthropological geography of law in society. Ashgate

Benkler Y (2007) The wealth of networks: how social production transforms markets and freedom. Yale University Press

Boaz A, Burak K (2017) Territorial designs and international politics: the diverging constitution of space and boundaries. Territ Politics Gov 5(2):115–130

Cannizzaro E (2020) La sovranità oltre lo stato. Il Mulino

Clopton Z (2016) Data institutionalism: a reply to Andrew Woods. Stanford L Rev. Online:69

Costabile A, Coco A (2018) Power relationships and social practices within contemporary democracies. The manipulation of institutional- normative processes. In: Saccà F (ed) Democracy, power and territories. Franco Angeli, pp 13–29

Daskal J (2015) The un-territoriality of data. Yale Law J 125:326

Eichensehr K (2017) Data extraterritoriality. Tex Law Rev 95:145–160

Heidegger (1927) Sein und Zeit. Erste Hälfte, Max Niemeyer

Mezzadra S, Cuppini N, Frappotti M, Pirone M (eds) (2024) Capitalism in the platform age. Emerging assemblages of labour and welfare in urban spaces, Springer

Spinoza B (2007) Etica, (Ethica Ordine Geometrico Demonstrata. De origine, et natura affectuum, 1662). Bompiani

Spinoza B (2021) Trattato teologico-politico (Tractatus theologicus-politicus). Bompiani

Todescan F (1979) Diritto e realtà. Storia e teoria della “fictio iuris”, Cedam

Woods AK (2018) Litigating data sovereignty. Yale Law J 128:328

Chapter 2
The Territory of Data or the Data of the Territorial State? The Shift of a Paradigm

2.1 The Ambiguity of the Internet as Everybody's Land

The Internet originally positioned itself as a coexisting space together with a physical space that is geographically and legally limited by territorial boundaries. The myth of a space which is free from states' prerogatives has dominated the birth of cyberspace in the 1990s (Polcák and Svantesson 2017, pp. 32–35). In reality, this resulted in a sort of duplication of spaces where territory has been used to exert sovereign claims, especially by US, whereas cyberspace has been fictitiously considered as a space without sovereigns (Kosseff 2019, pp. 77–78). As in the legal realm, it is not possible to conceive a space that is free from sovereigns—except theoretically for the outer space where there should be no claim for sovereignty—there has been an enormous debate on the legitimacy of sovereign claims over the internet (Land 2013, p. 393). The tension between the aspiration to regulation or cyberanarchy (Goldsmith 1999, p. 1250) has also drawn back analogies from offline world that essentially revolved around—after phases of over-regulation and deregulation—the alternative between territoriality and extraterritoriality (Polcák and Svantesson 2017, pp. 37–52).

The state is traditionally defined as the political and legal organization of a population settled over a limited territory. This principle was definitely consecrated with the Treaty of Westphalia with two corollaries: separation between secular and religious power and non-external intervention in sovereign matters (Besson 2011, § 13). This makes it a territorially based legal system. The territoriality principle enables a sovereign state to exercise exclusive jurisdiction over individuals within its territory. While the original Schmittian functions of territoriality are appropriation, division, and production of hearth, the ways of original acquisition of the sea and the rivers are similarly division and occupation for Grotius (Grotius 2012, p. 105). According to certain theories, political entities are aimed at realizing a contingent purpose as far as their action is oriented towards the land or towards the sea

M. Catanzariti, *Disconnecting Sovereignty*, Law, Governance and Technology Series 65, https://doi.org/10.1007/978-3-031-60734-9_2

(Del Vecchio 2021). In addition to the natural prerogative of a state being oriented towards a field of action, the lack of sovereignty over cyberspace is quite far from real. In the limits of compatibility with legitimate state sovereign claims, nation states can always exert claims over cyberspace.

As far as jurisdictional criteria can be used in an overlapping manner over the internet, states do not usually face conflicts of law. Although, as learned from international lawyers, the territoriality of law is a necessary requirement for political legitimacy, Besson argues that territoriality even in a globalized world can be understood as a jurisdictional basis that ensures equality before the law (Besson 2019, p. 120). This reveals too simplistic in fact, as it does not take into account the contingent character of territoriality and the different meaning that the exercise of sovereign prerogatives means to each state. However, it reveals to be a very powerful rationale in a context of mere exercise of territorial claims within states' borders with the exclusion of any forms of extraterritoriality. Besson's thesis argues that keeping the law far away from its many territories engendered a sort of private imperialism, a competition between uncontrolled powers. Territoriality has been—according to her reconstruction—a way to ensure a general application of the law to the members of a political community (Greco 2012, pp. 11, 101). Conversely, going beyond territory determines effects not only with respect to the physical frontiers that are overcome but also with respect to the laws of other territories: "what is unprecedented in this case is their combination in current circumstances of legal plurality and the overlap of different deterritorialized legal orders at the same time" (Besson 2019, p. 126). For example, one of the most relevant contradictions is the one between deterritorialization and universal human rights protection and in particular in the digital field, where for example, the regulation of online content raises issues of freedom of expression or hate speech, as well as data protection safeguards with respect to programmes conducted by state authorities outside their territories. Under human rights protection law, the exercise of jurisdiction is a necessary condition for individual protection. This requires contracting states to be held responsible for acts or omissions that give rise to an allegation of the infringement of rights and freedoms set forth in the European Convention of Human Rights. Classical examples are acts of consular and diplomatic agents over the foreign territory; consent, acquiescence and invitation; and individuals taken into the custody of a foreign state.

What complicated the framework is the fact that together with legal rules issued by states, over the Internet there is the coexistence of technical standards and norms of conduct set by non-state actors. In reality, there are definite criteria to solve controversial issues, but they always lie in the realm of jurisdictional powers connected to sovereignty over the state territory.

For instance, the principle of territoriality has gone hand in hand with the development of the opposite principle, extraterritoriality. However, extraterritoriality represents an exception in criminal jurisdiction that needs to be motivated under strict requirements (Ryngaert 2015, p. 85).

In the field of human rights protection, the ECtHR traditionally differentiated between two justifications of extraterritoriality, the former by applying the effective control principle (related to the power or to the effective control exercised by state's forces acting outside territory), the latter by applying the personality principle (depending on the status of the victim of crime or of the perpetrator as a national of the state exercising jurisdiction) (Giuffré 2021).[1] However, it seems to be peculiar recalling Judge Bonello's concurring opinion in the famous case *Al-Skeini* that ensures the extraterritorial application of ECHR. The opinion points out that states may ensure the observance of human rights in five ways: first, by not violating (through their agents) human rights; second, by having in-place systems that prevent breaches of human rights; third, by investigating complaints of human rights abuses; fourth, by scourging those of their agents who infringe on human rights; and, finally, by compensating the victims for breaches of human rights. These constitute the basic minimum functions assumed by every State by virtue of its having contracted into the Convention (§10). The opinion tries to decouple this taxonomy through the application of a functional test meaning that "*a State has jurisdiction for the purposes of Article 1 whenever the observance or the breach of any of these functions is within its authority and control*" (§11).

Interestingly, the opinion remarks that jurisdiction should be neither considered a territorial nor extraterritorial matter as far as it only needs to be functional, e.g., pursuing the objective for a State to exercise authority or control (Scheinin 2013, p. 212). This paradigmatic legal take disruptively opens a Pandora box based on the inconsistencies that have grounded conceptualizations and justifications of territoriality over time, such as the linkage between deterritorialization and universality. What is relevant is instead the exclusive effect of territoriality with respect to the production of a precise order that can be justified only per se without the need for any other rationale.

2.1.1 The Issue of Sovereignty in Cyberspace

The fact that cyberspace may compete or not with territorial spaces is relevant to understanding whether or not we can talk about sovereignty in cyberspace (Reed and Murray 2018). Sovereignty over the cyberspace has originally been placed as a shared competence among different actors without any prerogative of a state over the other, but quite soon it has resulted in a transposed space of national claims in the presence of any functional connection with the authority exerted by nation states: according to different criteria of international private law, sometimes it has

[1] For example, the ECtHR stated on the extraterritorial reach of the ECHR based on the following criteria: state's acts occurring within ECHR space but outside State's own territory, ECtHR, *Loizidou v. Turkey*, Appl. no. 15318/89; Judgment of 23 March 1995; military intervention not exercising effective control (denial), *Bankovic & Others* v. Belgium & Others, Appl. no. 52297/99, Judgment of 12 December 2001; military presence, *Al Skeini & Others v. UK*, Appl. no. 55721/07, Judgment of 7 July 2011; *Al-Jedda v. UK*, Appl. no. 27021/08, Judgment of 7 July 2011; State's acts occurring on territory outside of ECHR space, *Öcalan v. Turkey,* Appl. no. 46221/99, Judgment of 12 May 2005.

been based on residency or nationality, sometimes on where the harm that has been produced (so-called "effects doctrine") or on the basis of the effects of a certain conduct (Besson 2019, p. 118). However, when we talk in terms of sovereign rights, there is a presumption of legitimacy of sovereign powers, independence, constitutional and organizational autonomy, and territorial and personal jurisdiction within territorial boundaries (Goldsmith and Wu 2006).

What about sovereignty in cyberspace? For example, the EU Council decision of 2019 lists the following as the factors determining whether a cyberattack has a significant effect: the scope, scale, impact or severity of disruption caused, including economic and societal activities, essential services, critical state functions, public order or public safety; the number of natural or legal persons, entities or bodies affected; the number of member states affected; the amount of economic loss caused, such as through large-scale theft of funds, economic resources or intellectual property; the economic benefit gained by the perpetrator, for himself or for others; the amount or nature of data stolen or the scale of the data breaches; or the nature of commercially sensitive data accessed.[2] This means that the idea of control in cyberspace may overlap and also go beyond the scope of sovereign powers.

Whether and to what extent data fragmentation affects the principle of sovereignty is a matter of practice as well as of granular effects determined by the use of power and by its means: in the context of data usage, the capacity to fragment perceptions of reality utilizing certain data and not others, such as the full control over themselves or over our on-line life—that the law is able to transform into relevant legal facts. In this sense, the transformations of sovereignty need to be considered in light of changing legal institutions as well as changing modalities through which the law is deployed to assist social change (De Gregorio and Ranchordas 2020, p. 174; Pennisi 1990, 1997).

Territory is filled in of different meanings that crisscross functions of power. One of these functions is typically security, which has received enormous eco with technological development. Securitization has been the typical policy of most countries—the EU also—that has instrumentally used technology to fill in territory of instrumental practices that have separated an inside from an outside. This has somehow replicated the conceptualization of internal and external sovereignty in the territorial scope of digital laws or in the recognition of foreign orders and judgments, respectively, provided that international agreements are in place (Mitsilegas, Moreno Lax, Vavoula 2020, pp. 1–5).

Regardless of the scope of application of the law, territory has also represented a space to be surrounded by a wall that protects the state's power against its enemies. The logic friend/enemy has represented the rhetorical sublayer over which various strategies having different purposes—such as effective control, security, crucial infrastructures, and individual safety—found a common possibility in reinforcing territory (Schmitt 1972, p. 101). This also explains why territoriality does not conflate with the imaginary territory of cyberspace according to public international

[2] EU Council (2019), EU Council decision (CFSP) 7299/19 concerning restrictive measures against cyber-attacks threatening the Union or its Member States, 14 May 2019, https://data.consilium.europa.eu/doc/document/ST-7299-2019-INIT/en/pdf.

law because it has an inherent never-ended capacity to define given prerogatives (Massa Pinto 2023, p. 1211).

In a sense, while territory "certificates" the presence of legitimate powers, it is not said the contrary: legitimate powers can also be generated irrespective of territorial connections. This has been in a sense the case of Europe that has been saliently deemed to have a "parasitic territory", given its co-extensivity with the territory of Member States (Weinzierl 2021, p. 653).

2.1.2 *The Architecture of Internet Governance*

Internet governance can be considered a standardized data communication protocol that redefines the concept of space with respect to networks. Data governance offers an idea of data complexity as far as it reflects all groups of actors involved in the management of availability, usability, integrity and security of data. Data governance serves as an overall architecture that can go hand in hand through parallel routes not formally conflicting with jurisdictional claims. This means in practice that what lies on the layer of data governance is what happens with data and those actors who access data. What instead lies on the layer of data government necessarily needs to fit into issues related to jurisdiction and the state's sovereignty.

This observation is functional to understand how complex is reconciling the layers of data government and data government when one logic seeks to justify itself with respect to the other (Musiani 2013).

EU law has recently prompted a digital package in the context of the EU digital strategy: this package includes legislative instruments having a sectoral scope of law as well as a transversal normative instrument, which is the Data Governance Act. This legal tool fosters mechanisms of data sharing and data reuse even for altruistic purposes, chosen as the key actions of data governance. The general assumption is that good data management is useful to create better knowledge transfer between public sector and private sector data, but both need to be well equipped and have access to more data.

However, while governance is a term that allows cooperation between multiple actors, government is not. The data government denotes the particular role of the state in the regulation of the internet and regarding all that happens on the internet. All the activities occurring within territorial barriers need to be regulated by state rules that try to fit into the rules of data sharing and participation to the market's shares of different actors.

Fixing rules of data sharing is the main goal of data governance, but the apparent result, if we consider it in spatial terms, is that, in relation to territory, data governance overlaps with data government. Data occupy an imaginary space of power that is appropriated by government through unusual forms of governance. More often, public and private actors share means to achieve ends (Pupolizio 2019). Put in these terms, it apparently seems that one logic prevails over the other. In reality, actors involved in data sharing and those who have legitimate powers regulating data flows operate parallelly. Data transfers, for example, represent a technical means that makes it possible to transfer jurisdictional shares provided that some standards or conditions are met. The data government is always based on rules of access to data that can be put in practice throughout access to a physical infrastructure, e.g., servers located within territorial premises (Naef 2023).

If governance can be based on practices of cross-border and cross-sectoral data sharing, then data government is instead related to the use of data for certain states' specific tasks that are subject to the jurisdiction of states (Curtin 2009). However, as correctly pointed out by Obendiek, data generates a jurisdictional overlap between data governance and data government (Obendiek 2023, p. 51), as claims of control increase proportionally either in the public or in the private sphere. Issues related to digital contents, physical and virtual infrastructures, and data are increasingly connected to the state's jurisdictional claims either in the form of dependence or influence. This makes data governance a "crucial site of conflicts" where different forms of polarization are possible.

2.1.3 The Territorial Barriers for Data Governments

Data affect the order the law shall give itself in an unprecedented way. They aim to predict behaviors, taking part in the quintessential function of the law. However, the manner in which the law and data operate in creating order is not homogenous and tends to coexist, producing counterforces.

Data pervade everything so that one is naturally led to think that data are everything whatever they take, regardless of the context of harvesting (Crawford 2021, p. 95).

What is interesting, at a deeper glance, is that the way by which territory is codified and juridified greatly depends on the way to conceive territorial relevance for the law.

If data have by definition a global extent, however, emerging phenomena derived from data processing have a limited extent related to the space to which they are relevant.

What exactly data fragments? The territory or the law?

The debate is long-lasting, and this book aims to offer key points and understandings of the transformations of the law and how the law interacts with social change.

Territory aims not to be fragmented rather monolithic, in the sense that it relies on patterns that have their relevance according to their physical cohesion. What data manage to fragment, in reality, is not the physical space related to a territory but the normative space. Regulatory space is based on non-homogenous variables that are related to the conditions of the legal scope of application. This may create confusion because to face the sectoral parcellation of space, the monolithic character of territory stands in a way that it creates "shock waves". In other words, territory is not forced by data per se, but by the territorial use of data. Inevitably, digitization is one of the phenomena that has completely questioned the relationship of the law with territory (Koskenniemi 1989, p. 241). Traditionally, territory has been institutionalized not only as the core concept of state jurisdiction but also as the field of action of the law itself, which has ferried the history of power from the Middle Age to the Modern Age (Brunner 1983). Territorial borders define an inside as a difference from the outside and metaphorically can be reproduced for all purposes they serve. This efficient way to exert power has led technology to assimilate itself to various uses and concepts of space.

The territory is the place of synthesis where physical thresholds transform geography into history (Maier 2019). The historical and theoretical itinerary of powers developed around territory, along which jurisdiction and sovereignty have constituted the perfect combination of modernity in the West. As Carlo Galli reminds us, the red line that explains modern politics is sovereignty: any community in order to exist politically must be sovereign, and one can only be so within a territory (or more) (Galli 2019).

The founding core of international law conceptualized in political and legal theories of state sovereignty, in its seemingly monolithic character, reveals the fragility of contingency. It is never forever that it bears within itself the immanent character of transformation. State sovereignty can only be imagined where territory exists as a tangible sign of the expansion and change of an established power, which must be defended as a strategic interest in political and territorial integrity. Particularly appropriate is Maier's observation that 'territoriality does not arise outside the qualities of politics or economic or social relations that are organized with respect to their spatial extension in space' (Maier 2019, p. 9).

2.2 The Territories of the Law

In very simple words, not strictly related to any theoretical constructions, territory is relevant because it is the *locus* where all social interactions take place and has relevance for acts or facts that occur within a given space. However, the assumption of the necessity of territory as a legal rationale has been blurred among different rationales, and the reasons are not always coherent or conceptually convincing. Rather, they have to do with needs to face in an ordered way. Conversely, before the emerging *borderless law* in various ambits of global law ("borderless law", as Ferrarese calls it, 2006), the concept of territory continues to be misused for lack of conceptual alternatives (Costa 2013). Focus has been attached to different conceptualizations of supranational and transnational law or changing emerging actors such as private companies or individuals as users of global services. However, the reflection on territoriality has only been roughly criticized but not adequately addressed unless retrospectively either as a Schmittian historical dimension or as a normative Kelsenian space (Scaccia 2017, p. 6). However, both conceptualizations need to be profoundly adapted to the emerging context of data flows.

According to Kelsen, the primacy of international law, as the law including all legal systems, is inherently incompatible with the principle of territorial state sovereignty (Nitsch 2012; Zolo 2007). States are equal because they are sovereign the one with respect to the other. In fact, Kelsen contends that once state sovereign claims are recognized in their sovereign differences regarding different territorial extensions, populations and powers, territory can be identified only as a normative concept, e.g., the scope of application of the law (Kelsen 1989, pp. 73 and 103). What is interesting in this reconstruction is that there are abstractly not objective legal limitations of its discretional expansion both as for its territorial scope and its material scope of application (Kelsen 1989, p. 465).

This assumption brings Kelsen to radically deny the concept of sovereignty because it reduces it to the identification between sovereign and state as the final term of reference.[3]

Only temporarily does humanity divide itself into states formed in a more or less arbitrary manner. The idea of *civitas maxima* as an organization of the world, that is, of an objective universal international juridical order that places itself above states, overcoming the dogma of sovereignty and that does not depend on any recognition, is the political core of the legal hypothesis of the primacy of international law. It represents in the context of international politics the fundamental idea that pacifism is the inverted image of imperialism (Kelsen 1989, p. 468)

Data is one of the most disruptive concepts for the law, as we know it (Hildebrandt 2023, p. 30). While approaching this statement that is commonly shared, one should ask what is at stake in the control of data and what territoriality means in the context of data flows. We should be sure of what we are referring to and whether perhaps with the terms territory and territoriality, we refer to phenomena that are not particularly evocative of the impact of data on space and the law (Núñez 2020).

If, on the one hand, it is out of doubt that the law needs its own space to produce effects, it is not said that such a space of digital law—e.g., the space where data produces legal effects—should necessarily be a territory in the traditional sense. The problem with this is that the use of territoriality as a justification of a political and legal power cannot exit territoriality throughout other variables but only throughout the accumulation or disarticulation of territory. If one looks at the phenomenon in the contrary sense, in fact, the territorial rights, *Rechte am Gebiet*, have been conceptualized by Jellinek as an example of reflexive rights that cannot be defined as subjective rights themselves but as the consequence of precise State's prerogatives. The fact that the State does not exert *dominium* in terms of property but rather forms of *imperium* in terms of specific tasks is crucial to the institutionalization of jurisdictional power (Jellinek 1921). Grotius instead considers *dominium* and *imperium* as two possible forms of occupation with the difference that ownership is a prerogative of both citizens and foreigners. Territory has been then conceptualized in its different forms and usages as the classical means of state power, which essentially relates to the right to jurisdiction, the right to use territorial resources and the right to control borders (Miller 2012, p. 651).

[3] See the critique of Carl Schmitt to Kelsen's concept of sovereignty, Schmitt (1972a), pp. 44–48 see also Riccobono (2017).

According to Carl Schmitt, the land is tied to the law in a threefold way. It keeps it within herself, as a reward for her work; it shows it in itself, as a clear boundary; finally, it bears it on itself as a public mark of the legal system. The law is earthly and refers to the earth (Schmitt 1991, p. 20). The tension between the global character of the market and the terrestrial nature of the state does not run out the possibilities to better frame digitization. The state disaggregates and reduces itself to a bunch of sectoral functions to exit the limitations imposed by its own territorial jurisdiction (Scaccia 2017, p. 38). However, in practical terms, if the rationale to regulate data flows is the territorial scope of application, in case of conflicts, such a rationale cannot be than making this rationale stronger. However, this implies opposing a territory that becomes increasingly more functional to other territories that become increasingly weaker. However, the territorial means have nothing to do either with the forms of data circulation and of data accumulation. It does not justify any linkage with both, because data use terriorial routes in a very unpredictable way which does not follow the logic of approximation. The fiction of normative spaces sometimes creates such a strong abstraction that it is not easy to distinguish the metaphors of physicality from the physicality itself.

In the field of data governance, it is not clear enough whether territory can be considered a container for data or it is a fiction that ensures physical traction to control data flows then activating a sovereign claim. The question is far from non-relevant because if we rely on territory as a container, concepts such as data ownership, access to data and control become of most importance, representing different degrees of appropriation. In addition, as the case of a physical entity over a territory is based on a centralised approach, data can be stored in a database that is owned and/or controlled by a single party; even if data can be distributed over clusters of computers, data repositories are owned and controlled by that party. If territory is meant to be the container, data cannot be disassembled from its localization. As a container, territory is the threshold of two spaces: one internal and one external. As correctly commented by Besson: "If States were to remain ultimate authorities on the inside, they needed to be independent on the outside".[4]

Applying the two Schmittian elements (Schmitt 1991, pp. 19–29), orientation and localization—*Ortung* and *Ordnung*—to data flows may have an impact on the way by which data fragmentation works. Orientation allows a given organized power to recognize its own position towards the outside. This idea of *konkrete Ordnung* relies on a reality that is spatially localized, legally structured and historically determined by state institutions (Romano 2018; Gaudino 2017; Preterossi 2022). In this sense, every legal system is a spatial system. Space is, however, functional to decision-making in the sense that it means the field of action of the law. Carl Schmitt theorized how "the universalism of Anglo-American hegemony" was destined to erase all distinctions as well as the spatial pluralism in a nondifferentiated word—either deterritorialized or overterritorialized—totally administered by

[4] Against this backdrop, Besson gives account of those scholars who deny the identification of the concept of sovereignty with an idea of physical threshold (Besson 2011, § 78, Sovereignty).

transnational technology and economic strategies and subject to forms of international control. In Schmittian terms, a spatially neutral world, without partitions and without contrasts—and therefore without politics—is considered the natural place for technological progress (Schmitt 2005, p. 107; Schmitt 1972b, p. 161). In fact, modern political forms are concrete insofar as they are determined by original choices, i.e. decisions, about the orientation of politics towards the land or the sea or the lotus balance (Galli 2017, p. 7–32, p. 11).

Uprooted from its telluric foundations, this kind of geopolitical order loses its composite nature—ordered and oriented, better ordered as far as oriented—provided by the law. Schmittian's theory appeared not only as a prophecy for unterritorial data but also mainly to recognize the possibility of existence for entities founded and established, simply created by mankind, without the establishment of any connection with the territory. The author or originator of data counts more than the place where a certain power relation deriving from data flows so that origination and final destination of data ideally occupy many spaces all together (Catanzariti and Curtin 2023, p. 133).

2.2.1 Coding Borderless Data Along Territorial Trajectories

Data is increasingly becoming the new rationale for power relationships. Its accumulation often remembers or at least is assimilated to the debates on war in the relationship among states. In reality, the remit of data regulation itself has nothing to do with the law of war, but the purposes of data accumulation may achieve an objective that is quite overlapping with the use of expansive war to occupy territories. There is an enormous debate on information warfare (Floridi and Taddeo 2014). In fact, instead of gaining physical traction, states gain or lose in terms of power depending on how much data they can store, manage and control. The definition of space through data does not have a substantial meaning, as data do not have the ability to occupy space. They are intangible and not precisely countable. Of course, to store it, states need physical spaces to host servers, but it still does not have a territorial connection. The concept of politics is defined by Carl Schmitt as the maximum degree of a union within a political community as well as a separation from other political communities (Schmitt 1972b, p. 109).

In the reflection on data governance, the centrality of territory is misleading because territory has a historical function that is not entirely normative but is also factual. It can be replaced by other elements that over time ensure the accomplishment of some goals. Data governance does not need territory to anchor control upon data. The cross-border dimension of data often imposes on states that want to interact due to reciprocal obligations. Traditionally, sovereignty, as a limited legitimized power over territory, and jurisdiction, as the reach of a State's law, go hand in hand. This hendiadys has proven to be right, especially with regard to its concrete expression, the principle of territoriality. According to this principle, the right to prescribe and enforce laws is limited to the territory of the state towards other territories where the principle of territoriality applies in the same way.

There is an important legal and philosophical controversy revolving around the mismatch between private property and the state's sovereignty. On this approximation, Lockean's theory had been developed moving by the fact that the state was presented by an association of owners exercising sovereign powers (*Hersschaft-Genossenschaft*). However, this theory has been developed on a different pathway in the middle-age, as the *Grundherr* was considered sovereign over a territory in so far, for the fact of being owner of that territory, he also had the power to military defense of that territory (Nobili Schiera 2015, p. 221).

In the context of the general state's theory, territory has been conceptualized according to two opposite understandings: as a quality of the state (*Eigenschaftsheorie*) and as the object of a public property right of the state (*Eigentumstheorie*) (Fricker 1901). This tension between the two ideas of *imperium* and *dominium* still echoes today in a quite counterintuitive way (Michetti 2021).

Although this has been widely criticized and there is yet a well-distinguished separation between sovereignty and property (Cohen 1927, p. 8), in the digital debate, this error comes again to the forefront because it legitimizes at least partially the thesis that this book aims to question. This thesis revolves around the fact that data are physical and tangible things that can be appropriated and that have the capacity to occupy a space with their physical character.

Because of the lack of substantial connection between data and territory, it is misleading to apply the principle of territoriality to data. If we continue to consider data as the physical form they represent, we legitimize in fact a trend that creates an overlap between sovereignty and property.

Even in the physical domain, the effective overlap between sovereignty and property is due to the fear that the principle of territoriality shall avoid, the fear of lack of control over persons and goods that move around. As far as a sovereign entity exerts legitimate prerogatives because of a limited territory, it does not need to justify property or control over infrastructures that are included within physical territories. Should control over data exceed territorial borders, any exceeding power would need to be justified in a different way than on a territorial basis.

2.2.2 Decoding Territory Through the Law: What Challenges

Data has nothing to do with physicality or tangibility by nature. Legal fiction regards the linkage between data and its field of action/movement. Data deploys localization as far as it is needed to develop order and imputability. However, localization without a connection with orientation, e.g., without the meaning that is attributed to the space by a given legal order, does not achieve any goal. This is for some authors the case of European legal order (Mari 2011, p. 76; Scaccia 2017, p. 40). However, "not all historical polities have been territorially organized" (Roberts et al. 2021, p. 7). In the case of the European Union, for instance, the linkage with the historical constitutive event of spatial arrangement disappeared in favor of an idea of a common market and common values. In the lack of this linkage, talking in terms of regulatory trajectories of digital sovereignty is far from being real and effective. The Schmittian nomos is then the positioning of a command, but it does not necessarily overlap with its regulatory regime.

Rules in reality do not coincide either with abstract or universal precepts that are effective or with sovereign decisions, but they are the by-product of certain socio-historical situations and contexts that only ideally reflect a spatial dimension. Sometimes it is rather a conceptual dimension. In the international context, the most relevant research strand in the field of data governance has been described as a polarization between cyberspace and human rights. Whereas the concept of cyberlaw is usually applied to cyberspace in order to justify the conditions under which a state's power on the internet is legitimate to regulate the relationships to technological and electronic elements, including computers, software, hardware and information systems (IS), human rights protection is often opposite to it acting as limiting cyberlaw universally on the side of individuals.

Another dichotomy is related to the mimesis of data protection law by other regulatory sectors (De Hert 2023, p. 95). This has constantly produced an aftermath of regulations and policies duplicating the path towards personal data protection in a way that is not always coherent.

The perspective of this book is different, as it aims to offer an overall overview of the law regarding the regulatory mechanisms in relation to data. The examples offered refer more generally to the way by which regulating data flows in relation to the meaning of territory is conceived rather than to single results of sectoral regimes.

Inspired by the Schmittian theory that has been elaborated for physical world, the measurement of territory (that Schmitt calls "nomos") implies occupation, division and distribution. Occupation is for Schmitt is the "archetype of a constitutive legal process" that is inherently linked to the normative creation of space (Schmitt 1991, p. 25). However, the strength of the nomos consists in concretely positioning legal systems within a spatial framework, not only in dominating. Nomos is the immediate form in which political and social order become spatially visible (Schmitt 1991, p. 59). This implies occupying a given space by means of control together with the rules that are necessary to hold it. Therefore, territoriality is historically determined, in the sense that it is contingent, it is not temporally indefinite, and it limits a new spatial order of the earth. Nomos is the result of measurement and calculation, ultimately a spatial demarcation (Schmitt 1991, p. 65); therefore, the law is territorial by definition, as it represents a mixture of orientation and localization—*Ordnung and Ortung*, that mean constitution of a legal system and spatial localisation. These terms do not need to be considered under Schmittian lenses, as they represent one core issue altogether. As far as a set of rules is localized and specifically referred to certain subjects and temporally and spatially limited, it also gives rise to a concrete legal system. In the Schmittian theorization the sea is free, and there is no demarcation or possibility of calculation. All preglobal legal systems were terrestrian, whereas global legal systems are not, or better, try not to be terrestrian and ordered. Territory acts as a *katechon* and as a limit of arbitrariness. The nomos is the result of a concrete measurement that distributes entitlements, portions of power and pieces of land as far as there is a justified connection between such measurement and what needs to be measured. If this connection gets lost, then there is no reason—unless a reason that is only artificial one—to justify a criterion of governance. According to Schmitt, the *nomos* has an immediate strength that is not mediated by laws (Schmitt 1991, p. 63). Thus, the conquest of territory is an original act, whereas the division of territories is a consequence. This implies that foundational processes are spatially determined if an original situation where the state of nature is the land of nobody is assumed but not being technically a nonplace (Schmitt 1991, p. 96).

This book is not Schmittian nor Kelsenian in the sense that it does not apply to data either the highest version of spatiality represented by the idea of Grossraum—the pluriverse of large territorially determined spaces under a hegemonic power (Scalone 2017, p. 179)—or the idea of planetary plain space to the issue of jurisdiction over data. This book is also not a study on the conflicts on law emerging by data regulatory schemes (Hörnle 2021; Obendiek 2023).

The Schmittian theoretical construction is used to reflect upon the case of data flows and their impossibility to occupy a territory physically but at the same time their expectation to determine a concrete territorial scope of the law; Kelsen's theoretical take is helpful in deconstructing the paradigm of sovereignty throughout the deconstruction of its normative variables. Both theories show how fragile can be the alternative between sovereign prerogatives and global order and from radically different perspectives envisage the possible conditions of international relations. The different degrees of conceptualization of territorial fragmentation offer a preview on how the paradigm of sovereignty can be reduced in a nutshell to a set of competences (Cannizzaro 2020, p. 113). This is particularly relevant if applied to sectoral regulation enshrined in the EU digital strategy.

2.2.3 Connecting the Dots, Differentiating the Branches of the Law

Based on its capacity to represent as many dimensions as possible, data can also be fictitiously territorial as far as it is the object of a seizure or if we rely on physical control over a network architecture, e.g., as far as it is considered and interpreted according to rules based on physicality (Woods 2018, p. 328). This kind of architecture usually requires compelling compliance by states, but in the case of conflicts of law, one of the most utilized means is sovereign deference.

However, data can be all—material and nonmaterial—but what is interesting is that this happens in nonmediated forms. Data can be entirely commodified and multiply used to achieve objectives. States have closer possible interest in data exploitation and usage and must exercise jurisdiction on them often for necessity; otherwise, many of the related phenomena remain uncovered. Therefore, the urgency to go in depth in the analysis of disconnecting factors and effects of what precisely puts together data and territory is crucial.

However, how to disconnect *Ordnung* and *Ortung* in the field of data regulation? (Schmitt 1991). Is it just utopian to create a unified world without underlying conflicts under the sword of technique? (Tucker et al. 2017). It aims to dig into different stories of territoriality. This helps to shape the roadmap on which certain phenomena are ascribed to the power over the land. The double movement between deterritorialization and reterritorialization moves along tension axes and states' actions (Della Morte 2018). The most frequent solution has been to locate intangible assets somewhere both from a theoretical and an applicative dimension. Which is the real problem to such a configuration? The problem is that as far as territory is not used as a metaphor being instead a real mechanism of recognition, this is performative in its effects. The law reterritorializes and deterritorializes itself—operating self-reproduction—and applies this mechanism to all its objects (Deleuze and Guattari 1997; Andronico 2002). In relation to data it is a hybrid operation and this is challenging because it is not always recognizable where physicality does apply or not. It is made evident by the linkage between sovereignty and jurisdiction as sovereign right and duty (Besson 2011, § 118, § 123). Jurisdiction was the Latin word including both meanings: an authority over persons and goods within a territory. According to this definition and under certain requirements, jurisdiction is the legal authority to state the law (Hörnle 2021, p. 4). There has always been a linkage between jurisdiction and sovereignty. There is a large literature strand that questions the tenet of sovereignty for globalization (Kalmo and Skinner 2010, pp. 132 and 186; Ryngaert and Zoetekouw 2014, p. 185).

2.3 By Nature or by Law? Data and *fictio iuris*

The *datum* is different according to nature or according to law. According to nature, data can be everything based on their representative capacity and therefore are neutral; according to the law, data's representative power profoundly affects the legal construction of reality.

According to emerging studies on holistic data regulation, "data embeds security into trade and trade into security and changes the face of institutionalization, creating the need for cooperation, needs for trust, governance and rigour" (Fahey 2022, p. 1).

However, datum is a term that recalls an activity that has been concluded and that it shows up as a fact-finding. This logical nuance is not insignificant even considering digital data that are interconnected. In fact, the activity of collection and analysis crystallizes reality, contextualizing it into spatial and temporal coordinates. This, however, has nothing to do with the nature of data that, because of its fragmentation, e.g., incapacity to fully reflect a phenomenon unless throughout aggregated forms, is fluctuating (Humphreys 2018, p. 191).

Data production increasingly creates a favorable framework where the law itself is made of data and for this is interchangeable. Then, data production by law quite often risks being confused with law production by data. I specifically refer to phenomena that require the production of data as a basis for the legal knowledge to be opposed to phenomena that create the law based on the need to control data flows (Schiavello 2023). For this, it is very important to differentiate between the two situations as far as data may meaningfully activate legal fictions. One of the most overarching legal fictions is the one created surrounding the principle of territoriality. This is peculiar because the flexible and versatile nature of data impacts territory in an exactly opposite way with respect to the law. Whereas the law shapes its own scope over space, data instead fragment space and its relevance depending on what exactly they represent in a given moment. Such a reconfiguration of space produces an enhanced divarication between law and nature based on which legal fictions have the function of framing the uncontrolled movement of data. However, the argument for which data trajectories are determined by physical constraints, in other words, by the location of cables, is certainly not novel. However, even when that is assumed, the idea of consequential spatiality, which is related to a relationship with a given place, loses its relevance.

Data not only exceeds territories but also has to do substantially with them. The ambiguity may, however, emerge from the fact that territory may ideally be the place where data are stored in a server and all the activities involving data and occurring outside the premises of the territory, but thanks to the functionalities of the server materially located, it is deemed to be territorial. The tension between territorialization and deterritorialization has been at the core of various attempts to inscribe the essence of power within physical limits. The more capitalism follows its tendency to 'decode' and 'deterritorialize', the more does it seek to awaken or reawaken artificial territorialities and residual encodings, thus moving to counteract its own tendency (Deleuze and Guattari 1997, p. 224). According to Guattari and Deleuze, rhizomatic structures—which could be one of the interconnected data—do not belong to any jurisdiction, and any point of them can be connected to any other. "A range of theorists argue that the uncoupling of law and state reveals that territoriality is a merely contingent feature of law; globalizations, in particular economic globalization, drive the processes by which law becomes increasingly deterritorialized, or so we are told" (Lindahl 2018, p. 14).

Having territoriality as a term of reference means bearing in mind that power establishes a relationship with data in the sense that it fills in territory with data in various senses.

Filling in territory with data or using territory to reach out to data are both ways to explore what *Ordnung* and *Ortung*—orientation and localization, the two Schmittian legal and political categories—mean when applied to data. The increasing data flow that constantly crosses territories offers a dichotomic picture of territories of data—as inevitable objects of territory—and data of states—as entitlements representing goods.

However, the fact that data means something different depending on what it represents and whether it is static or interconnected makes their relationship with space profoundly mutable. This changing character affects the relevance of territory for digital phenomena. As long as territory is permeable to data, it is evident that it does not limit states' prerogatives. As pointed out by Crawford, "The way data is understood, captured, classified, and named is fundamentally an act of world-making and containment" (Crawford 2021, p. 121).

The metaphor of territory is powerful as far as it performs in an equal and generalized order. This means that any sovereign power, being constructed over a territorial logic, cannot be understood outside this framework. In legal terms, it also means that any power that is not based on the limitations of territory is non-legitimate. The performativity of data-driven constructions has the ability to overcome territory using territorial logic. As far as technologies reterritorialize data, territorial logic is predominant as a tool to ensure sovereignty indiscriminately, not as a tool to exert sovereign prerogatives for a certain goal (Pistor 2019, pp. 108, 205). Of course, the neutral character of technology—the relevance for it of uses and targets as well as of justifications—in this way is transferred into a territorial neutrality of data that increases physical porosity towards data. This can be understood as a unit of contiguous space used, organized, and managed by a social group, individual, or institution to restrict and control the access for people to places and goods.

Sometimes the word is used as a synonym for place or space, but territory has never been such an original or generic word as the other two in the canonical use of geographic terminology.

Globalization has imposed territory to gradually become just one type of spatiality, or the way space is used, rather than the exclusive way it is used.

From this perspective, territoriality is the strategic use to achieve organizational goals.

One cannot claim to associate modernity with territoriality in the global era. The process of state construction always has two crucial attributes. One is exclusivity, according to which all political entities that have not been able to achieve a reasonable size of sovereignty over a contiguous territory cannot aspire to the role of major political actors. The other is mutual recognition, meaning that the power of states is resided considerably by the recognition each state receives from other states through non-interference in so-called international affairs. We must think of territory as an extremely efficient way to achieve organizational results, but changeable and replaceable.

2.3.1 *Juridification of Data and Regulation of Flows*

Let us start from a radical opposite hypothesis. The alternative to a model centered on territoriality is applying a theory that is not nomothetic with regard to data—in the sense that data does not create any legal representation in relation to a territory because of its non-static nature. Nonetheless, this may input an irregular element in the organization of the terrestrial space.[5]

Global data flows moves and circulates all over the world and beyond. With respect to the unambiguous relationship between territories and data, imagining data flows crossing the globe means the possibility of generalizing into one unique flow of data over territories.

Territory is not necessarily essential to the definition of sovereignty. It has a historical dimension limited to its specific function as an organizational form of spatial order. Because states recognize themselves as limited by territories, jurisdiction of states is based on the principle of territoriality. Between terrestrial immobility and fixity and maritime mobility, data-driven technologies use territory as an instrumental tool to facilitate movement and data circulation.

If we try to make a parallel between digital law and the law of war, the war of *jus publicum Europaeum* can be considered a war between states, conducted by one regular state army against another. Jus publicum Europaeum is then the by-product of interstate law between European sovereigns that used the law of territoriality all over the world. The peculiarity of this parallelism is whether or not data management can be a vehicle of imperialism, as was the case in the European conquest of the non-European world and the conquest of the free sea by the United Kingdom. Schmitt contends that the territorial state's sovereign task consists in putting the war on shape not necessarily with rules, but through the principle of territorial sovereignty that makes the law between specific orders, spatially organized (iusti hostes) based on the principle of "par in parem non habet jurisdictionem" (Schmitt 1991, pp. 186–187).

Digital competition, conversely, cannot be compared with a war because territorial traction is not necessarily aimed at gaining control over data, and the shares of control over data flows cannot be comparable or measurable through quantitative methods that are similar to physical measurement over a territory. The Schmittian idea, according to which the advancement of technology will only determine a greater intensity of the new conquests, divisions and productions and will only exacerbate the old problems, is hardly applicable to digital environments. There is not a perfect equivalence with the concept by which those who dominate the earth, which has apparently become so tiny, will occupy and exploit the new spaces. However, it is worth noting that for Schmitt, territoriality ensures regularity and recognition in the lack of which disorder dominates the scene out of control. Territory cannot only represent—as pointed out by Kelsen (Kelsen 1934, p. 52)—a factor of the normative content of legal system eventually resulting in the field of application of the law (*Geltungsbereich von Rechtsnormensystemen*) and substantially implying a denial of the space (Ruschi 2019, p. 366). Territory has meaningful relevance. It points out a telluric fixity and maritime mobility. This bipartition has

[5] In this sense, the territorial use of data can be assimilated to the Schmittian theory of partisan according to which the partisan holds a terrestrial configuration but alters and expands the territory forcing the conflict on irregular layers. See Schmitt (2005).

been described by Carl Schmitt in the *theory of partisan*, where new solutions are considered the masks that show new problems.

We can agree that state sovereignty is not a universal concept that is valid for every age and population but a historical concrete phenomenon that is linked to a specific time (Schmitt 1991, p. 142). If we consider this assumption from the perspective of data regulation, the universal character of globalization aims to make all objects uniform to make the same standards applicable. The modern order—what Schmitt calls "nomos"—is based on the division of European land into state sectors with specific borders and precise competences. This organizational form of the spatial order resisted over two centuries from limiting European wars. Is it truly war in terms of division of the land and entitlement to exert sovereign powers a term that can be associated with data? Concepts are never entirely overlapping for different phenomena.

Data is the new ontological territory itself. Its capacity moves rapidly and represents any form of reality. It is, however, not enough to embrace a radical opposite hypothesis, the one that leads to the theorization of partisan as irregular and not recognizable under the physicality of the world (Schmitt 2005).

The fact that data can blend into various dimensions and camouflage represents the ambivalence of data that lies between its non-terrestrial nature and its capacity to represent whatever. In contrast to the partisan, data is not recognizable because of the lack of linkage with territory. The partisan instead is not recognizable because it completely mimics the earth. From the parallelism we can conclude that technological development transforms spatial structures and spatial orders and questions the foundational concept of sovereignty, which is the equality of states.

The issue here is that the technological universalism of the West has radically replaced the logic of territory. If the sea is left outside any spatial order, is cyberspace comparable with the sea? Even the premise is that separately talking about peace and war for Schmitt is like losing the unitary character of the nomos, which is the one with the other, we assume that the state logic is inherently related to localization by definition. Conversely, the logic of the sea is naturally oriented to disorder, which opposes the State against private entities (Schmitt 1991, p. 413; Ruschi 2012). The logic of data lies in-between: fluctuating nature aimed at producing stable effects.

2.3.2 *Data Connection Through Physical Spheres*

The Schmittian thesis sounds peremptory. Even according to the most tellurian view, every very international juridical order that does not want to deny itself must protect not the territorial status quo of a given historical moment, in its several peculiarities, but its own fundamental spatial structure (nomos), the unity of order and localization (Schmitt 1991, pp. 226–227). However, building on the terrible Schmittian thought, it is possible to approach the data regulation by trying to apply it. According to this thought, what is extremely relevant is terrestrial fragmentation when one is able to "feel" the sea (Cassano 2005). Feeling the sea also means incorporating the vulnerability of physicality at different layers. If physicality opens up to other spaces the difference between fixed and borderless structures loses its relevance (Malgieri 2023, p. 47; Pino 2003).

The idea of territory is inherent to the law in its metaphorical meaning. The law defines itself in relation to its field of application. The field of application is the metaphor of a territory, not necessarily considered as a physical entity but rather as an ambit of action. As an artificial architecture that is functional to connect ambits of action, the law must also establish stable connections within the areas that are covered. The logical scheme is always tailored upon the spatial scheme. The law is divided into micro-territories that are functionally connected to each other but independent of one another.

Territorial logic is fundamentally a comfortable way to assess who and to what extent one entity has the power to exert legitimate prerogatives within a limited frame.

This is true irrespective of the fact that data can be the object of digital rights (data protection, property rights, online freedom of expression) or the means of governance (the Data Governance Act[6] provides examples of how data can be used to regulate different regulatory segments, e.g., laying down conditions for the reuse of data held by public authorities), because both perspectives are part of the big picture where EU law plays its bet in the global order.

The Data Act (Regulation EU 2023/2854) instead poses its basis for data sharing, reaching out to three actions: access to private sector data for the public sector; data access and use in public relationships; and new rules allowing customers to effectively switch between different cloud data-processing service providers.

This dichotomy reflects the fragmentation deriving from the multifaceted character of data under the lenses of the law that often blurs its syntactic and semantic layers, e.g., not only the way by which data is put together through its components but also how it is structured to be meaningful.

The juridification of data has been enabled in various ways: connecting the use of data with emerging rights or expanding the linkage between regulation and the potential usage and interpretations of data. In many cases, the relevance of data emerged in relation to the fundamental rights' status of data protection and the right to privacy. If we think, for example, of cases on mass surveillance, the overarching character of data flows is the result of activities of wiretapping and collection that need to be relevant globally to compel rights protection globally. This has been, for example, the case of *Big Brother Watch v. United Kingdom*[7], as well as many other cases that have extraterritorially triggered the protection of rights, where the ECtHR has ascertained the violation of the right to a private life outside UK because of activities of bulk collection perpetrated outside national borders. The universal

[6] Regulation (EU) 2022/868 of the European Parliament and of the Council of 30 May 2022 on European data governance and amending Regulation (EU) 2018/1724 (Data Governance Act) (Text with EEA relevance), PE/85/2021/REV/1, *OJ L 152*.

[7] Applications nos. 58170/13, 62322/14 and 24960/15, Judgement 21 May 2021.

character of human rights has enormously expanded in the field of mass surveillance.

As far as data is relevant globally, its connection with territory is unrelevant. Conversely, the attempt to reconcile data with territory is to force the nature of data into narrow binaries. Digital flows can assume a territorial or extraterritorial nature depending on what kind of rules they are attached upon.

In the mentioned case, the bulk interception is generally directed at international communications (that is, communications physically travelling across State borders), and while the interception and even examination of communications of persons within the surveilling State might not be excluded, in many cases, the stated purpose of bulk interception is to monitor the communications of persons outside the State's territorial jurisdiction, which could not be monitored by other forms of surveillance. In so far as the Court has considered targeted interception, it has, for the most part, been employed by respondent States for the purposes of investigating crime. However, while bulk interception may be used to investigate certain serious crimes, Council of Europe member States operating a bulk interception regime appear to use it for the purposes of foreign intelligence gathering, the early detection and investigation of cyberattacks, counterespionage and counterterrorism.

While bulk interception is not necessarily used to target specified individuals, it evidently can be—and is—used for this purpose. However, when this is the case, the targeted individuals' devices are not monitored. Rather, individuals are "targeted" by the application of strong selectors (such as their email addresses) to the communications intercepted in bulk by the intelligence services. Only those "packets" of the targeted individuals' communications that were travelling across the bearers selected by the intelligence services will have been intercepted in this way, and only those intercepted communications that matched either a strong selector or complex query could be examined by an analyst.

The paradoxical effect is that, for example, conversations within one state may be more protected than if such conversations occur between a citizen of one state and a citizen of another state. This implies an ambiguous difference between territoriality in the strict sense and effects theory.

The task of sovereignty is to place oneself within an unfounded instance of order: to bring to light the origin of an order. This original act makes sovereignty: working on a void that forces you to do something you cannot do at all.

The breaking through of sovereignty, which is a load-bearing pillar and which remains not because it is a relic but because it is load-bearing, is the original act. In the Schmittian modality, not the land, but the taking of the land is the quintessential characteristic of sovereignty.

However, it is not possible to assert the existence of customary law specific to cyberspace or even obligations descended from international agreements.

2.3.3 Sovereign Claims over the Data Sphere

In the case of a cyber-attack at the state level, the consequences of which are comparable to those of an armed attack, it is possible to invoke the right of self-defence enshrined in the UN Charter. In the case of cyber operations in the context of an armed conflict, international humanitarian law must be respected, while for operations aimed only at obtaining information, human rights principles apply. More urgently, states are exerting sovereign claims over cyberspace that they try to justify. The creation of the Open Ended Working Group (OEWG) through resolution 73/27 by General Assembly on security of and in the use of information and communications technologies has confirmed the application of international law to cyberspace. For example, rules and principles of international law—be they customary or treaty-based—applicable to activities in cyberspace should not be limited to those pertaining to the prohibition of the use of force in international relations, but they should also prohibit cyber operations conducted by a State, which produce harmful effects over the territory of another State, irrespective of the physical location of the perpetrator, or cyber operations conducted from the territory of another State without its express authorization.[8]

The process of EU integration cannot expand to the limit of requiring limitations or expansions of state sovereignty based on specific subject-matters or single topics (Amato 2012, p. 9). Analogical operations such as handling cyberspace as outer space are far from being realistic. The main criteria that are utilized are strictly related to the nationality or residency of subjects affected by the use of data (not necessarily data subjects).

However, there are activities such as bulk interception that do not fall per se outside the margin of appreciation of states, as stigmatized in the *Big Brother* case. In particular, regarding general clauses as national security, for example, national authorities enjoy a wide margin of appreciation in choosing how best to achieve the legitimate aim of protecting national security and therefore may in principle engage in strategic surveillance of foreign communications (Kuner et al. 2018, p. 1).

Indeed, divergent levels of protection from unwarranted state intrusion exist, based on whether the intercepted material is domestic or foreign in nature, thereby setting out separate standards for targeted and bulk interception of communications. At the domestic level, an assessment should be made at each stage of the process of the necessity and proportionality of the measures being taken; bulk interception should be subject to independent authorization at the outset, when the object and scope of the operation are being defined; and the operation should be subject to supervision and independent ex post facto review.

In general, the standards enshrined in *Weber and Saravia v. Germany*[9] apply. According to those safeguards, the domestic law authorizing surveillance must

[8] Italian Position Paper on International Law and Cyberspace, https://www.esteri.it/MAE/resource/doc/2021/11/italianpositionpaperoninternationallawandcyberspace.pdf.

[9] Application n. 54934/00, Judgement 29 June 2006)

specify (1) the nature of the offences, which may give rise to an interception order; (2) a definition of the categories of people liable to have their telephone tapped; (3) a limit on the duration of the telephone tapping; (4) the procedure to be followed for examining, using and storing the data obtained; (5) the precautions to be taken when communicating the data to other parties; and (6) the circumstances in which recordings may or must be erased or the tapes destroyed (§ 95 Big Brother).

The *Big Brother* case integrates two additional standards: (7) the procedures and modalities for supervision by an independent authority of compliance with the above safeguards and its powers to address noncompliance; and (8) the procedures for independent *ex post facto* review of such compliance and the powers vested in the competent body in addressing instances of noncompliance. Judgment means that bulk surveillance in the UK and across Europe will require prior independent or judicial authorization, checking for adequate "end-to-end safeguards", from the initial collection of data to the selection of items for storage.

The government admitted that the purpose of bulk surveillance "is not to search for the communications of identified targets" but to gather mass data and decide "who should be a target".

On this paradigmatic admission that confirms the predetermined activity of data collection, there is a relevant dissenting opinion that is worth noting: "Admitting nontargeted bulk interception involves a fundamental change in how we view crime prevention and investigation and intelligence gathering in Europe, from targeting a suspect who can be identified to treating everyone as a potential suspect, whose data must be stored, analysed and profiled (…) a society built upon such foundations is more akin to a police state than to a democratic society. This would be the opposite of what the founding fathers wanted for Europe when they signed the Convention in 1950" (Judge Pinto de Albuquerque's dissenting opinion, *Big Brothers case*).

Margin of appreciation is one more time then a delicate issue because data blurs information.

2.4 Exclusive Control Within On-line Fragmentation

As stressed by Elden in the *Birth of Territory*, territory is not a natural feature but a technique of power to exert control. It is a very successful notion (Elden 2013).

The continuity of territory allows data to be fragmented and spread over states and jurisdictions in a very flexible way. This means that data fragments situations and facts provide for different segmentations of reality. However, this may be done because of the continuity between territories.

Data perform a mimetic activity with respect to territory throughout which it is able to fragment spaces moving over a physical continuity. Paradoxically, data fragmentation is possible because of territorial continuity and in relation to it; otherwise, without the territorial relevance of any given legal order, even data would be not capable of acting in a fragmentary fashion. One example is the triangulation of data throughout satellites and countries. Such a triangulation makes it possible for data to exit territory and be vehiculated over another territory throughout a non-territory, e.g., the outer space that is nonrelevant to the concept of jurisdiction because, pursuant to the Outer Space Treaty, national sovereignty cannot be exerted over it.

Data control is the goal that reshapes legal institutions. Trying to make technology and the law territorially converging facilitates this goal. However, this means that territorializing data reconfigures an expansion of geography that is useful to exert control as far as data is accessed, stored and processed. Entrepreneurial actors gain traction over activities carried out on the globe based on how many data shares and across which spaces, fictitious or material, they are able to move. Access to data and capacity to handle data are sides of the same moon.

The idea of exclusive control that is not anchored to data but to physical entities—such as bodies and lands—overcomes fragmentation only apparently.

The law cannot respond to data fragmentation in a fragmented way—by enlarging the legal notion of territory as a matter concept—to ensure its exclusive control. Quite paradoxically exclusive control in a widespread manner tries to functionally preserve an idea of continued physical space that does not correspond to reality. In Humphreys's words: "Data are rendered in a form [data] from which they may be in turn epistemically recombined" (Humphreys 2018, p. 193).

Territory of data or data of the territory at the end?

The lack of territoriality for data implies a series of other issues: how to deal with ubiquity, intangibility, and immateriality. The medium counts more than the contents. For example, the domain name system, or DNS, makes the Internet accessible throughout the use of IP addresses corresponding to different devices. IP addresses are usually made of a list of digits linking a series of letters with a series of numbers. Their infrastructure is flexible, as it ensures quick changes between certain domains and IP addresses and allows a certain domain name not to be necessarily tied to a particular computer.

One of the most well-known regulatory issues is that related to data location in cloud computing. Andrew Keane Woods, in a very famous essay *Against data exceptionalism* related to American law, tries to address the issue of the limits of government access to personal data stored in the cloud, arguing that data are not exceptional in nature and that potential conflicts of law may be solved based on data location (Woods 2016).

The materiality of infrastructures enables the exercise of power, although the way by which cables work and are connected is not based on any physical proximity. Cables are owned and operated by both private actors (some state-owned) and large conglomerates of public and private actors. Even in the cloud, the issue of data location is highly problematic because data can be freely accessed all over the world but stored locally.

2.4.1 Digital Rights and Limits of Jurisdictions

Conceiving the link between data and rights as a possibility to create digital rights—such as online freedom of expression, data protection, and database protection—allows conceptually justifying rights and their attached "digital" character as a limit to jurisdictions.

With the words by Humphreys, the inherent character of data is the combination of infrastructural ubiquity and semantic fungibility (Humphreys 2018, pp. 191–202). This cannot completely overlap with a physical structure. The book does not have the ambition to systematize this old debate but rather to ask whether there are possible alternative strategies to territorial logic.

The challenge is to configure the right space for intangible things that have the ability to flow across borders and not stay unmoved. The concept of residence is contrary to the logic of data.

Sometimes data are not related to a territory of a nation state. One may think that data are in the cloud, but they are instead in the ocean that are owned by web giants such as Amazon, Google, Facebook and Microsoft. Bits of code that move around the world are the functional means that connect the dots.

Undersea cables are critical infrastructures. Submarine cables have been connected to the world for years. Therefore, the question is whether the connection of realities through data—which is in fact achieved through data sharing, data transfers and data circulation broadly speaking—can also be realized in the lack of territory.

If we try to respond to this simple question, we can easily realize that territory is the point of reference of a way of thinking of legal order. Based on a different perspective from the one discussed so far, it may also be a fiction to think of data in terms of unterritoriality if they exploit territorial coordinates.

In non-territorial spaces, there is a logical substitution of territoriality with concepts such as property/management/control that are counterintuitive because of the lack of object on which it is possible to exert rights. Suddenly, this contrast determines a prevalence: to exert sovereignty, the territory has to occupy the space of data so that data is in a sense encapsulated into a space.

However, in real terms, this does not have anything to do with the legal category of property that can be hardly referred to data in the European context (Calabresi-Melamed 1972).

This has to do with the concept of location, although we are not arguing that data location is exhaustive of any jurisdictional claim over data.

Following Svantesson's reasoning, territoriality needs to be rethought as the only possible legal framework for sovereignty, but this depends on the purpose that territoriality serves (Svantesson 2017, pp. 14 and 124–126; Svantesson 2015, p. 518). With the words of Samantha Besson, "When territorial jurisdiction is mentioned, it should not be therefore understood to mean that jurisdiction is territorial in nature, but only that territory is used as a shorthand to the function of jurisdiction" (Besson 2012, p. 863).

The logic to relate data to territory is misleading. It can often refer to a physical space but not always. This means that the underlying mechanism of power referred to as spatial appropriation and occupation is also used, often irrespective of the contingency, to identify a center of imputation of certain facts. However, the change of focus from the idea of a place that contains data into a mechanism to increase the capacity of a state to exert control over space is not to be underestimated. Focusing on the occupation of the physical space has allowed legal theory to consider territory as a metaphor for space and to build on the related legal category. This scenario seems to be logical if we have in mind the territoriality of the physical space as a point of reference, but if we move to data, things may change.

Data instead may compose a fictitious territory because it only apparently passes through territory. The territory expects to own its data only because it is a space where they circulate, although data do not occupy any territory. In this sense data may become a prerogative of a sovereign power over a territory as far as this is justified from the perspective of territorial connection. This means that jurisdictional claims over data can be treated as regarding a physical object without reference to the real physical impact of data over the territory.

When we talk of and deal with data, it is not clear enough if data may represent a disruptive phenomenon that seems to produce a bundle of consequences to which traditional categories can be applied or if it is in fact so disruptive that it completely needs new legal categories. The problem of sovereignty about data is preliminarily this: whether it is possible to find legal spaces for data other than territorial ones where exerting rights or withdrawing authority.

Sometimes territory only represents a valid umbrella capable of covering all existing phenomena. However, because of the lack of causality between territory and data, often the overuse of territoriality cannot be justified precisely for its lack of legitimacy.

While proprietary attitudes create confusion with the idea of *imperium*, which is a jurisdictional authority and not an object of proprietary ownership, jurisdiction is instead truly only one possible specification for power relationships (Abizadeh 2016). In the case of data, such specification is not peculiar itself.

The relationship between territory and data, on the one hand, as well as between rights arising from the use of data or from violations perpetrated over the internet, is another application of the same reasoning when the relevance of the phenomenon to be regulated is not so peculiar from a territorial perspective. The diffusion of digital content as well as data protection of internet users are not, for example, rights that have territorial significance, but they may be relevant territorially only with respect to specific focus on the establishment of providers, on the residency of nationals, etc., that substantially have nothing to do with the effective protection of those rights.

2.4.2 The Resilience of the Authority Principle

In a famous work *Law and Borders. The Rise of Law in Cyberspace*, 1996, Johnson and Post view cyberspace as a separate space (Johnson and Post 1996). This view has legitimized nonstate orders that allow states to exert jurisdiction beyond their limits. Why does the Internet need a sovereign? The traditional answer is that global Internet would not deserve a national jurisdiction but rather a global jurisdiction (Wu 1997). The opposite position advanced by Goldsmith points out the necessity of legitimate sovereignty over cyberspace.[10]

There is then an apparent tension between an illusion of cyberspace as a space without sovereigns and of the Internet as a global phenomenon. Nonetheless, the reality is that phenomena made global through the Internet are incardinated on material boundaries, and the result is territorial, although the cause is not.

Sovereignty cannot be shared, but the internet does not have sovereigns. However, the principle of sovereignty applies to states' cyber activities through the ability of a state to regulate such matters within its territorial borders and to exercise independent state powers.

The reality in its pure simplicity is that the internet is a technical protocol that cannot be the object of sovereign powers, but the infrastructure is material and subject to the rules defined by the states (Zeno Zencovich 2016, p. 14).

That's the reason for the territories of data, because the Internet does not have its own territory, but it is helped by the territories across which it operates for its specific function. The problem is that exerting sovereign powers seems to block the regulation of different phenomena.

Territory as legitimacy means is still how the law is. The law needs to occupy various areas, as the link with space legitimizes its authority. However, the territories of the law are many as much as they result in sectoral fragments of regulation. It is not a unique and continuous flow.

The boundaries and relevance of territory as a rationale help to identify whether it is a substantial or a formal rationale.

What behavior ought to come in a given place? Even the space is given as well as data. The typical construction of the law is that "states' territorial rights are held in rem against all persons". Saskia Sassen perfectly centered the point observing that even while globalization can be considered "denationalization," it continues to be shaped, channeled, and enabled by institutions and networks originally developed with nations in mind, then as a process of state making expanded outside the states' borders (Sassen 2006).

She correctly points out that the main issue related to territoriality is "what kind of a "territory" is constituted through such a network of multiple localities in matters of law". This depends on the fact that digital networks are embedded in nondigital environments or at least non-entirely virtual environments.

---

[10] Goldsmith (1998): "A nation possesses territorial sovereignty in the sense that it exercises the principal means of authority within a given territory. The Internet is not, as many suggest, a separate place removed from our world" (p. 476).

In the end, the real problem is what institutions have in mind when they think of processes. Globalization is a novel localization of social interactions and therefore is a theoretical frontier (Sassen 2006, p. 289). In the words of Sassen, territory, authority, and rights are then transhistorical because they are flexible to changing realities (Sassen 2006, p. 351). However, the system of interpretation is embedded within nondigital environments. Globalization "takes place literally" (Lindahl 2018, p. 22).

The attempt of legal theory to justify the government of digital flows through the principle of territoriality has been applied to jurisdictional claims. It has needed to write down data along territorial trajectories and to define the space occupied by data through material coordinates. The use of automation has put together algorithms and data over physical borders, trying to apply the principle of territoriality to heterogeneous things, representations of reality on the one hand and algorithms on the other. We can think, in particular, of virtual borders that have been activated for the securitization of Europe and border management. Enabling borders of functionalities means creating legal performativity through advanced technologies (Mezzadra and Neilson 2013). However, this implies a reterritorialization of territories that adds a further powerful logic to the logic applied normally as a territorial limitation. Enabling smart borders means fostering territorial approximation in such a way that territories can proliferate and power accordingly. The AI Act classifies AI systems in the area of migration, asylum and border control management as high-risk AI systems[11] because they 'affect people who are often in particularly vulnerable position and who are dependent on the outcome of the actions of the competent public authorities' (Malgieri and Niklas 2020, p. 37; Malgieri, 2023; Corso 2019, pp. 3–14).

Decoding territoriality then requires replacing territory with alternatives to it, allowing the principle of territoriality to alternate differences in the legal solutions that are based on it. Differences related to the use of territoriality help in drawing applicable solutions. However, it is not easy to differentiate the use of territory according to a different interpretation of territorial connections. In fact, territoriality denotes a monolithic approach to the scope of application of the law that is only apparently flexible in terms of possible consequences. In other words, using territoriality as an operational way only means expanding the scope of application of the law in various areas of the law regulating digital flows. In other words, this requires dissecting the principle of territoriality through its functional factors that are related, e.g., to the elements constituting a fact that is relevant for the law, such as space, harm, establishment of a company, data protection, right to redress, access to data and digital contents.

Bits of realities incorporated in data are both representations and rules (Humphreys 2018, p. 193). Data are metaphors for everything, but even their unterritorial nature reflects the absence of a dimension that is fundamental to legal thinking.

The so-called "tension axes" around which the law of data is built reflect the way by which the law reflects this absence (Della Morte 2018).

[11] Recital 39 Ai Act.

Regulatory models of data in different sectors, such as data protection, competition, and IP, reveal how data are a metaphor of a legal source. Not all legal spaces are occupied by data, but the law expects to occupy all spaces where data can transit. The issue is not merely theoretical or strictly legal. It is logical. If data are juridified, they are subject to space and time constraints and not to their own time and space. This represents a sort of drag effect.

What is then the place for data-driven law? Is it a completely online environment or is it an offline modality applied to the online world?

References

Abizadeh A (2016) Sovereign jurisdiction, territorial rights, and membership in Hobbes. In: Martinich A, Hoekstra K (eds) The Oxford handbook of Hobbes. Oxford University Press, pp 397–431

Amato G (2012) Il costituzionalismo oltre i confini dello Stato. In: Costituzionalismo e Globalizzazione, Annuario AIC 2012, p 9

Andronico A (2002) La decostruzione come metodo. Riflessi di Derrida nella teoria del diritto. Giuffrè

Besson S (2019) Why and what (state) jurisdiction. Legal plurality, individual equality and territorial legitimacy. In: Klabbers J, Palombella G (eds) The challenge of inter-legality. Cambridge University Press

Besson S (2011) Sovereignty, max Planck encyclopedias of international law. Oxford University Press. https://opil.ouplaw.com/display/10.1093/law:epil/9780199231690/law-9780199231690-e1472?prd=EPIL

Besson S (2012) The extraterritoriality of the European convention on human rights: why human rights depend on jurisdiction and what jurisdiction amounts to. Leiden J Int Law 25(4):857–884

Brunner O (1983 or.ed. Land und Herrschaft: Grundfragen der territorialen Verfassungsgeschichte Österreichs im Mittelalter, Rohrer, 1939), Terra e potere: strutture prestatuali e premoderne nella storia costituzionale dell'Austria. Giuffrè

Calabresi G, Melamed AD (1972) Property rules, liability rules, and inalienability: one view of the cathedral. Harv Law Rev 85:1092

Cannizzaro E (2020) La sovranità oltre lo stato. Il Mulino

Cassano (2005) Il pensiero meridiano (2nd edn, 2021). Laterza

Catanzariti M, Curtin D (2023) Beyond originator control of personal data in EU interoperable information systems: towards data originalism. In: Curtin D, Catanzariti M (eds) Data at the boundaries of law. Oxford University Press, pp 133–174

Cohen MR (1927) Property and sovereignty. Cornell Law Q:8–30

Corso L (2019) 'Vulnerabilità e concetto di diritto'. In Corso L, Talamo G (eds), *Vulnerabilità di fronte alle istituzioni. Vulnerabilità delle istituzioni*, Giappichelli, pp 3–14

Costa P (2013) Riflessioni su alcuni aspetti teorici della territorialitá. Costituzionalismo.it 1

Crawford K (2021) The atlas of AI. Yale University Press

Curtin D (2009) Executive Power in the European Union. Law, Practices and the Living Constitution. Oxford University Press

De Gregorio G, Ranchordas S (2020) Breaking down information silos with big data: a legal analysis of data sharing. In: Cannataci J, Falce V, Pollicino O (eds) New legal challenges of big data. Edward Elgar, pp 174–203

De Hert P (2023) Post-GDPR lawmaking in the digital data society: mimesis without integration. Topological understandings of twisted boundary setting in EU data protection law. In: Data at the boundaries of European law. Oxford University Press, pp 95–132

Del Vecchio A (2021) La legge nell'Oceano. Ugo Grozio e le origini dello spazio politico moderno. Il Mulino
Deleuze G, Guattari F (1997) Millepiani. Capitalismo e schizofrenia, sez. I, Rizoma, Castelvecchi
Della Morte G (2018) Big data e protezione internazionale dei diritti umani. Regole e conflitti. Editoriale Scientifica
Elden S (2013) The Birth of Territory. The University of Chicago Press
Fahey E (2022) The EU as a global digital actor: institutionalizing global data protection, trade, and cybersecurity. Hart
Ferrarese MR (2006) Diritto sconfinato: inventiva giuridica e spazi nel mondo globale. Laterza
Floridi L, Taddeo M (2014) The ethics of information warfare. Springer
Fricker KV (1901) Gebiet und Gebietshoheit. Mit einem Anhang: Vom Staatsgebiet. Verlag der H. Laupp'schen Buchhandlung. Tübingen
Galli C (2017) Introduzione. Schmitt e Hobbes: una strana coppia?, in Carl Schmitt. Sul Leviatano. Il Mulino.
Galli C (2019) Sovranità. Il Mulino
Gaudino U (2017) Carl Schmitt e la critica geografica contemporanea. Geopolitica. Rivista semestrale dell'Isag 7(2)
Giuffré M (2021) A functional-impact model of jurisdiction: extraterritoriality before the European court of human rights. Questions of International Law 82:53
Goldsmith J (1998) The internet and the abiding significance of territorial sovereignty. Indiana J Glob Leg Stud, p 475
Goldsmith J (1999) Against cyberanarchy. Univ Chic Law Rev 65:1250
Goldsmith J, Wu T (2006) Who controls the internet?: illusions of a borderless world, vol 2006. Oxford University Press
Greco T (2012) Diritto e legame sociale. Giappichelli
Grotius H (2012) In: Neff SC (ed) Hugo Grotius on the law of war and peace. Cambridge University Press
Hildebrandt M (2023) Boundary work between computational 'law' and 'law as-we-know-it'. In: Curtin D, Catanzariti M (eds) Data at the boundaries of EU law, pp 30–65
Hörnle J (2021) Internet jurisdiction: law and practice. Oxford University Press
Humphreys S (2018) Data. The given. In: Hohmann J, Joyce D (eds) International Law's object. Oxford University Press, pp 191–202
Jellinek G (1921) Allgemeine Rechtslehre. Springer Nature
Johnson DR, Post D (1996) Law and borders: the rise of law in cyberspace. Stanf Law Rev 48(5), pp. 1367–1402
Kalmo H, Skinner Q (2010) Sovereignty in fragments. The past, present and future of a contested concept. Cambridge University Press
Kelsen H (1934) Reine Rechtslehre. Einleitung in die rechtswissenschafttliche Problematik, Leizpig-Wien 1934, trad.it. Lineamenti di dottrina pura del diritto, Torino 1952, p 52
Kelsen H (1989, or.ed. Das Problem der Souveränität und die Theorie des Völkerrechts: Beitrag zu einer reinen Rechtslehre, Mohr Siebek, 1920), Il problema della sovranità e la teoria del diritto internazionale. Contributo per una teoria pura del diritto. Giuffrè
Koskenniemi M (1989) From apology to Utopia. The structure of international legal argument. Cambridge University Press, pp 241–242
Kosseff J (2019) The twenty six words that created the internet. Cornell University Press
Kuner C, Cate F, Lynskey O, Millard C, Ni Loideain N, Svantesson D (2018) An unstoppable force and an immoveable object? EU data protection law and national security. Int Data Priv Law 8(1):1–3
Land M (2013) Towards an international law of the internet. Harv Law J 54(2):393
Lindahl H (2018) Authority and the globalization of inclusion and exclusion. Oxford University Press, p 14
Maier C (2019) Dentro i confini. Territorio e potere dal 1500 a oggi. Einaudi
Malgieri G, Niklas J (2020) Vulnerable Data Subjects. Computer Law & Security Review 37:105415

Malgieri G (2023) Vulnerability and Data Protection Law. Oxford University Press
Mari L (2011) Ordinamento, localizzazione, uniformità: quale nomos, dopo Schmitt, per l'Europa? Teoria del diritto e dello Stato, 1-2/2011, pp 76 ss
Massa Pinto I (2023) Territorio e potere. In Enciclopedia del Diritto. I tematici, pp 1211–1232
Michetti M (2021) Organizzazione del potere e territorio. Legittimità dello Stato e livelli di governo. Giappichelli
Miller D (2012) Territorial rights: concept and justification. Polit Stud 60:252
Mezzadra S, Neilson B (2013) Border as Method or, the Multiplication of Labor. Duke University Press
Mitsilegas V, Moreno Lax V, Vavoula N (2020) Securitising Asylym Flows Deflec tion. Criminalization and Challenges for Human Rights, Brill Nijhoff, pp 1–5
Musiani F (2013) Network architecture as internet governance. Internet Policy Rev 2(4):2013. https://doi.org/10.14763/2013.4.208
Naef T (2023) Data Protection without Data Protectionism. The Right to Protection of Personal Data and Data Transfers in EU. Law and International Trade Law, Springer
Nitsch C (2012) Diritto e forza nella comunità degli stati. Studi su Hans Kelsen e la teoria del diritto internazionale. Satura Editrice
Nobili Schiera G (2015) A proposito di una traduzione di un'opera recente di Otto Brunner. Scienza e politica XXVII:221–237
Núñez JE (2020) Territorial disputes and state sovereignty: international law and politics. Routledge
Obendiek AS (2023) Data governance: value orders and jurisdictional conflicts. Oxford University Press
Pennisi C (1990) La costruzione sociologica del fenomeno giuridico. Giuffrè
Pennisi C (1997) Istituzioni e cultura giuridica. I procedimenti come strutture di comunicazione, Giappichelli
Pino G (2003) Il diritto all'identità personale. Interpretazione costituzionale e creatività giurisprudenziale, Il Mulino
Pistor K (2019) The Code of Capital. How the Law Creates Wealth and Inequality. Princeton University Press
Pupolizio I (2019) Pubblico e privato. Teoria e storia di una grande dicotomia, Giappichelli
Polcák R, Svantesson DJB (2017) Information sovereignty. Data privacy, sovereign powers and the rule of law. Edward Elgar
Preterossi G (2022) Teologia politica e diritto, Laterza
Riccobono F (2017) Antikelsenismo italiano, Giappichelli
Reed C, Murray A (2018) Rethinking the jurisprudence of cyberspace. Edward Elgar
Roberts H, Cowls J, Casolari F, Morley J, Taddeo M, Floridi L (2021) Safeguarding European values with digital sovereignty: an analysis of statements and policies. Internet Policy Rev 10(3). https://doi.org/10.14763/2021.3.1575
Romano S (2018) L'ordinamento giuridico. Quodlibet
Ruschi F (2012) La terra, il mare, il diritto secondo Carl Schmitt. Giappichelli
Ruschi F (2019) Spazio. La questione del territorio statale. In: Andronico A, Greco T, Macioce F (eds) Dimensioni del diritto. Giappichelli, pp 345–368
Ryngaert C (2015) Jurisdiction in international law. Oxford University Press
Ryngaert C, Zoetekouw M (2014) The end of territory? The re-emergence of community as a principle of jurisdictional order in the internet era. In: Kohl U (ed) The net and the nation state: multidisciplinary perspectives on the internet governance, pp 185–201
Sassen S (2006) Territory, authority, rights: from medieval to global assemblages. Princeton University Press
Scaccia G (2017) Il territorio fra sovranità statale e globalizzazione dello spazio economico, 3, rivistaaic.it
Scalone A (2017) Schmitt's theory of Grossraum: a post-statal perspective? Scienza&Politica XXIV(56):179–205

Scheinin M (2013) Just another word?: jurisdiction in the roadmaps of state responsibilities and human rights. In: Langford M, Vandenhole W, Scheinin M, Van Genugten W (eds) Global justice, state duties: the extraterritorial scope of economic, social, and cultural rights in international law. Cambridge University Press, pp 212–232

Schiavello A (2023) Conoscere il diritto. Mucchi

Schmitt C (1972a) Definizione della sovranità. In: Miglio G, Schiera P (eds) Le categorie del politico. Saggi di teoria politica. Il Mulino

Schmitt C (1972b) Il concetto di 'politico'. In: Miglio G, Schiera P (eds) Le categorie del politico. Saggi di teoria politica. Il Mulino

Schmitt C (1991, or. ed. Der nomos der erde im Völkerrecht des Jus Publicum Europaeum 1950), Il nomos della terra nel diritto internazionale dello "ius publicum europaeum". Il Mulino

Schmitt C (2005) Teoria del partigiano. Integrazione al concetto del politico. Adelphi

Svantesson DJ (2015) A jurisprudential justification for extraterritoriality in (private) international law. Santa Clara J Int Law 13(2):518–571

Svantesson, D. J. (2017), Solving the internet jurisdictional Puzzle. Oxford University Press

Tucker A, De Bellis DP, Puydt PE (2017) Panarchy: political theories of non-territorial states. Routledge

Weinzierl J (2021) Territoriality beyond the state: the EU's territorial claims and the search for their legitimacy. German Law J 22:650–672

Woods AK (2016) Against data exceptionalism. Stanford Law Rev 68:729

Woods AK (2018) Litigating data sovereignty. Yale Law J 128:328

Wu TS (1997) Cyberspace sovereignty? The internet and the international system. Harv J Law Technol 10(3):648

Zeno-Zencovich V (2016) Intorno alla decisione nel caso Schrems: la sovranità digitale e il governo internazionale delle reti di telecomunicazione. Il diritto dell'informazione e dell'informatica 31:683–696

Zolo D (2007) Kelsen: la pace internazionale attraverso il diritto internazionale. Jura Gentium. Rivista di filosofia del diritto internazionale e di politica globale. https://www.juragentium.org/topics/thil/it/kelsen.htm

Chapter 3
The Off-line Juridification of an On-line Space

3.1 What Cables Stand for?

The legal rationale surrounding sovereign powers has been constructed to replicate the offline world.

The different rationality of the law and the technique to recenter the relation "ought/be" has represented a general justification having relevance within a given space. Territoriality had the function of setting up those limits, recentering the relationship between facts and rules. It is not certainly a novelty for the law to face challenging objects such as data in our case to regulate shifting landscapes. Data, however, present the peculiarity of being covered by the common legal mechanisms related to jurisdictional claims only if data itself manages to be subject to a legal fiction. Considering data as a physical object—and not according to its immaterial and intangible nature—represents an issue as far as the fiction of physicality does not manage to overcome the potential of its nature.

In other words, even though the law produces legal fictions, in the case of data, legal fiction cannot completely embrace the functioning of data. As correctly pointed out by Julie Cohen, "In their different ways, both networked media infrastructures and legal institutions sit between truth and power. They can be means for resisting domination or vehicles for embedding it, but even that formulation is too simple. Through their capacities to authorize, channel, and modulate information flows and behavior patterns, code and law *mediate* between truth and power. The terms of the dialogue are shaped by the technological and institutional settlements that emerge as struggles to shape the emerging networked world wind their way toward resolution" (Cohen 2021, p. 5).

Reasserting territorial state control (Daskal 2020, p. 956) gives the apparency to limit the expansion of networked infrastructures, but the borderless nature of data is stronger than territorial constraints. Why is territoriality still a rationale for digital law? If we look at the practice of human rights, territory is a way to exert

M. Catanzariti, *Disconnecting Sovereignty*, Law, Governance and Technology Series 65, https://doi.org/10.1007/978-3-031-60734-9_3

responsibility and imputability: "Jurisdiction" under Article 1 is a threshold criterion. The exercise of jurisdiction is a necessary condition for a contracting state to be held responsible for acts or omissions imputable to it that give rise to an allegation of the infringement of rights and freedoms set forth in the European Convention (§ 74, see Ilaşcu and Others v. Moldova and Russia [GC], no. 48787/99, § 311, ECHR 2004-VII).

Is physical infrastructure adequate to incorporate and explicate the relationships arising from data?

Physical control over the network and the internet infrastructure that is located within states' borders is the functional equivalent pattern of the principle of territoriality in the context of data governance (Woods 2018, p. 361). As data per se is nonterritorial, regulating data flows needs a connection with infrastructure where data lie. Most of the controversies on the regulation of interconnected data flows are based on the regulation of infrastructures (Zeno-Zencovich 2016, p. 683). However, unlike a pure physical infrastructure, data infrastructure is made of different components: data assets, such as datasets, identifiers, and registers; standards and technologies used to provide access to data assets; policies that inform the use and management of data assets and the data infrastructure itself; organizations that govern the data infrastructure; targeted subjects involved in contributing to or maintaining it; and those who are impacted by decisions that are made using it.

The physical component of infrastructures incorporates data. Network infrastructures include the hardware and software resources of an entire network that enable network connectivity, communication, and management of an enterprise network. It is the physical equipment (hardware) and the software applications that support the entire lifecycle of technologies.

3.1.1 *Data Between Territories*

The centrality of territory in data governance currently informs two different models: digital sovereignty, which implies keeping and storing data domestically, and extraterritoriality, which envisages the exercise of state sovereignty over data worldwide (Christakis 2020, pp. 22, 52). In both models, territory acts as a landmark concept: the former uses technology to replicate physical territories through digital borders (for example, local storage and processing requirements and geo-blocking), whereas the latter seeks to escape physical territory by expanding its legal notion (for instance, extraterritorial orders and global injunctions). Both models are the expression of a will to expand the influence of territorial states, either by attracting data to their territories (for example, by requiring companies to store, process and copy data exclusively on servers located within the national borders) or by expanding their territories in order to reach data outside borders (for example, by granting the public and private sector access to data worldwide). In contrast to existing studies, I accept that data is nonterritorial in the sense that its legal status is not inherently dependent on connecting territorial factors to the physical infrastructures of data cables.

This position supports the idea that inevitably, sovereignty needs to disconnect from physicality to pursue its objectives in a field such as regulation of data that is substantially not based on physical connection.[1] This aspect is common to all areas of sectoral legislation—such as data protection, intellectual property, telecommunications and infrastructures, and regulation of digital contents. Regardless of the fact that the substantive core of rights in such situations changes, what is relevant to note is that data would deserve regulation only in relation to its function. The functional approach may better address the purpose of data usage and the justification of the competence over certain sector data.

Once sovereignty is established, sovereign claims can also perform without some factors that justify their effectiveness in relation to a precise purpose. Because justification is generally provided *ex post* throughout the exercise of a claim, the main function of sovereignty is ensured by the fact that functional factors can be used as a shorthand to allow its function.

This functional approach is generally accepted in the context of human rights protection but not as regards the general exercise of states' jurisdiction, which is predominantly based on the linkage with territoriality.

Conversely, what should be relevant in light of a functional approach is the normative relationship that unites state parties to rights holders. What is worth noting is that, however, the concept of state jurisdiction under domestic law may not necessarily overlap with the concept of jurisdiction under human rights' international law (Besson 2012, p. 869). One thing is thinking that data vehiculates some human rights that can be protected universally; one thing is to locate data as an object of jurisdictional claims.

The borderless nature of data implies the fact that even digital rights—those deriving from the regulation of data flows—should not have a domestic scope of application but rather a global scope (Moreno Lax 2020, p. 385). In the context of human rights protection, for instance, extraterritorial claims may or may not follow a functional approach based on situational control or in general forms of control other than merely territorial or personal control; however, jurisdiction always realizes the "sovereignty-authority nexus" that is normative (Moreno Lax 2020, p. 396). In any event, jurisdiction is generally related not only to the scope of courts' judgement but also to "the spaces in which a country can legislate and enforce its own laws and decisions" (Michaels 2017). However, state jurisdictional claims over data cannot always be justified by the universal character of human rights protection or by the unterritorial nature of data. These nuances depend on what data stands, e.g., the semantic potential of data. Even sectoral legislation on data is inspired by the contents that data represent. What data stands for informs the logic of the need for

---

[1] A research strand on digital disconnection is recently emerging. Elaborating on it, we propose a theory of sovereignty that adapts to digital objects paradoxically in a disconnected manner to exert resistance. Legal performative forms have the ability to connect or disconnect from some variables to pursue their goals. See Lomborg and Ytre-Arne (2021), p. 1529.

regulation. Paying attention to this means abandoning common places based on the alleged mismatch between digital regulation and the physical limitations of space because of predefined ideas. The need for physicality is equal to the counterneed to exceed the nonphysical space. *Extraterritorium* has always been translated into extraterritorial obligations as a theoretical dimension of the comfort zone both for states and for individuals who have been used for exceptional uses, although very limited (Altwicker 2020, p. 234; Benton 2010, p. 222; Tilmann 2020). In the Grotian perspective, the effectiveness of transnational natural rights that are disentangled by the territory of a state is symmetrical to the possibility of state agents being "extra-territorial" in their immunity (Hildebrandt 2013, p. 196). However, it is worth noting that the dynamics of the law surrounding territory are related to the logic of inclusion and exclusion with respect to which jurisdictional claims become measurable throughout territorial accumulation. Territory depicts the area of possible and concrete power that is easier to justify (Del Vecchio 2021). Something very important should be specified. Even Grotius is convinced that the modality to exert sovereignty does not differ on the land and on the sea: "sovereignty over a part of the sea is acquired in the same way as sovereignty elsewhere, that is … through the instrumentality of persons and territory" (Grotius 2012, p. 112).

Grotius's theorization of mare liberum as global law, however, precisely represents the test case for Schmittian land law, i.e., the conquest of the territories delimiting it and the need for border stabilization (Grotius 2012, pp. 105–115). This historical need determined the transition to the space of states, inaugurated by the Peace of Westphalia, which sanctioned the end of religious disputes as a cause of war and the recognition of an international system based on the autonomy and equality of states.

The use of territorial resources is certainly instrumental to the state's policy of self-assertion and expansion. Indeed, profound changes in our concept of territory usually bring fundamental political and economic changes and are also accompanied by changes in the scientific and philosophical spatial and temporal concepts (Maier 2019, p. 16). Depending on how one imagines space, therefore, the possibilities of coexistence within it change completely.

Sovereignty according to Ferrajoli (Ferrajoli 1997) has a natural law origin, as it serves to satisfy a practical need: that of providing a legal foundation for the conquest of the New World. The three main ideas of Francisco de Vitoria's doctrine of sovereignty, that of the equality of states, the affirmation of a set of sovereign natural rights, and finally the theory of war as sanction, all manifest an aporia according to Ferrajoli. However, they, even in their ambivalence, have been enormously successful because they have been used as doctrines of legitimation of existing arrangements. De Vitoria equates states with orders by arguing that civil laws obligate legislators and especially kings. The failure of this idea was caused by the antinomy, which soon proved insoluble, between the forms historically assumed by the sovereignty of states and the idea of their subjection to law. First, the idea of the societas gentium as a community of free and independent peoples but subject to law entered into crisis. In particular, the coverage of conquerors' interests behind "values" proclaimed as universal: first the mission of evangelization, then the conquest. The ius communicationis and ius commercii theorized by Francisco de Vitoria as natural rights opened the path to the "mission of civilization" during the colonial era, up to today's globalization of "Western values". In the beginning, the exercise of sovereignty is expressed in the conquest of territories to which the categories of private law apply (the so-called inventio): *sui juris, esse suae potestatis, superanus or summa potestas* (De Vitoria 2005). However, sovereignty soon no longer needs the additional justification of property and becomes an autonomous concept related to the unity of the nation-state.

If territoriality is therefore the only modality consecrated also by international law, the existence and subsistence of states is even more dependent on the function that the use of this concept shall ensure. Where territory can no longer represent the purpose of regulated conflict between states, even security once offered by territory becomes precarious everywhere, and the impression is that it can only be maintained by applying constant surveillance (Maier 2019, p. 3).

It is then visible how the failures produced by the loss of significance of territoriality affect all concepts used to trigger its overuse, such as, for example, securitization and surveillance in this case.

This urgently shows the clash between a territory that is congruent with its measurable contents throughout the algebraic sum of parts and a territory materially limited but traversed by unlimited intangible flows. To what extent can the West's most deeply rooted architecture resist in an era defined as post-territorial (Praet 2010, p. 169), in which flows of all kinds—people or things—are in stark contrast to the finitude of space?

If, therefore, the acquisition of territory has, up to a certain historical phase, been the most important instrument for rationalizing sovereign power, its representative capacity has become completely permeable to all that is contrary to its logic.

Power relations are no longer intelligible only by means of a horizontal line demarcating an inside versus an outside but can be understood and managed according to an acentric, non-hierarchical rhizomatic logic that Deleuze and Guattari, for example, attempted to neutralize through the double bind of deterritorialization and reterritorialization and that Maier reproposes as a possible reconfiguration of space through the politics of filling space with infrastructures (Deleuze and Guattari 1997). Applying this reasoning in the data field means coupling territory with infrastructures that are either physical or digital where data can pass through. Very often, for instance, when territory has proven inadequate, the answer has been the use of extraterritoriality, i.e., the expansion of certain territorial prerogatives outside the territory, i.e., onto other territories. Faced with the well-known question of the need to develop global spaces for global phenomena, forms of adjudication nevertheless follow regulatory models that hinge on the territory circumscribed and limited by borders. Flows make use of space by dilating and shrinking it. Flows of any kind—migratory and digital—are representative forms of reality that increasingly come into conflict with the legal foundation of sovereignty and in relation to which spatiality becomes a field of interaction that is no longer objectively valid for providing security and peace. In such an architecture, the sedentary space is striped, by walls, fences and paths between fences, while nomadic space is smooth, marked only by strokes that erase and move with the journey (Deleuze and Guattari 1997, p. 530).

3.1.2 Data as the Wealth of Nations

Territorial relevance has a large impact on the idea of belonging. To whom belongs data after all? This misleading question, together with the pervasive character of territorial relevance, draws the practices of data regulation along some tensions, basically represented by this option: data belong to the state as the "owner" of the territory where cables lie or to companies that generate that data or build the hardware where data are stored. Interestingly Arash Abizadeh pointed out that territory is not necessarily related to sovereignty. The Lockean model grounds jurisdictional authority in private dominion over things, while the Hobbesian model derives property rights from sovereign authority. Jurisdictional authority relies on the object of proprietary ownership: the state's territorial rights are held *in rem* against *all* persons (Abizadeh 2016, p. 397).

A good starting point to approach this very long-lasting controversial debate would be reformulating the question into this. What is the effect of the misuse of territory? Why should territory be taken seriously? Is it possible to disconnect sovereignty from territory and how?

Data reshapes the law because the legal fiction of territorial continuity cannot entirely cover digital controversies. Sovereignty goes hand in hand with data as far as it does not disrupt it.

However, there are advanced technologies such as blockchain, for example, that completely avoid linkage with territory. Commentators have talked in terms of "alegality" because of the lack of connection with territory (De Filippi et al. 2022, p. 358) and "interlegality" referring to regimes that tascend national sovereignty (Klabbers and Palombella 2019, p. 1; Palombella 2021). The weak connection of blockchain technologies with territory may certainly enhance elusive mechanisms but cannot ground the theoretical assumption that blockchain is unrelevant to the law because of this. Our claim does not go in this direction. The law has been traditionally based on territory but can also draw its legitimacy from other factors if territory is no longer representative of factual linkages, as in the case of data. Legitimizing discourses on grey zones without legal constraints does not solve the issues at stake and is theoretically misleading, as all phenomena in order to legally exist need to be regulated regarding the effects they produce.

Data governance is quintessential to the wealth of nations because of its capacity to be commodified. Not only the possibility to pay with personal data as contractual counterperformance (Metzger 2017; De Franceschi 2021) but also the entire datafication of the world and relationships.

The possibility of reducing all relationships to data flows determines a shift of representative forms towards new meanings and contexts of relevance. This phenomenon is represented by emerging transitioning rights that testify to two additional reflexive phenomena: language in transition and law in transition. On the one hand, legal language tries to keep pace with change by adding new meanings that catalyze emerging trends, uses and legal concepts (for example, smart contracts).

For example, personal data can be used for exchanging digital content. Certain apps advertise their users about the possibility of retaking control over their personal data and prompt individuals to have a cut of the sale of their personal data. However, the personal data economy is presented as the possibility for users to obtain value from their data in response to changes in the free or discounted provision of digital services. This phenomenon is amplified by some cognitive distortions: availability cascades, consisting of a self-growing process by which the collective trust in something becomes stronger as much it is confirmed by society; bandwagon effect; fear of missing out; fears of missing out; anchoring/framing; and herd behavior (Malgieri and Custers 2018, p. 289).

Among the pricing factors, we count reuse, discretion in attributing value, completeness, accuracy, identifiability, and calculation of infringements. In certain cases, revenues may also depend upon data assets appropriated through ubiquitous automated operations that may produce surveillance assets (Sartor and Lagioia 2020; Sartor 2015).

This is made possible by two factors: the ownership of the means of behavioral modification and the unilateral declaration that accumulates surveillance assets throughout hyperscale to avoid lack of reciprocity and informational asymmetry. However, in Europe, the legal basis for the possibility of deploying data as a counterperformance is controversial. While the General Data Protection Regulation (GDPR) provides that personal data cannot be considered *a counterperformance* where data processing is necessary for the execution of a contract in which the data subject is not a contractual party, the Directive on certain aspects concerning contracts for the supply of digital content (Directive EU 770/2019, DCSD) of December 2015 covers all cases in which service providers use personal data of consumers as a basis for the refunding of its service. According to DSCD, only data processed to comply with a legal obligation cannot be used as counterperformance.

However, goods with digital elements are excluded from the application of DSCD because to them, the Sale of Goods Directive (Directive EU 2019/771) applies. They can be defined as goods that incorporate or are interconnected with digital content or a digital service in such a way that the absence of that digital content or digital service would prevent the goods from performing their functions (Recital 21). Regarding location data, IoT devices rely on them to properly function, but the consumer protection layer of the DCSC/SGD does not apply to the cases where there is no transfer of ownership for a price.

A frequent example of data used as contractual counterperformance is location data that provide the basis for mobility data and are included in the range of personal data (Efroni 2020, p. 257). Sharing location data can sensitively enhance the technological performance of devices.[2]

---

[2] The e-privacy Directive defines location data as 'data processed in an electronic communications network or by an electronic communications service, indicating the geographic position of the

Although, for example, Art. 7 GDPR provides a bundling prohibition stating that when assessing whether consent is freely given, the utmost account shall be taken whether, inter alia, the performance of a contract, including the provision of a service, is conditional on consent to the processing of personal data that is not necessary for the performance of that contract. However, once an individual pays with data—personal or nonpersonal pursuant to Directive 770/2019—she can hardly withdraw her consent freely (Rodotà 2018, or. ed. 1973, p. 43; Rodotà 1995, pp. 41–100).

3.2 Controlling Data Flows: Data as Fictitious Commodities?

The commodification of reality is exacerbated by the bulk collection for differentiated usages. Data represent the most mimetic form of economy and knowledge. In the context of information-based economies, data and other commodities share the possibility of being extracted to produce data. However, there are differences between basic goods and data. Data extraction serves to identify behavioral trends and gain insights about the people under study. Of course, data commodities are not immediately usable and tradable, as they need to be analysed with cutting-edge technologies. They can be considered valuable data-based objects only as far as they are embedded in digital ecosystems, including infrastructures. As a commodity, data can be the object of jurisdiction but also in search of jurisdiction. In particular, the mimetic capacity of data to represent all dimensions of life and existence—including nature, money and labor—makes it possible to handle them differently according to different uses. The capacity of the law to differentiate its objects addresses data always based on its capacity to be a metaphor of existing legal categories. If data is linkable to a legal category in the way by which they are deployed, then it is easier to expand the scope of the law by approximation. In practical terms, this means that if data is attached to the context of goods and services offered within a relevant market, as is the case of data protection in the EU, then the linkage produced by data with some activities is related to the concept of establishing an enterprise for which what can be done with those data becomes relevant from a legal perspective. In the field of IP, for instance, nonpersonal data can be treated as a good when it gains a representative capacity that reaches the status of property rights for which the law provides a precise taxonomy and a limited number. In the field of health data sharing for research purposes, data can be used and reused for reasons

terminal equipment of a user of a publicly available electronic communications service'. Recital of this Directive includes as examples of location data those related to the latitude, longitude and altitude of the user's terminal equipment, to the direction of travel, to the level of accuracy of the location information, to the identification of the network cell in which the terminal equipment is located at a certain point in time and to the time the location information was recorded (emphasis added).

of public interest as a public good, and the way by which the law interacts with data is based on the lawfulness of the processing.

How territorial connections can shape legal culture and economic strategies much depends on the fact that territory has traditionally represented a space for wealth's production (Celata 2009; Bathelt et al. 2011) where means of power produce and enhance power. This mechanism has inspired the idea of data spaces as functional spaces for data regulation and data sharing to enhance the market's possibilities crossing sectoral regulation.

3.2.1 No-Rights to Data?

Data can represent different things depending on the legal status they have. If data are useful to represent certain phenomena or facts, this means that data can reach all points of the planet in a very limited time. At the same time, the legal nature of data draws different realities according to what data may represent.

Law production by data may give rise to the creation of digital rights. This depends on whether data represent a given content to be protected—such as the case of personal information or digital contents—or a communicative structure—for example, an algorithmic code.

One of the main authors who has engaged in the attempt to enlarge the conceptualization of the meanings of property is in the American context Paul Schwartz, considering property as "*any interest in an object, whether tangible or intangible, that is enforceable against the* world" (Schwartz 2003, p. 2058). The main three arguments for justifying a property right on data are the following: liability regimes do not protect users as well as property rights and do not create incentives (Bergelson 2003, p. 379); data property would enhance the development of technologies, as companies that use that data would have an incentive to respect and enhance the protection of privacy so they could be considered reliable in such business. This positive externality would benefit privacy regulation in general (Lessig 2002, p. 247); property rights have an *erga omnes* effect and are hence better legal tools. Unlike liability rules, property rights allow data holders to protect their data against everyone. In contrast, the most relevant grounds for opposing such construction are the following: ownership rights may increase data fragmentation and prevent the realization of economies of scope due to high transaction costs (Duch-Brown et al. 2017); they cannot play an adequate function in protecting privacy; on the side of individuals, a right on property does not add anything as they do not have either commercial powers vis-à-vis companies or political and legal powers vis-à-vis states; and licensing all personal data is possible only in the field of commercial transactions and is costly and time-consuming (Prins 2006, pp. 247–248; Poullet 1990, p. 161). Recognizing any property right needs an economic justification as revenues through sales in the case of intellectual property, whose function is to permit the storage of value over time and allowing durable investments. In the field of law enforcement, any public interest in sharing data is hardly justifiable as a property right; conversely, the right to data protection has never been defined as data ownership but rather as the right to control one's own data flows to ensure informational self-determination (Wenderhost 2017, p. 327). Scholars argue that the creation of a new system of data ownership is not advisable, as factual control of data supported by technical protection measures allows data holders to exclude third parties or charge them a price for making data available (Stepanov 2020, p. 65).[3] One thing is in fact that data are non-rival in consumption; another is to postulate that digital infrastructure should be non-excludable. They also argue that there is no economic justification for the creation of a new system of data ownership based on the incentive argument (Drexl 2017a, p. 223). Others suggest that the incentive function may be less important for scenarios where data can be produced at virtually zero marginal cost. In this light, ownership can only protect against commercial infringements, not against noncommercial reuse of the data. This is the reason why there has been an attempt to define a right as much as possible tailored to an overarching definition of property (Purtova 2009b, p. 507). In fact, she argues that by adjusting some elements of property rights, such as the commercialization of data, it is possible to create valuable allocative choices in terms of rights.[4] In this direction, for example, the statutory system in the UK does not provide any real ownership of information but rather monopoly rights on the reproduction and exploitation of information. Interestingly, criminal law provides for a notion of "stolen information" that recalls the idea that something that was of someone at a certain moment it is no longer available.[5] Nonetheless, in the European context, it is not immediate to think in terms of commercial appropriation of personal data, as giving an economic value to attributes of personality is considered against dignity (Whitman 2004, p. 1151). Two are the main arguments surrounding this idea: the right to personal data protection is a personality right that cannot be "ownable"; it is also a fundamental right that is not compatible with any other exclusive right over data. Individuals' right to data protection means that they have the right to control their data flow, e.g., information relied on them. They do not own data containing that

---

[3] According to Stepanov, the exclusion of third parties consist of (1) Right to exclusive possession; (2) The right to personal use and enjoyment; (3) The right to manage use by others; (4) The right to the income from use by others; (5) The right to the capital value, including alienation, consumption, waste, or destruction; (6) The right to security (that is, immunity from expropriation); (7) The power of transmissibility by gift, devise, or descent; (8) The lack of any term on these rights; (9) The duty to refrain from using the object in ways that harm others; (10) The liability to execution for repayment of debts; and (11) Residual rights on the reversion of lapsed ownership rights held by others.

[4] Purtova (2009a), pp. 225–243: "*In case of a mere property, "the idea of property comprises the notion that something that pertains to a person is, maybe within drastic limits, his to use as he pleases and therefore his to permit others to use gratuitously or for exchanged favours. ... It embraces some open-ended set of use-privileges and some open-ended set of powers of control over uses made by others." That has also been referred to as erga omnes effect or trespassory rule*".

[5] See https://ec.europa.eu/digital-single-market/en/news/study-emerging-issues-data-ownership-interoperability-re-usability-and-access-data-and (25th April 2018).

information (Drexl 2017a, p. 257).[6] IP scholars use to distinguish the semantic level of information to indicate what is the object of a property right: the object of a property right is the content of information to be distinguished from its embodiment (syntactic level). Personal data are the object of an explicit allocative choice that protects identified or identifiable natural persons to whom information refers from unlawful external interferences, not property. The issue is that data cannot be handled as commodities. The nature of data protection as a fundamental right has been deeply embedded in European culture. Rec. 1 of the GDPR provides that "*The protection of natural persons in relation to the processing of personal data is a fundamental right*".

Legal understanding assumes a different and more precise notion of ownership, as generally owning a certain good implies that nobody else can own that good at the same time; that not everything is "ownable" but only certain goods that are generally tangible; that only a limited number of property rights exists (*numerus clausus*); and even according to a legal basis, new property rights can be created only if they fit in that limited number. Against the notion of digital property, the main arguments stress that factual control is relevant when referring to tangible resources. The non-rivalrous nature of immaterial entities such as data is understood as the justification for the *numerus clausus*. Non-rivalrous nature means that an actor can have something at disposal for use, while another actor has without it costing me any of the original good. Furthermore, the adjective "personal" is a dynamic concept: what is today not personal data could be considered in the near future to be personal data if changes mean that it can be used to identify an individual. Last but not least, it is not conceivable in most of the cases a data possession, as it is not possible to provide the evidence of de facto control. The case of data creates troubles in the use of the notion, at least because it is necessary to ask whether data are goods; if yes, what kind of goods they are; and if they are ownable; which kind of advantages does the recognition of data ownership produce for individuals or for the state? Are there potential disadvantages? Using the term ownership as applied to data, one may encounter first of all problems in the definition; in the strict term, it refers to a specific exclusive right over something (*res*), which includes any form of own disposal and excludes any form of use by third parties. Most legal systems exclude the notion of ownership for intangible goods such as digital data, as the right of disposal in an absolute manner is referred to as physical goods (Barbero 2017). German legal authors have proposed to accept the concept of "data property" (*Dateneigentum*) by an analogy to "property of things" (*Sacheigentum*) (Hoeren 2019), arguing that granting immediate relief to the victims of unlawful interference with personality on the basis of the general clause of tort can improperly use the notion of property of the name or of the image. The problem is not showing that commercial appropriation of personal data is not legitimate but rather that if a property right on data is recognized, it is not allowed to provide for different entitlement regimes or

[6] Drexl (2017b), p. 267: "Protection of personal data is neither vested in the natural person for economic purposes, nor is it an absolute right. Personal data protection does not allocate economic value".

restrictions depending on the actors involved. The use of "*personal data cannot be viewed in the isolated perspective of one single piece of information to be used by one organization for a very specific* purpose" (Prins 2006, p. 256). Depending on the different options available—such as, for example, no exclusive rights on data; exclusive control on data and non-consensual access regime; nonexclusive control on data and consensual access regime—it must be borne in mind that if we engage with the idea of data property, so that rules should be equal for all players, as property does not provide for subjective limitations of rights. The issue of data ownership can be built on top-down theories that emphasize the initial constitutive moment in the collection of personal data or on bottom-up theories that focus on the legal creation of certain rights. Every subsequent transfer would produce derivative rights of property according to the one who possesses it for the first time. Recently, an interesting debate has been generated across Europe approaching the idea of data property in the digital market, which recalls some ideas arising beyond the Atlantic (Litman 2000, p. 1286; Samuelson 2000, pp. 1136–1146).

Many voices among scholars and stakeholders around Europe share the idea of dismissing such an operative solution, as there are studies showing the scarce capacity of ownership to represent a valuable operative solution for regulating data flows. Amongst the possible risks, it is to mention the creation of monopolies for the concentration of data in the hands of large private companies, particular public policy issues to be pursued, and the need for economic value to justify a proprietary asset.

3.2.2 Data Governance and Data Jurisdiction

The international scholarship agrees to point out that "it is common to identify a tension between legal plurality and the concept of jurisdiction, understood for now to mean the right or power to enact, enforce or adjudicate law. More specifically, the legal order whose jurisdiction can be questioned by legal plurality is presumably one that is comprehensive in scope or, at least, exclusive in its power to rule" (Besson 2019, p. 94). According to Besson, this is because the concept of jurisdiction is normally associated with the state's prerogatives that are personally and spatially limited. However, changing phenomena have determined important paradigm shifts. First, nonterritorialized regulatory forms; overterritorialized through the extraterritorial reach of domestic jurisdictions or the creation of large "legal ensembles like the EU". A very clear definition of the distinction between sovereignty and jurisdiction is that "sovereignty describes the power to rule, whereas jurisdiction describes the authority of a state to rule" (Hörnle 2021, p. 9).

In the long run, digitalization has then determined a separation between governance and jurisdiction; despite having different scopes, they could overlap.

While data governance refers to the use of communication and information technologies to create communication channels putting specific stakeholders in contact with the political and institutional world, data jurisdiction refers to the power to adjudicate rights related to data flows.

Data governance is then generally a borderless concept because it is the expression of power relations that are not typically hierarchical but also between cooperatives between public and private actors. Data jurisdiction instead always involves a vertical dimension within which the power of a state is exerted over many relations.

One of the most useful definitions of data governance describes it as a "structure of global governance through which some states govern transboundary markets – an often-oligarchical structure in which a few powerful countries wield the capacity to set and implement rules" (Krisch 2022, p. 482).

As pointed out by Besson, "The legal orders whose norms may be overlapping in the domestic order, may range from infranational orders (e.g., the law of federated entities, indigenous law or religious law) to transnational orders (e.g., *lex mercatoria* or *lex electronica*), international orders (e.g., international criminal law, international trade law or United Nations [UN] law), supranational orders (e.g., European Union [EU] law) or even other foreign domestic orders (e.g., foreign tax, competition or environmental law)" (Besson 2019, p. 93).

The creation of digital borders has been a means to enhance the securitization of physical territory through advanced technologies, but this usage has affected all orders together. For example, if we look at the European order, the effects produced by the technologization of borders are intuitive because European borders overlap with the national borders of some member states. There are many other examples in the field (Mezzadra - Neilson 2013).

Rules and control over data management should circulate along with data. Jurisdiction must go hand in hand with governance in this respect. However, reality shows that data sharing considerably relies on power relationships among authorities and thus requires rules of sharing and usage to prevent misuses or appropriation of data. Datafication of persons and life should comply with a model that differentiates between the legal status of data as well as its format—whether it is relevant according to the contents it vehiculates or to its representative potential. Governance for the digital sphere requires a nonterritorial dimension because territory does not represent the salient aspect in relation to data. For example, Art. 32 COE Convention of Cybercrime Data represents a measure to assess power in the capability to control and manage metaphors of goods and knowledge. The two common regulatory options to achieve this objective are, on the one hand, offering competitive technologies to emerging markets, basically requiring companies to locate data within the premises of hosting the Beijing effect; on the other hand, regulating digital markets by imposing companies compliance with standards of protection (Brussels effect). In both cases, the exportation of a cultural model is the common aspect between the forms of technological or legal imperialism. Both models present critical aspects (Fahey 2022), but the technological trigger is definitely based on an on/off process by which, once a solution is operationally undertaken, the process cannot be interrupted unless the objective is not achieved. Legal design is instead not sufficient to nuance the effect of technological imperialism, which can also be defined as data production by law.

The factors that affect this process are various and blurred purposes and scopes of data management. On the one hand, large-scale data gathering is becoming an essential way to access and process public sector data on a regular basis. On the other hand, law enforcement authorities are increasingly processing personal data during investigations in a manner that becomes most relevant in scope if considering the targeted individuals involved in criminal proceedings. This then represents a trend that blurs together operational, technical, and informal aspects of the way by which law enforcement authorities use enormous amounts of data that they have at their disposal in one way or another. The use of data to conduct investigations, detection and prosecution of crimes completely disrupts the criminal categories related to evidence that are peculiar to each national legal system. The lack of trust depends on the fact that data are considered proprietary assets. Dealing with data, it is worth imagining a model of sovereignty that can be tailored to different regulatory sectors and profits from the flexible format as well as from the flexible legal status of data. Then, of course it is to be borne in mind with kind of data we deal with.

3.3 Towards a Legal Status of Data

Pursuant to the definitions provided by the Data Governance Act and Data Act, data gained their autonomous legal definition as "any digital representation of acts, facts or information and any compilation of such acts, facts or information, including in the form of sound, visual or audio-visual recording". Data are then powerful because they manage to represent interconnected information, but in Europe, the right to data is generally excluded. Only a *sui generis* right to database has been enshrined in the Database Directive for the producer who makes an investment in the collection of data. The Database Directive[7] (96/9/EC) defines two different regimes that are exceptions to this general principle: copyright, dedicated to databases that 'by reason of the selection or arrangement of their contents … constitute the author's own intellectual creation';[8] and *sui generis* right, which assigns to 'the maker of a database which shows that there has been qualitatively and/or quantitatively a substantial investment in either the obtaining, verification or presentation of the contents' the right 'to prevent extraction and/or reutilization of the whole or of a substantial part, evaluated qualitatively and/or quantitatively, of the contents of that database'.[9] As we can read in the Executive Summary of the Data Act "The Court of Justice of the European Union has sharpened the understanding of substantial investments in a database, clarifying that the *sui generis* right aims at protecting the investments in the collection, not the creation of data as a by-product of another economic activity. This reflects a specific choice of the EU in not protecting the

[7] Directive 96/9/EC, OJ 1996 L 77/20 consolidated version 6/6/2019 (hereinafter 'Database Directive').

[8] Ibid. Art. 3.

[9] Art. 7 Database Directive.

creation of data as such in order to achieve a perfect interchangeability between users and data holders".

However, the data's legal status is far from being defined consistently. This determines a puzzling way to perceive its potential from a legal perspective, which is also reflected in the way by which the law justifies its scope. Physicality is the main rationale used because it is certain and objective, as territorial boundaries are generally recognized by the international community. Finding different ways to justify the linkage between the law and data can be problematic if the connection with physical entities is always remarked upon. As a result, locational data only have the possibility to be as much as possible metaphors of tangible things and places. Whereas usually the law has interacted with data starting from this capacity to be relevant for many kinds of relations, now the codification of data that is functional to its representative capacity clears the way by which the law approaches data, not directly but with respect to its representative capacity.

3.3.1 Functional Definitions for Multiple Actors

Technologies undeniably can be used to make territories more functional, increasing their potential connectivity. However, as much as data are considered in relation to their capacities to move assets, the control over them is also deployed in relation to the physical portions of territories vaguely interested in data usages of any kind.

Amy Kapczynski warns that "Data are a social product, one that can be transformed into a commodity but that does not exist in the world without us, waiting for collection and exchange. Control over data and its production is socially and legally determined. The tendency instead to see data as a thing that springs from a person and that enters the world as a transcendent object misapprehends what data is and obscures how it came to serve as a critical form of capital in the current age" (Kapczynski 2020, p. 1460).

The more the law is connected throughout mapping different territories, the more the law needs to be differentiated within small branches of sectoral application. This allows connecting dots and data by differentiating the areas of the law. How is it feasible? The interconnected nature of data permeates borders in such a way that makes the very concept of limit, frontier, border neutral and sometimes useless. Data itself, for its very nature, is able to overcome every border so that the same concept of physical limit is not conflicting but nonrelevant.

Logical and spatial connections can be achieved differently if we do so through technologies or legal constructions. To be complementary, law and technology need to flow on parallel routes that do not conflict with each other, as they involve differentiated spheres of action.

Is it then possible that the law questions the territoriality principle? The only mechanism for coding and decoding the normativity of territory is the law. It is a reflexive mechanism. As far as the law uses territoriality to handle data in movement, the law does not manage to decode the monolithic structure of territory. To disassemble it, the law needs to cope with the purposes of territoriality.

Competing actors try to influence how spaces will be 'imagined' and/or governed. The exercise of territorial design is composed of three factors: physical components, territorial demarcation, and the political and social function of demarcated space. This dynamic involves the interaction of actors and phenomena that are not homogenous either in terms of effects produced within certain areas of the law or in terms of the global extent of these effects.

There is an interesting take regarding the European legal paradigm related to jurisdiction, which is described by Ralph Michael as *horizontal*: "Jurisdiction is justified *vis-à -vis* other states with a plausible claim to jurisdiction, not *vis-à -vis* the defendant and its interest in protection from the court" (Michaels 2006, p. 1047).

For this reason and to this extent, European jurisdiction is also international, in the sense that jurisdiction can be seen as a matter of international law. Jurisdictional rules are, at least potentially, universal. Michaels correctly states that "the role of state boundaries in the international European paradigm is one of allocation: the locus of an event or a party defines the place that has jurisdiction in a multilateral fashion" (Michaels 2006, p. 1058).

This model well explains the trend of the EU in judging the world regarding compliance with European standards. Europe has embarked in the attempt to enclose all digital phenomena that occur within its digital market into its legal outreach.

This represents a hyperbole because Europe does not possess its own territory but only boundaries, in the sense that the external boundaries of its Member States overlap with its own external boundaries. This oxymoron is extremely interesting if we look at it in the context of the legal paradigm to which it belongs. It in fact belongs to a legal paradigm, i.e., to an epistemic background for analysis, that explains how it is possible in the lack of a physical territory to expand a territorial scope out of the European external boundaries. For Europe, jurisdiction means jurisdictional venue (Zaccaria 2022; Pannarale 2012). This implies a reflexive process involving certain patterns. For example, most European countries think of jurisdiction as a keyword that enables the impossibility of being out of legal boundaries. Other experiences, such as the US, for example, identify jurisdiction as a group of prerogatives that are related to powers that have positive content. Michaels interestingly discusses these two modalities of dealing with jurisdiction: "Europeans preferred to unify both the law of recognition and enforcement and the law of jurisdiction in a "double convention," in which every imaginable basis of jurisdiction would be either needed or prohibited for purposes of jurisdiction and enforcement. In contrast, Americans supported a "mixed convention," which would have included agreement on both needed and forbidden grounds of jurisdiction but would have retained a third gray zone of bases that are neither needed nor prohibited but merely permitted. Clearly, such a model works well in the framework of a bargain-bases on which agreement cannot be reached are left in the gray zone, which represents the state of nature" (Michaels 2006, p. 1066).

3.3.2 *Beyond the Public/Private Divide: Competitive and Cooperative Dimensions of Information Control*

In the last two decades, public sector data access has been enhanced by the cooperation of private sector control. The capacity to handle enormous flows of data has been made possible throughout the basic infrastructures made available by private providers.

Both cooperative and competitive dimensions are the test bench offered to governments for rethinking new forms of sovereignty more akin to the digital world. More often, social control is the result of the interaction between the private and public sectors, based on a collaborative model, which is often carried out via mandatory disclosure orders issued by courts or administrative bodies towards large companies that sometimes seek to balance the interests of their customers through proactive activities.

What is crucial is that throughout the cooperation between private and public sector data, democratic principles are not undermined.

This was clarified by the European Court of Human Rights in two leading cases involving Russia and Hungary (*Zacharov v. Russia [GC] App. 47143/06, Judgement 4/12/2015* and *Szabó and Vissy v. Hungary, App. 37138/14, Judgement 12/01/2016o cases*). Ensuring privacy increasingly makes it possible to prevent threats to other rights from political power against freedom of expression and freedom of the press, for example but also freedom of assembly, association, and, therefore, the freedom of citizens to freely form critical political thought (and vote accordingly). Privacy and data protection represent a paradigmatic example of the interdependency of human rights and fundamental rights. Ensuring privacy and respect for personal data helps has prevented discrimination of individuals on the basis of sensitive characteristics and thus has helped ensure the free exercise of their rights (political, civil, social). Avoiding massive collection of personal behavioral data has prevented online campaigns of personalized mental manipulation of voters.

The cultural approach to use data protection safeguards to avoid the violation of other rights is emblematic. For instance, in the field of data access, the Court of Justice has sharpened the requirements for companies regarding the disclosure to data subjects of personal data disclosed to recipients.[10] This requires companies to review their internal processes and their templates for responding to access requests to avoid fines and damage actions for failure to provide access.

In particular, where personal data have been or will be disclosed to recipients, there is an obligation on the part of the controller to provide the data subject, on request, with the actual identity of those recipients.

Pursuant to the principle of interdependence between fundamental rights, the Court points out that the data subject's right of access is necessary to enable the data subject to exercise other rights conferred by the GDPR, namely, his or her right to

[10] See Case C-154/21, 12 January 2023.

rectification, right to erasure ('right to be forgotten'), right to restriction of processing, right to object to processing or right of action.

3.3.3 *Justiciable Data on a Global Scale*

A jurisdictional model based on an idea of civitas maxima overcoming state jurisdiction implies a correspondence between an organizational model of *civitas maxima* and the concept of peace. While generally data refers to underlying concepts and rights that have their own scope of application, quite often the territorial relevance of data seems to be neutral unless it is related to situational aspects.

This means for data to be enshrined in related rights that can be considered globally thanks to universal forms of protection. This is the case, for example, of digital rights triggered by massive phenomena such as mass surveillance that activate forms of protection irrespective of territorial constraints under certain conditions (Milanovic 2015, p. 81; Bignami and Resta 2015, p. 231). The extraterritorial reach of fundamental rights has also been recently claimed at the constitutional level by the *Bundesverfassungsgericht* in the BND's case (BVerfG 19 May 2020, 1 BvR 2835/17) in application of the principle of dignity without any restriction. Pursuant to Article 1(3) of *Grundgesetz*, fundamental rights are directly applicable and binding for all state authorities (executive, legislative and judicial) without any territorial limitation. This implies that all state authorities are bound to respect fundamental rights protection within or outside German jurisdiction (Rojszczak 2021, p. 69). Recently, the case of echo chambers has been significant in terms of how the problem of online clusters is relevant. Echo chambers provide environments where people are more comfortable misbehaving, as they are surrounded by other misbehaving people. This phenomenon is truly paradoxical because it is an example of delimitation without physical boundaries.

3.3.4 *International Law or Transnational Law for Data?*

The Outer Space Treaty of 1967 runs out the applicability of the principle of territoriality. The outer space, including celestial bodies, is allegedly not appropriable and shall be free for exploration and use by all states. In fact, outer space is not subject to sovereign claims of states, by means of use or occupation, or by any other means, and shall be free for exploration and use by all States. However, far from being pacific, this principle seems to be rather abstract because a race of states for space resources has started yet (Zannoni 2020, p. 329; Zolea 2020, p. 1). However, when the qualification of space as a "common heritage of mankind" appeared in the Treaty of 1979 treaty, many States turned away from international space law and gave up ratifying this treaty.

Emerging debates have been raised on the application of data protection laws in outer space. Whereas satellite operations carried out by the ESA seem to be not under the umbrella of the GDPR, instead in cases such as those where a controller or processor is located in the EU and processes personal data via a satellite located in outer space; satellite Internet, GPS, and media providers that offer their services to customers in the EU; and a space data centre that is based in the EU or processes data about individuals located in the EU. In all of these situations, the GDPR seemingly applies. Pursuant to Art. 38 of the Statute of the International Court of Justice, the legitimacy of extraterritorial claims may be assessed in light of "*international conventions [...] establishing rules expressly recognized by the contesting states; international custom, as evidence of a general practice accepted as law; (and) the general principles of law recognized by civilized nations [...]*". (Goldsmith and Wu 2006, p. 159).

What seems to be unconvered by the GDPR is the transfer of satellites to outer space where data are generated, as technically, the GDPR does not apply outside of the Earth but only for transfers to third countries (Figg 2019). An object-driven approach suggests moving the attention from the space occupied by data to their function. According to the predominance of some values or cultural models, the EU positions itself in its external action towards the globe as a standard setter (Bradford 2020; Cremona 2018, pp. 3–30; Schiavello 2023).

The space surrounding the Earth between planets and stars is far from being comparable to what we experience as Earth. The main difference is that we never experienced a possession of it. Structural principles of external relations the EU cannot make a convincing claim to sovereignty *under international law.* The issue is functional: as far as a State can control data within its territory, there is no need to resort to concepts other than territorial jurisdiction.

Sending data to space is now becoming a way to circumvent territorial restrictions due to the exercise of jurisdiction. Data gained from satellites cost sensibly less than other things. The advantage is, as outlined by the project CODE-DE (Copernicus Data and Exploitation Platform, Germany), to access all of the data and process them directly.

Last, data localization policies have spread around the world, affecting the capacity of global trade.

Local Data Mirroring, Explicit Local Data Storage, De Facto Local Storage and Processing, Explicit Local Data Storage and Processing, Explicit Local Data Processing and Routing are all strategies to keep data locally.

Any idea of law applied to data exceeds the states' lines. However, I completely share Szigeti's thesis. In a digital context, there is no difference between strict territorial decisions and extraterritorial decisions, as they are identical. If geography does not truly matter, it is dangerous to abuse geographical meanings without geographical references (Szigeti 2016, p. 398).

There have been many ways to handle the problem of territoriality, the most relevant of which are comity or obligation theory. However, the most commonly used practice has been value sharing for data protection.

This has generated, for example, in the field of data protection, something like a subsequent legislation, a kind of legislation that I define as such in so far it realizes the effects that it wants to promote. In other words, the territorial scope of EU data protection law is complemented with the regime of data transfers that means for the EU to delegate jurisdiction over cross-border data flows to "adequate" jurisdictions.

As a matter of fact, also drawing from international customs, the more widespread thesis was the one by Goldsmith and Wu, "*with few exceptions, governments can use their coercive powers only within their borders and can control offshore Internet communications only by controlling local intermediaries, local assets and local persons*" (Goldsmith and Wu 2006, p. 159).

Starting from the well-known definition of transnational law by Jessup that identifies it "to include all law which regulates actions or events that transcend national frontiers. Both public and private international law are included, as are other rules which do not wholly fit into such standard categories", what can be relevant in the law of data is the mixture of different layers of regulation. This is certainly the way by which different legal orders can be recomposed into a systematic path of understanding digital phenomena. "Functionally, for purposes of private international law, the law of jurisdiction can be defined as those rules and principles that determine the circumstances under which a court is entitled to adjudicate and render a substantive judgment with regard to the international and/or interstate connections involved" (Michaels 2017).

A theoretical grid for practical issues related to territorial claims should however be valid globally and for many sectoral regulations.

Julia Hörnle points out how the notion of jurisdiction depends on the different contexts, which may be (1) public international law, (2) private international law, (3) the criminal justice system, and (4) regulatory jurisdiction. The first function of jurisdiction in the context of public international law aims at restricting a state's power to its territory, and it allows each state to assert power over its territory. However, it has two more functions: jurisdiction also allows a state to represent its people (and those under its control) at the international level (second function of jurisdiction), and especially in the modern (post-World War II) sphere of international human rights, it may also imply state responsibility (third function of jurisdiction).

In private international law, instead, jurisdiction has a different function. In particular, first, it covers the competence of a domestic court to hear and decide a particular dispute (court jurisdiction); second, it covers the question of which legal system's law that court uses to decide the case (applicable law); and third, it covers the question of whether a particular court decision will or will not be recognized and enforced (enforcement).

In the field of criminal justice, investigative jurisdiction refers to the competence of the police and prosecution authorities to investigate crimes. Cross-border cooperation in criminal investigations also raises difficult questions as to which country's criminal procedure law applies to the investigation to ensure due process (this was one of the issues in the *Megaupload* case). Enforcement jurisdiction is concerned with jurisdiction in extradition cases (where the requesting state must show that it has jurisdiction to try the case) and the principle of *ne bis idem* as well as jurisdiction in the context of seizure of foreign assets. Regulatory jurisdiction is about the question of when a regulatory body is competent to apply its powers to a foreign entity (Hörnle 2021, p. 7).

3.4 Jurisdiction in Search for Sovereignty

Data creates a powerful mismatch between sovereignty and jurisdiction, since sovereign claims over data do not truly correspond to any jurisdictional power. Data make it possible in reality that sovereignty does not have its interface in the jurisdiction and vice versa that jurisdiction acts without sovereignty, and this hendiadys has traditionally, as pointed out by Hörnle (Hörnle 2021, p. 20), "exclusive territorial jurisdiction is not inevitable or immutable: jurisdiction based on a territorial basis may not be exclusive, allowing for pluralist legal systems coexisting within the same territory. Which system of jurisdiction prevails (exclusive territory or pluralism within the territory) depends on the relative power of the sovereign in a territory and the external forces reaching into that territory. To the extent that the process of globalization leads to a weakening of state sovereigns' exclusive power, it may cause a return towards a more pluralist system of jurisdiction in state territories".

The need to overcome territoriality stems from the problem to outreach everything outside. Without it, territoriality would continue to be an efficient mechanism for the exercise of jurisdiction. Whereas extraterritoriality, i.e., the expansion of territory out of its borders, increasingly in a functional manner, technically makes sense in its accepted meanings under international law if it is only limited to acts or conduct that have some physical repercussions that justify the apprehension of the state through the expansion of its territory. In relation to data things are quite different, and both territoriality and extraterritoriality run the risk of a legitimacy flaw. The demise of the state monopoly should not be confused with the end of sovereignty.

Sovereignty arises contingently with the state, but this does not mean that sovereign forms outside the modern world cannot be assumed. Such a strong claim takes on the weight of its responsibility. Law is revealed in its essence, as it is close to its application. Digital flows profoundly blur the mechanisms of legal causation as well as imputability. The direction of infringement and enforcement, for example, is also the result of the activity of Internet gatekeepers who not only determine access to data and thus how it circulates, most often owning the digital infrastructure, but can also restrict or influence the dissemination of digital content (Maroni 2022; Hörnle 2021, p. 35).

Law, in the hermeneutic perspective, is nothing more than a social practice continually led in search of its unity of meaning (Viola 1990). New tools are needed to govern new phenomena. Legal understanding is contingent and provisional, as it is valid for that particular legal issue or specific case.

The demise of the state monopoly should not be confused with the end of sovereignty. Sovereignty arises contingently with the state, but that does not mean that sovereign forms outside the modern world cannot be assumed. Such a strong claim takes on weight. Law is revealed in its essence close to its application. Law, in the hermeneutic perspective, is nothing more than a social practice continually led in search of its unity of meaning.

Europe is adopting a model that has nothing to do with the territoriality of data infrastructures (as Europe does not have by definition any territorial digital infrastructures under the form of cables) but with a construction of legal territorialities that overlap with the scope of application of law. The legal notion of territoriality then becomes broader than the physical notion.

3.4.1 Kelsenian Normativism vs. Schmittian Decisionism

According to the Kelsenian normativist thesis, the primacy of international law on state law is provided by the fact that international legal order does not have any executive means. According to this theory, the unity of legal order is based on international subjectivity and states' equality.

Kelsen, however, points out that the spatial interpretation of jurisdiction is only one of its specifications. According to a normativist perspective, jurisdiction means competence or legal power. According to Schmittian theory, the plurality of legal orders is not possible without a plurality of localizations. This lays down the basis for the theory of *Grossraume*. *Ordnung* is not possible without *Ortung*. However, in the case of borderless data, which *Ordnung* is possible if *Ortung* is lost? Only religion, with its mystical foundation, allows something like this. Technology and opacity of algorithms. Instead, the secularized version of the world urges to be embedded in a history where the act of occupation is the archetype of a foundational process. This process consists of the division and redistribution of the land.

Extraterritoriality is "another way of saying that the possibility of jurisdiction outside the state's territory, as implied by the notion of 'extraterritoriality', continues to depend on a spatial closure that gives rise to an inside as opposite to an outside: territorial jurisdiction" (Lindahl 2018, p. 13).

One of the traditional ways to assert control over data has been mapping territory through the infrastructures where data flows.

As correctly commented by Zencovich, the problem, in fact, is not that of establishing which private law should apply to the legal relationship and who is the competent judge. What is at stake in these cases, however, is the public regulation of the networks, which cannot be resolved through the rules applicable to private entities (Zeno-Zencovich 2016, p. 683).

In addition to amity lines, safety belts or competing spaces, in light of Kelsen's theory, international law should be the reconciling factor of state order, not its opposite. Its sanction for the violation of the international order is war. Sovereignty is a mere legal category, whereas according to Schmitt, it is empirical. Legitimacy and authority should rely on the legal system itself as the supreme as well as the ultimate authority within a territory that ensures absolute independence and freedom.

In the *Problem of Sovereignty and the Theory of International Law*, Kelsen argues, "Only temporarily, and by no means forever, does contemporary humanity divide itself into states, which, moreover, were formed more or less arbitrarily. Its legal unity is the civitas maxima as the organization of the world: this is the political kernel of the primacy of international law, which is at the same time the fundamental idea of that pacifism which in the sphere of international politics constitutes the inverted image of imperialism" (my translation, Kelsen 1989, p. 468).

Danilo Zolo argues that Kelsen embraces the monistic theory according to which there is no differentiation between domestic and international law and that the latter encompasses all national laws.

For Kelsen, the source of international law is not the obligation of mutual recognition between states but a source other than the state, which establishes its primacy over the domestic legal system. This means that the validity of the state must be sought in international law that determines the conditions of validity of state law. The problem of state sovereignty consists of the fact—for Kelsen—that international law is a legal system conferring obligations and rights on the state.

If we disregard the monistic hypothesis, it is logically inconceivable according to Kelsen what for him is the very essence of the international order, namely, the idea of a community of states endowed with equal rights despite their diversity in terms of territorial extent, population and power.

For Kelsen, on the contrary, the subjects of international law cannot but be, in addition to states, individuals, and hence, the rules of international law must also regulate the activities of individuals, exerting direct consequences on them. Kelsen is concerned above all with establishing that all human subjects are bound to obey international norms (even if, in passing, he maintains that international law is also competent to deal with a state's duties towards its citizens).

The main critique to Kelsen has been the fact that the monistic theory by which the international order should represent the confirmation of the domestic order. The unity of the law and the primacy of international law is represented by the civitas maxima as the organization of the world where war is only considered a sanction.

This means, applied to digital flows, that the digital jurisdiction should reflect the sovereign domestic jurisdiction of all countries (what Carl Schmitt calls *Weltbürgerrecht*).

Then, the idea of oriented law is composed of a contingent international law that brings a remembrance of origin. The relationship between order and orientation is not simply decision-making, but it is called Nomos.

Nomos, according to Carl Schmitt, is the combination of Ordnung und Ortung, order and orientation that gives rise to concrete historical orders, which arise from something, are for someone and against someone (very different from the Ciceronian idea of lex). The liberalist creed believes that because its contingent character politics is private, the contingent character of Nomos has nothing to share with the private use of politics, for which technique is its typical tool. Contingency means being able not to be. Said in the language of politics, it means that the principle of equality can be twisted, giving place to the deconstruction of the modern. Conversely, Kelsen mantains that the problem of sovereignty derives its validity not from the real world but from a theoretical architecture.

The term "Entscheidung"—which for Schmitt means cutting, partitioning, and producing (Schmitt 1972c, pp. 205–312)—serves to remove necessity from politics. Schmitt is an oppponent of the concept of a liberal democratic West. What does the West mean then?

Common sense, even scientific common sense, for Carl Schmitt, follows the winners. The history of the Western hemisphere is the history of shifting of a line. The West is indeterminate because it provides no orientation. The ius publicum europaeum is the counter-history of the state: it is anti-universalism. The state is a concrete detail; it can never be the universal political form extended across the planet. For example, exporting democracy means that the world is a smooth space. However, what about data flows across borders? One may argue that the answer depends on what data means and represents.

The only form of order is division: at maximum, it is possible to talk in terms of large spaces. Universality produces uncontrolled effects. The unconditioned is a conditioned that ignores itself. One thing is the physical appropriation of the space where it is not the space to create the political order, but it is quite the opposite. One thing is the control of data flows, and one thing is anchoring the Internet to physical geography. The former does not imply the latter (Braverman et al., 2015). When more than one state claims jurisdiction over digital flows, conflicts of law may arise. All EU regulatory pieces share a very broad scope of application.

The Data Act for instance applies to data generated by the use of machines or services and data held by public sectors that are intended to be made available for data recipients.

What worries truly if states can rule on all that happens within its territory. Well, the fact is that data does not happen but data represents and is given. The territorial character of the phenomenon that is determined by data representation is not real. Problems related to the cloud are mainly connected to national security.

An availability concern can also arise when public sector data reside on cloud infrastructure outside the jurisdiction that could be rendered inaccessible at some point in the future through accident or deliberate interference if a copy is maintained within the territory. Usually, the criterion is the linkage between the conduct of subjects to regulation and the territory of the Union (Saluzzo 2019, p. 22).

In the European Union's view, from the perspective of public international law, when a public authority requires a company established in its own jurisdiction to produce electronic data stored on a server in a foreign jurisdiction, the principles of territoriality and comity under public international law are engaged, and the interests and laws of that foreign jurisdiction must be considered (European Commission, Brief on the Microsoft Case).[11]

[11] However, the EU did not take any position in the case, see Brief of the European Commission on behalf of the European Union in support of neither party, https://www.supremecourt.gov/docket-

It is visible how territoriality is "a dysfunctional concept"—as correctly pointed out by Polcák and Svantesson (Polcák and Svantesson 2017, p. 80). Territory should be taken seriously as the way to cut and then create order.

3.4.2 Disconnecting Sovereignty, Jurisdiction and Territory

Sovereignty can be disconnected by elements that are no longer useful to assert its power. Territory in the context of digital flow regulation is one of the elements from which sovereignty can be disconnected. This assertion may seem counterintuitive considering that lawyers are used to identify.

Disconnection from territory—where data are is an operation that is apparently of fundamental importance. The difference between sovereignty and jurisdiction is that "sovereignty describes the power to rule, whereas jurisdiction describes the authority of a state to rule" (Hörnle 2021, p. 9).

Europe is adopting a model that has nothing to do with the territoriality of data infrastructures (as Europe does not have by definition any territorial digital infrastructures under the form of cables) but with a model of legal territory that overlaps with the scope of application of a certain rule. The legal notion of territoriality can be broader than the physical notion.

Jurisdictional authority as the object of a proprietary ownership the state's territorial rights are held *in rem* against *all* persons.

In the government of data, the traditional distinction between property and sovereignty even intuitively reacquires a peculiar meaning. As argued by Ryngaert, jurisdiction allows States to give effects to sovereign independence. This is not sufficient in the realm of data government if not associated with the property of infrastructures (Ryngaert 2015).

If this is the truth, then sovereignty without jurisdiction cannot achieve its objectives and is theoretically not possible. However, sovereignty can be based on alternative criteria that ground its jurisdictional scope. The problem is to treat data as a natural resource and as good.

As far as data are considered a commodity, property or other entitlements are more adequate than the idea of control over a physical sphere of influence (Rodotà 2004 or. ed. 1997, p. 45; 2012, p. 378).

Disentangling this issue allows us to be more flexible in the reasoning about sovereignty without forcing the rationales of what we aim to contend.

One issue is exerting a sovereign power over a physical space; one issue is the regulation of what happens in this physical space.

It is not the first time that regulators cope with immaterial objects. This has been the case for financial transactions, but in cyberspace, the reality is that the strongest

---

pdf/17/17-2/23655/20171213123137791_17-2%20ac%20european%20commission%20for%20filing.pdf.

technological power dictates the rules (Wu 1997, p. 647). Europe does not accept this state of the art and tries to promote its own way. However, it is not clear enough if it is possible to exert a sort of defensive jurisdiction without leading to conflicts of law.

The incoherence is that digital sovereignty is a vague concept that does not mean anything in legal terms unless sovereignty and then jurisdictional claims. Europe should be more concrete in appropriating sovereign expectations on its own digital infrastructures. This is comprehensible if we think that Europe cannot expect to exert sovereignty over any territorial premise.

As noted by Humphreys, "Binary digits are just numbers, but they are numbers whose purpose is to take on representative values that will provide a means of distinguishing everything from everything else: to represent something in digital format, we just need to work out a means of counting it" (Humphreys 2018).

Legal Sources

BVerfG 19 May 2020, 1 BvR 2835/17)

ECtHR case law

Zacharov v. Russia [Grand Chamber] App. 47143/06
Szabó and Vissy v. Hungary, App. 37138/14

References

Abizadeh A (2016) Sovereign jurisdiction, territorial rights, and membership in Hobbes. In: Martinich A, Hoekstra K (eds) The Oxford Handbook of Hobbes. Oxford University Press, pp 397–431

Altwicker T (2020) Justice beyond borders – extraterritorial obligations from Thucydides to Grotius. Rechtsphilosophie - Zeitschrift für die Grundlagen des Rechts (RphZ) 6(3):234–248

Barbero M (2017) Study on emerging issues of data ownership, interoperability, (re-)usability and access to data, and liability. European Union

Bathelt H, Feldman MP, Kogler DF (2011) Beyond territory. Dynamic geographies of knowledge creation, diffusion, and innovation. Routledge

Benton L (2010) A search for sovereignty. Law and geography in european empires, 1400-1900. Cambridge University Press

Bergelson V (2003) It's personal, but is it mine? Toward property rights in personal information. U C Davis Law Rev 37:379

Besson S (2012) The extraterritoriality of the European Convention on Human Rights: why human rights depend on jurisdiction and what jurisdiction amounts to. Leiden J Int Law 25(4):857–884, 869

Besson S (2019) Why and what (state) jurisdiction. Legal plurality, individual equality and territorial legitimacy. In: Klabbers J, Palombella G (eds) The challenge of inter-legality. Cambridge University Press

Bignami F, Resta G (2015) Transatlantic privacy regulation: conflict and cooperation. Law Contemp Probl 78:231–266

Bradford A (2020) The Brussels Effect: how the European Union rules the world. Oxford University Press

Braverman I, Blomley NK, Delaney D, Kedar A (eds) (2015) The expanding spaces of law: a timely legal geography. Stanford University Press

Celata F (2009) Spazi di produzione. Una prospettiva relazionale. Giappichelli

Christakis T (2020) "European Digital Sovereignty": successfully navigating between the "Brussels Effect" and Europe's quest for strategic autonomy. Multidisciplinary Institute on Artificial Intelligence/Grenoble Alpes Data Institute: Studies on Digital Governance

Cohen J (2021) Between truth and power. The legal constructions of informational capitalism. Oxford University Press

Cremona M (ed) (2018) Structural principles and their role in EU external relations law. Hart

Daskal J (2020) The opening salvo. The CLOUD Act, e-evidence proposals, and EU–US discussions regarding law enforcement access to data across borders! In: Bignami F (ed) EU law in populist times. Oxford University Press, pp 319–341

De Filippi P, Mannan M, Reijers W (2022) The alegality of blockchain technology. Policy Soc 41(3):358–372

De Franceschi A (2021) Personal data as counter-performance. In: Senigaglia R, Irti C, Bernes A (eds) Data protection in software services. Giuffré, Milano, pp 153–176

Del Vecchio A (2021) La legge nell'Oceano. Ugo Grozio e le origini dello spazio politico moderno. Il Mulino

De Vitoria F (2005) De iure belli (Galli C ed.). Laterza

Deleuze G, Guattari F (1997) Millepiani. Capitalismo e schizofrenia, sez. I, Rizoma, Castelvecchi

Drexl J (2017a) On the future EU Legal Framework for the digital economy: a competition-based response to the 'ownership and access' debate. In: Lohsse S, Schulze R et al (eds) Trading data in the digital economy: legal concepts and tools. Nomos, pp 223–244

Drexl J (2017b) Designing competitive markets for industrial data. Between propertisation and access. JIPITEC 8:267

Duch-Brown N, Martens B, Mueller-Langer F (2017) The economics of ownership, access and trade in digital data. European Commission, Joint Research Centre. https://www.econstor.eu/bitstream/10419/202223/1/jrc-dewp201701.pdf

Efroni Z (2020) Location data as contractual counter-performance: a consumer perspective on recent EU legislation. In: Finck M et al (eds) Smart urban mobility. MPI Studies on Intellectual Property and Competition Law, vol 29. https://doi.org/10.1007/978-3-662-61920-9_13

Fahey E (2022) The EU as a global digital actor: institutionalizing global data protection, trade, and cybersecurity. Hart

Ferrajoli L (1997) La sovranità nel mondo moderno. Laterza

Figg R (2019) The application of data protection laws in (outer) space. www.iclg.com

Goldsmith J, Wu T (2006) Who controls the Internet? Illusions of a borderless world. Oxford University Press

Grotius H (2012) In: Neff SC (ed) Hugo Grotius on the law of war and peace. Cambridge University Press

Hildebrandt M (2013) Extraterritorial jurisdiction to enforce in cyberspace? Bodin, Schmitt, Grotius in cyberspace. Univ Toronto Law J 63(2):196–224

Hoeren T (2019) Datenbesitz statt Dateneigentum? MMR 1

Hörnle J (2021) Internet jurisdiction: law and practice. Oxford University Press

Humphreys S (2018) Data. The given. In: Hohmann J, Joyce D (eds) International law's object, pp 191–202

Kapczynski A (2020) The law of informational capitalism. Yale Law J 129(5):1460–1515

Kelsen H (1989, or.ed. Das Problem der Souveränität und die Theorie des Völkerrechts: Beitrag zu einer reinen Rechtslehre, Mohr Siebek, 1920), Il problema della sovranità e la teoria del diritto internazionale. Contributo per una teoria pura del diritto. Giuffrè
Klabbers J, Palombella L (2019) (eds) The challenge of inter-legality. Cambridge University Press
Krisch N (2022) Jurisdiction unbound: (extra)territorial regulaton as global governance. EJIL 33(2):481–514
Lessig L (2002) Privacy as property. Soc Res 69:247–270
Lindahl H (2018) Authority and the globalization of inclusion and exclusion. Oxford University Press, p 14
Litman J (2000) Information privacy/information property. Stanf Law Rev 52(5):1286
Lomborg S, Ytre-Arne B (2021) Advancing digital disconnection research: introduction to the special issue. Convergence 27(6):1529–1535
Maier C (2019) Dentro i confini. Territorio e potere dal 1500 a oggi. Einaudi
Malgieri G, Custers B (2018) Pricing privacy: the right to know the value of your. personal data. Comput Law Secur Rev 34(2):289–303
Maroni M (2022) The right to access the Internet: a crititical analysis of the constitutionalisation of the Internet. Unigrafia
Metzger A (2017) Data as counter-performance. What rights and duties do parties have? https://www.jipitec.eu/issues/jipitec-8-1-2017/4528/jipitec_8_1_2017_metzger_data%20as%20counter-performance.pdf
Mezzadra S, Neilson B (2013) Border as method or, the multiplication of labor. Duke University Press
Michaels R (2006) Two paradigms of jurisdiction. Mich J Int Law 27:1003
Michaels R (2017) Jurisdiction, foundations. In: Basedow J et al (eds) Elgar encyclopedia of private international law. Edward Elgar
Milanovic M (2015) Human rights treaties and foreign surveillance: privacy in the digital age. Harv Int Law J 56:81
Moreno Lax V (2020) The architecture of functional jurisdiction: unpacking contactless control—on public powers, S.S. and Others v. Italy, and the "operational model". German Law J 21:385–416
Palombella L (2021) Interlegality: On interconnections and 'external sources. The Italian Law Journal 7:2
Pannarale L (2012) Il diritto che guarda. Rischi della decisione giuridica, Franco Angeli
Polcák R, Svantesson DJB (2017) Information sovereignty. Data privacy, sovereign powers and the rule of law. Edward Elgar
Poullet Y (1990) Data protection between property and liberties. A civil law approach. In: Kaspersen HWK, Oskamp A (eds) Amongst friends in computers and law. A collection of essays in remembrance of Guy Vandenberghe. Kluwer Law International, The Hague, p 161
Praet P (2010) Prolegomena to the post-sovereign *Rechtsstaat*. In: Kalmo H, Skinner Q (eds) Sovereignty in fragments. The past, present and future of a contested concept. Cambridge University Press, pp 169–185
Prins C (2006) Property and privacy: European perspectives and the commodification of our identity. Inf Law Ser 16:223–257
Purtova NN (2009a) Property in personal data: a European perspective on instrumentalist theory of propertization. In: de Filippi P, Gomes de Andrade NN, Fernandez-Barrera M (eds) Law and technology: looking into the future - selected essays. European Press Academic, pp 225–243
Purtova N (2009b) Property in personal data: learning from the American discourse. Comput Law Secur 25:507–521
Rodotà S (1995) Tecnologie e diritti, Il Mulino
Rodotà S (2004, or. ed. 1997) Tecnopolitica. La democrazia e le nuove tecnologie della comunicazione. Laterza
Rodotà S (2012) Il diritto di avere diritti. Laterza
Rodotà S (2018, or. ed. 1973), ed. Alpa G, Elaboratori elettronici e controllo swociale, Jovene

Rojszczak M (2021) Extraterritorial bulk surveillance after the German BND Act Judgment. Eur Constitutional Law Rev 17:53–77
Ryngaert C (2015) Unilateral jurisdiction and global values. Eleven
Saluzzo S (2019) The principle of territoriality in EU data protection law. In: Natoli T, Riccardi A (eds) Borders, legal spaces and territories in contemporary international law. Within and beyond Springer, pp 121–141
Samuelson P (2000) Privacy as intellectual property? Stanf Law Rev, 52, pp 1125–1173
Sartor G (2015) Il diritto nell'informatica giuridica. Rivista di filosofia del diritto, Special Issue, pp 71–92
Sartor G, Lagioia F (2020) The impact of general data protection regulation on artificial intelligence. Study European Parliamentary Research Services, STOA
Schiavello A (2023) Europa, diritti, democrazia in tempi difficili. Diritto & questioni pubbliche 2:211–219
Schmitt C (1972c) Appropriazione/Divisione/ Produzione. Un tentativo di fissare correttamente i fondamenti di ogni ordinamento economico-sociale, a partire dal «nomos». In Le categorie del 'politico'. Il Mulino, pp 295–312
Schwartz PM (2003) Property, privacy, and personal data. Harv Law Rev 117:2056, 2058
Stepanov I (2020) Introducing a property right over data in the EU: the data producer's right – an evaluation. Int Rev Law Comput Technol 34(1):65–86. https://doi.org/10.1080/13600869.2019.1631621
Szigeti PD (2016) The illusion of territorial jurisdiction. Tex Int Law J 52(3):369
Tilmann A (2020) Justice beyond borders—extraterritorial obligations from thucydides to grotius (March 30, 2020), Rechtsphilosophie - Zeitschrift für die Grundlagen des Rechts (RphZ), Forthcoming, Available at SSRN https://ssrn.com/abstract=3564495 or https://doi.org/10.2139/ssrn.3564495
Viola F (1990) Il diritto come pratica sociale. Jaka Book
Vol. 52, No. 5, Symposium: Cyberspace and Privacy: A New Legal Paradigm? (May, 2000), pp 1125–1173, pp 1136–1146
Wenderhost C (2017) On elephants in the room and paper tigers: how to reconcile data protection and data economy. In: Lohsse S, Schulze R et al (eds) Trading data in the digital economy: legal concepts and tools. Nomos, Baden Baden, pp 327–356
Whitman JQ (2004) The two western cultures of privacy: dignity versus liberty. Yale Law J 113:1151
Woods AK (2018) Litigating data sovereignty. Yale Law J 128:328
Wu T (1997) Cyberspace sovereignty? The Internet and the international system. Harv J Law Technol 10(3):648
Zaccaria G (2022). Nuove fonti, nuove categorie. Il Mulino
Zannoni D (2020) The dilemma between the freedom to use and the proscription against appropriating outer space and celestial bodies. Chin J Int Law 19(2):329–358
Zeno-Zencovich V (2016) Intorno alla decisione nel caso Schrems: la sovranità digitale e il governo internazionale delle reti di telecomunicazione. Il diritto dell'informazione e dell'informatica 31:683–696
Zolea S (2020) Esplorazione spaziale e nuove forme di appartenenza: spunti comparativi. Cardozo Electronic Law Bulettin 26:1

Chapter 4
Codifying Digital Extraterritoriality

4.1 Transforming Un-territoriality into Extra-territorial Rationale

The nation state is no longer the relevant community for digital law because the linkage to territory is no longer strictly relevant to the digital phenomenon. It may be but it may not. The possible alternatives shed light on how territoriality is no longer necessary to regulate data flows and to avoid conflicts of law. '[T]he point today', as Gunter Teubner puts it (Becker and Teubner 2022), is to rationalise the 'nation-state tradition' and constitutional theory with 'three current major trends – digitisation, privatisation and globalisation'. The state, in other words, now operates as one of many administrative platforms within a global marketplace of economic, political, and social transactions in which extraterritoriality is the norm rather than the exception (Haskell 2019, p. 22).

Digitisation represents, of course, only one of the multiple challenges faced by the nation state in approaching cross-border phenomena. This has enhanced the consideration of extraterritorial rationales as merely technical means rather than as a substantive functionality. Substantively extraterritoriality does not have any rationale, as it is not logical to justify it: it is only a surplus of power attached to additional reasons: "Thinking of 'extraterritoriality' as a particular kind of scholarly frame encourages us to understand the concept not as a description of the world that can be shown to be objectively true or false, but as a set of criteria developed within scholarly literature and governed by the social rules of the discipline and its literary conventions" (Haskell 2019, p. 13).

Drawing from pre-existing unitary interests, Goldsmith and Posner (*The Limits of International Law*, 2007) point out how sovereign interests drive international agreements as far as this is functional to preserve the state's interests, often against a vision of legal pluralism or cosmopolitan choice of law (Berman 2005 and 2012, pp. 61 and 244).

M. Catanzariti, *Disconnecting Sovereignty*, Law, Governance and Technology Series 65, https://doi.org/10.1007/978-3-031-60734-9_4

However, most recent studies on extraterritoriality show how the expansion of territorial scope of application or the use extraterritoriality (when the first mechanism fails) do not present many differences, especially in data protection law (Taylor 2023, p. 261).

This paragraph aims to answer this question: why is extraterritoriality a compelling rationale for unterritorial data, although the non-territorial character of data has nothing to do with the extraterritorial claims over data? Traditionally, extraterritoriality has been the mechanism to handle legal phenomena occurring outside the premises of territorial states. The indispensable nature of territory for any conception of sovereignty has been broadly accepted so that any alternative to territoriality has failed. Nonetheless, although from a conceptual perspective, this has implied that no alternatives have been sought with respect to territoriality, the mismatch between data and territory has visibly created a parallel way of lawmaking based, on the one hand, on the possible extension of territory depending on the instrumental nature of its reach and, on the other hand, on the immateriality of data that is capable of mimicking whatever is the place where it goes through.

The overwhelming jurisdictional logic of modern law has imposed its determinacy over all objects of jurisdictional claims—material and immaterial—forcing the nonterritorial nature of data into the legal fiction of territoriality. This means that although legal fiction technically works to produce applicative solutions that do not fail in terms of the effectiveness of the law, this is not enough to ensure the stability of the global order. Our hypothesis is that if territory is not helpful in achieving a specific objective that proves to be quintessential to the justification of any exerted power, then it can be replaced by another uniform criterion. The way by which the *fictio iuris* works is, however, in terms of assimilation, not in terms of approximation. As extraterritoriality represents a broad mechanism deployed by territoriality in regard to contact with objects that do not have a territorial nature, nonterritorial objects receive extraterritorial solutions. One does not often think that a fictio iuris may not present externalities. In the case of territoriality as applied to nonterritorial things, this is particularly true because it is, after all, nonmotivated.

4.1.1 *Approximating Territory:* quasi extra territorium

Jurisdictional claims have developed around the core of territory by approximation. This implies that what lies before or after territory represents something that is defined approximating by excess or by defect to territory. A special fiction of immunity has been then elaborated in regard to jurisdictional accumulation (Päl 2021). The concept of *quasi extra territorium* has been elaborated in the Grotian doctrine to attribute a decree to different cases of derogation to territoriality. In particular, it referred during the seventeenth and eighteenth centuries to the privileges and exemptions of diplomats. They consisted of treating diplomats, their residences, and their goods as though they were located outside the host country. However, since the global reach of their mission exceeds the territory of the state that legitimises their power, the conceptualisation of *quasi extra territorium* tries to answer the problem related to the limits of territorial activities even in the specific context of diplomatic immunity (Altwicker 2020, p. 234).

However, the concept of quasi extra territorium is interesting as applied to data flows because of its expandable nature that justifies, on the one hand, the application of rules and exempts some individuals or situations from the application of other rules.

Data are not only noncoherent with a Westphalian frame but also noncoherent with one single nature. As observed by Crawford, "Data began to be described as a resource to be consumed, a flow to be controlled, or an investment to be harnessed" (Crawford 2021, p. 56). Value has always been extracted from physical resources, no matter whether it has been done through the control over the related territory or the property of resources themselves. Depending on how treating data, whether as physical resources stored within physical premises or as an unmaterial entity, makes it useless to distinguish between territorial and extraterritoriality regarding data (Szigeti 2019, p. 30).

4.1.2 Towards a Functional Approach?

Is a one-fits-all solution possible? The idea of a functional approach as applied to jurisdictional claims is not intended in relation to sovereignty but to territoriality. We depart from the idea of a functional approach mainly aimed at "regaining control and independence in the management of the digital ecosystem" (Celeste 2021, p. 224), where "territory apparently loses its centrality".

Conversely, our idea is that because of the centrality of territory informing all choices, even those that are extraterritorial, we should determine alternative mechanisms to territoriality, not alternative mechanisms ensuring sovereign claims. The most relevant threshold to be overcome is territoriality in fact, since the connection with territory still represents at the moment the legitimising factor for any jurisdictional claim in the digital world (Yildiz 2019, p. 215).

However, exploring the pathways of a functional approach to digital jurisdiction means enabling different criteria that are alternatives to territoriality and that may justify jurisdictional claims. We propose functional criteria that, in relation to different controversies, may better address the substantial connection between data and power over it.

As noted by Nicolini, "Whereas territory refers to a tract of land under the domain of a political authority, territoriality points to a territory made politically meaningful through processes of spatial production" (Nicolini 2022, p. 24). However, what territoriality represents is just a function that can be replaced as far as it finds a "functional equivalent". The illusion of replacing territoriality with extraterritoriality is something that cannot fit any purpose for the inescapable ubiquity of digital services.

In Europe, the scale effect of the EU market has amplified the scope of digital regulation starting from the GDPR. However, the indifferent use of territoriality and extraterritoriality just to subject the world to a cultural model does not reveal sustainability in the long run.

Material issues (i.e., infrastructures) cannot be easily sifted out from immaterial issues (i.e., contents), as they interact and interpenetrate; traditional international relations are ill-equipped to deal with these issues because they are fundamentally grounded in territoriality.

A postulate in contradiction to what constitutions establish must be overcome: the nexus between constitution, people and sovereign state that has remained in the dominant culture, in contradiction to the inherently universal character of fundamental rights protection. As Ferrajoli warns, there is no alternative to global constitutionalism, the development of a constitutional sphere that is compatible with global powers (Ferrajoli 2022, p. 185; see also Pollicino 2023, p. 569).

However, two centripetal forces move the one towards the other: massive transfer to supra-state headquarters of powers and processes of disintegration. We then doubt the purely technical character of jurisdiction as well as the uncritical acceptance of changing law as valid because it is in force.

Like all self-reflexive mechanisms, the idea of disconnection does not mean disintegration at all. In fact, one should not confuse the planes of cause and effect.

Indeed, the fragmentation wrought by data does not affect sovereignty but only the principle of territoriality. In this respect, the rise of new dimensions of rights amplifies this phenomenon. Indeed, one must not confuse the planes of cause, i.e., fragmentation. of phenomena operated by data, and of effect, disconnection. This book proposes an idea of disconnection from territoriality that in each case presupposes sovereignty and preserves it by implementing alternative strategies.

The issue of the erosion of sovereignty by globalisation and digitisation has been addressed from many angles, and the response has been from many voices to point out the inadequacy of the sovereignty paradigm. However, what in my opinion has not been stressed clearly enough is the crisis of sovereignty read through categories that can no longer be used, such as territoriality.

This does not mean that territoriality is no longer relevant to sovereignty in the age of data flows. Instead, it means that it is not possible to understand data regulation rationales if only models based on physical location, modelled on the so-called theory of Beale's "vested rights" (Beale 1935, pp. 938 and 1091), are applied.

Since territoriality does not even entirely overlap with territory, as it represents its reflexive mechanism, thinking about the relationship between sovereignty and data in different application cases without anchoring on the principle of territoriality may also somehow imply the possibility of saving different uses of territory.

Indeed, territory has traditionally been regarded as a hypostasis of law: there is law only where there is territory. However, one must imagine something different, namely, that law is preexistent to territory to the extent that it serves as the enforcement mechanism of its *jurisdiction*.

The question, then, is to identify the borderline point of disconnection. To what extent can sovereignty disconnect from territory to remain effective? The argument here is that territory in relation to data, not necessarily being representative of an essential element inherent in regulation, can be replaced by different functional criteria. However, one should not make the mistake of approaching the topic using the consequences inherent in not applying the territoriality principle. If one abandons territoriality in relation to data, one must also abandon its rationale. For this reason, the widespread use of extraterritorial claims only perpetuates the inadequacy of the territoriality principle with respect to digital phenomena. Moreover, by virtue of the immaterial and placeless nature of digital data, it is baseless to distinguish between territoriality and extraterritoriality when we do not deal with the physical objects or with the location of persons, as argued by Szigeti (Szigeti 2019, p. 30). Additionally, this distinction has implied a sectoral approach to digital law depending on the areas dealt with and the contexts of reference on a case-by-case basis, effectively transforming the geographical space into a space of competence and thus merely legal. This does not in principle entail any interpretative problems but nevertheless implies a forcing of the various legal systems gradually involved in equipping sovereignty with erroneous categories, i.e., on requirements that are not compatible with the immaterial character of data flows. In essence, decoupling data from territory implies not thinking in terms of critical infrastructures and where they are located nor only in terms of jurisdictional accumulation. Moreover, this would not be unique in history, since rationalisation processes have constantly followed one another and progressively moved away from their original use. Such would be, in the case of territoriality, a reformulation of it in terms of an exception vis-à-vis the digital phenomenon. However, institutions change to survive, and this is radical because the institutionalised process itself is built by the same institutions that are established. As pointed out by Fahey, the "institutionalisation of the EU constitutes the joint processes of formalisation and stabilisation of procedures, institutional coordination, with the ability of individual actors to influence institutional development" (Fahey 2022, p. 8).

4.2 The Multiple Facets of Extraterritorial Jurisdiction

The justification of overstepping territoriality is to produce local effects of the global internet. Embracing the territory is a conceptual operation: not only to apply its legal normativity but also to map future strategies. The knowledge of territory has been in fact one of the core issues of strategic planning.

Some contend that online disputes inevitably lead to the exertion of extraterritorial claims by states against internet law firms. Examples would be many—from takedown orders of unlawful contents to delisting and right to be forgotten, law-enforcement data production requests—to indicate that often the clash is not between different laws and different states but between states exerting powers and intermediaries resisting with these powers with their business (Woods 2018, pp. 128, 328, 356).

State control over the internet means "physical control over the network architecture" (Woods 2018, p. 361). What was pointed out by this author is not perfectly convincing when he argues that powers to compel compliance and powers to control the means of compliance are different things (Woods 2018, p. 364). In reality, they are both means of exerting sovereignty pursuant to a certain legal basis, but the second means is strictly related and depends on the technological capacity. Controlling the means of compliance implies controlling the ways by which a technological infrastructure may work and produce effects.

Always justified in terms of exception from territoriality, extraterritorial jurisdiction has always been deployed in the field of criminal law to cover as much as possible actions occurring outside the premises of the legitimate state. However, some scholars have distinguished between extraterritorial jurisdiction and territorial extension depending on whether there is a territorial connection with the regulating state that should take into account conduct or circumstances abroad (Scott 2014a, p. 87).

As correctly observed by Nicolini, the exercise of bordering cyberspace is cyberlaw, for which topological descriptors, such as the IP address, are important, although geographical coordinates are functional to domestically enforce the law of the internet (Nicolini 2022, p. 271). Data disrupts the legal order insofar as they fragment the reality subject to legal analysis by camouflaging its essence in the process. In fact, depending on their representative spectrum, law changes even simultaneously with its regulatory activity.

The problem with the extraterritorial relevance of data is the seemingly extraterritorial relevance of certain digital phenomena. We can think of electronic surveillance, which by its very nature and purpose exceeds the limits of territory. Surveillance, which is not targeted directly at individuals, therefore has the capacity to have a very wide reach, both inside and outside the territory of the surveilling State. Safeguards are therefore pivotal and yet elusive.

4.2.1 Prescriptive and Judicial Extraterritorial Jurisdiction for Data

Pursuant to the Harvard Draft Principle, the customary international law bases for the exercise of jurisdiction were set up as the following: territorial principle involving jurisdiction over conduct within territory, persons present within territory and conduct generating within territory; nationality principle, determining jurisdiction based on the nationality of persons committing the offence (active personality principle) or based on the nationality of the persons injured by the offense even committed by aliens (passive personality principle); protective jurisdiction applying jurisdiction over threats to vital interests of a State, such as for example the extraterritorial conduct against national security; universal principle over crimes not depending on a linkage with the State that represent serious international offenses.

There is a vast literature on private international law in the field, and the aim of the book is not to recall it as it exceeds its goals (Ryngaert 2015a). However, what is interesting is a position that envisages unilateral action as a tool to provide global corrective justice in the common interest (Ryngaert 2020, p. 92),[1] especially in the field of human rights protection (Pariotti 2004; Ollino 2022, p. 81). This seems to be an attempt to split the effects of extraterritorial claims into positive and negative: extraterritoriality pursued in light of universal values' protection could be positively evaluated because its exercise would be allegedly claimed in the common interest. However, this optimistic view, although suitably structured and theoretically sophisticated, risks not giving account of unitary conceptualisation of jurisdiction, including its practice.

There is a factual ground that deserves to be highlighted: as observed by Svantesson, we are so used to think in terms of territoriality that a dispute regarding two citizens using the Internet within a country is by default dealt with resorting to the territoriality principle, whereas things can no longer be considered under the territorial lenses if the conduct occurs whether the Internet is used outside the country. Tension territoriality/extraterritoriality represents a "definitional conundrum" that confirms the inadequacy of the territoriality principle (Svantesson 2015, p. 518).

In a so-called "dysfunctional system", there are other criteria that are additionally used to address the problem of internet regulation: some additional components are (territorial) sovereignty, comity, due diligence, and the duty of noninterference. Translating these components into reality is not an easy task. For example, while it is uncontroversial that a territory is subject to the sovereignty of one state, it is not certain that a person or a matter is subject to one single authority. The problem is then the impossibility of a perfect overlap between territory as a container and life, acts, facts, and persons as contents. The imperfection of the fiction is shown by the fleeing nature of data.

Additionally, comity is not a one-fits-all solution to be used generally, as it allows the recognition of the authority of another country within the territory of a country. It is obviously discretional and not related to objective grounds. Conversely, the principle of non-intervention means that a state refrains from exercising jurisdiction over a conduct considered essential to its interest but perpetrated in another country. Finally, according to the principle of due diligence, a State is bound to use due

[1] Very interestingly Ryngaert summarises the debates on sovereignty "sovereignty, jurisdiction, and territory are enduring cognitive scripts that may require reconceptualisation in light of current governance challenges. These capacious scripts have in fact historically been 'sites or spaces of enunciation' that allow powers and authorities to concretise multiple political discourses, to include or exclude persons or events, and to realise material justice. They are 'legal constructs whose meanings and uses vary depending on the context in which they are employed', that are subject to conceptual manipulation, have little essentialist meaning, and are not socially neutral. Reinterpretations and innovations of these notions, which favour action to tackle novel problems, may well be possible within the current structure of international law. This depends on the evolution of international relations such as the increasing interdependence between states and international justice conceptions".

diligence to prevent the commission within its dominions of criminal acts against another nation or against its people.

Based on this puzzling situation, extraterritoriality often becomes a way for over-regulation over all, regardless of the fact that there are certain phenomena that are incapable of being localised in one country or another. After all, extraterritoriality means that one country acts as it would apply the territoriality principle of another country (Scott 2014b, p. 1343).

That's why we should stop thinking even in terms of "replacement of location" at least conceptually, although operationally, the substitution of a location-based approach represents a suitable option (Szigeti 2019, p. 44).

Commentators have tried to distinguish jurisdictional claims according to the effects produced by rules: while prescriptive jurisdiction is the ability to make laws that can validly purport to regulate people and situations, regardless of their location, judicial jurisdiction for example means the power to rule on controversies within national premises.

4.2.2 Adapting Territorial Exceptionalism to Data Flows

Data nationalism or territorial extension seem to be the two options related to the models of data governance.

A consequence of a randomly organised model of jurisdictional claims over data inevitably leads to opposite solutions sometimes noncoherent with the way by which territorial connection is interpreted and applied.

As correctly pointed out by Eichesener, many can be jurisdictional criteria such as the place where data are located, the place where data are accessed, the nationality of the target of a certain activity or the location of the target of a certain activity, but this criterion can also be the complex of circumstances or the place where data are meant to be accessible by the state that accesses it. As Eichensehr correctly observes "One test is the location of the data itself, as Microsoft urged. Another is the location where the data are accessed, as the U.S. government argued. Yet another approach would establish a test that takes into account the nationality of the target of the investigation or the nationality and location of the target. Still another approach would rely on a "totality of the circumstances" evaluation to determine extraterritoriality. Finally, the Tallinn Manual suggests that the determinative factor is whether data are "meant to be accessible" from the State that wishes to access the information (Eichensehr 2017, pp. 154–155).

Four branches of the law would be relevant for internet jurisdiction: private international law (domestic rules in civil and commercial disputes), public international law (competence of the state on its territory), criminal justice (investigations, power of police and criminal courts), regulatory administration (Hörnle 2021, p. 5).

If it is true that cross-border data flows need at least three regulatory segments—private international law, public international law and transnational law—it is also true that sectoral regulation of data flows reiterates territorial models (Velasco et al. 2016, pp. 465–476).

4.2.3 Enforcing Digital Rights Across Jurisdictions

Digitalisation is disruptive from several perspectives: the deep transformations produced in labor markets, the granularity of tasks related to human activities, the disintermediation in various sectors of the economy, the platformization of public opinion, the fragmentation of human behaviors and identities into bits and pieces of data and their multiple uses. In a more substantial way, digitalisation profoundly affects one of the pillars of modern law and legal thought: the notion of state sovereignty (Rodotà 2004, or. ed. 1997, p. 45; 2012, p. 378).

Digitalisation has in this respect triggered two different regulatory models. The first is the trend towards extraterritorial claims over data, exemplified by several situations such as law enforcement's access to data located abroad, global injunctions, and the territorial extension of domestic law. The second, often a reaction to extraterritoriality, has resulted in the development of forms of data nationalism such as local storage and local processing requirements issued by governments and the establishment of national clouds for various types of data.

These two options appear to be opposites, but in fact, they converge in many ways because they are both based on the centrality of territory. The first option expands the legal notion of territory, whereas the second replicates the notion of territory digitally.

Both options are based on a "territorial logic" that is inconsistent with the nonterritorial nature of data. The misuse of territory has led to forms of retaliation by nation states that risk undermining geo-political relationships. The tension between territorial and extraterritorial claims has been made increasingly visible and tangible because of the intangible and ephemeral nature of data. Deactivating data's territorial connecting factors from jurisdiction may avoid distortive effects in the multiple and multipurpose ways data is used.

This reconceptualisation is not merely theoretical. It has immediate consequences both on the limits of extraterritorial claims in digital matters and on the legal architecture for the establishment of an EU cloud infrastructure. The latter has mainly been associated with the idea of bridging the technological gap between Europe and the main international actors, such as China and the US, by achieving technological autonomy. This has also been presented as the path towards European digital sovereignty to oppose different models of extraterritoriality perpetrated by China and the US, the first based on the idea of digital territorial sovereignty, the other consisting of long-arm jurisdiction (Huo and Yip 2021, p. 328).

Practical issues related to digital rights are data protection, antitrust, human rights, and the liability of providers (Ryngaert and Taylor 2020). Many legal phenomena in sectoral areas of EU data governance show how the nature of data is disruptive with respect to physical territory. In the field of data protection, the right to dereferencing (e.g., the removal of links related to personal information) has sometimes been imposed only for data located within the EU (CJEU, *CNIL* case), but it has also been granted to individuals vis-à-vis companies established outside the EU to which EU data protection law has been applied (CJEU, *Google Spain* case). In disputes related to electronic commerce, the imposition on intermediaries to remove illegal content has operated worldwide (SCC *Equusteek* and CJEU *Facebook* cases). In the field of law enforcement's access to data, some warrants have been issued by public authorities to service providers to release data irrespective of their location storage (*U.S. v. Microsoft* case). In intellectual property law, the orders directed by national courts towards operators of online marketplaces that advertise and offer goods for sale on their websites targeting consumers outside the EU also aim to prevent the infringement of intellectual property rights in third countries (CJEU, *L'Oréal SA* case). For the global protection of human rights, transatlantic mass surveillance programs of individuals violate the right to respect private life under the European Convention of Human Rights (ECtHR, *Big Brother Watch v. UK* case). For the global reach of the European Charter of Fundamental Rights, the Safe Harbor Agreement in ruling Schrems I and the Privacy Shield in ruling Schrems II, two schemes related to a system of voluntary self-certification and self-assessment of US companies of fulfillment of data protection safeguards,[2] were declared invalid under EU law for violating Mr. Schrems' fundamental right to data protection after his data were transferred and physically relocated in the United States (CJEU, *Schrems I and II* cases).

4.3 Sectoral Regulatory Frameworks: Surveillance, Law Enforcement Data Access, Shut Down of On-line Contents

Data protection law has acted as a push for the territorial extension of EU law (Celeste 2021, pp. 9–26) to rebalance the effects of foreign programmes that intercept data of European citizens (cases *Schrems I*, C-362/14 and *Schrems II*, C-311/18). However, data protection has been only one of the most relevant triggers for Europe in competing with other models of data governance. What is at stake is the need to keep valuable data secure from industrial espionage, unauthorised disclosure and more general violations of intellectual property. The rationale for data protection is, for example, promoting the free flow of data with a high degree of protection to enhance international trade and international cooperation (Zeno Zencovich 2021, p. 173). The underlying lack of trust in data processing and continued use by third countries has driven a series of initiatives that aim to export the model based on fundamental rights as a standard setter (Bradford 2020) by

[2] While the Safe Harbor included as for privacy safeguards, the Privacy Shield also included law enforcement purposes.

imposing, for example, strict requirements for data transfers (*Schrems* II, C-311/18). This is the famous Brussels effect, a term coined by Anu Bradford in 2012 (Bradford 2012) and refreshed over the years (Bradford 2020 and 2023), essentially to indicate the regulatory unilateral outreach of EU law and power to shape global markets. For Bradford, "Unilateral regulatory globalization occurs when a single state is able to externalize its laws and regulations outside its borders through market mechanisms, resulting in the globalization of standards. This process can be distinguished from the political globalization of regulatory standards, where regulatory convergence results from negotiated standards, including international treaties or agreements among states or regulatory authorities. It is also different from unilateral coercion, where one jurisdiction imposes its rules on others through threats or sanctions. Unilateral regulatory globalization is a development where a law of one jurisdiction migrates into another in the absence of the former actively imposing it or the latter willingly adopting it" (Bradford 2012, pp. 3–4). Then, she helpfully distinguishes de facto and de jure Brussels effects: "While the EU regulates only its internal market, multinational corporations often have an incentive to standardize their production globally and adhere to a single rule. This approach converts the EU rule into a global rule—the "de facto Brussels Effect". Finally, after these export-oriented firms have adjusted their business practices to meet the EU's strict standards, they often have the incentive to lobby their domestic governments to adopt these same standards in an effort to level the playing field against their domestic, non-export-oriented competitors—the "de jure Brussels Effect" (Bradford 2012, p. 6).

In other words, transferred personal data maintain a jurisdictional "EU label" wherever they go to avoid violations of the right to data protection by third countries. In practice, this means that where third countries are not considered adequately safe to receive data, the only way to send data to them is to encrypt their format, making them nonreadable for the recipients (Recommendation 1/2020 and 2/2020 EDPS, Saluzzo 2019, p. 121).

Data protection law has been a regulatory field in which the EU has resorted to the extraterritorial use of jurisdiction to limit the interference as well as the impact of other regulatory models in the EU. This has been very clear in the case law of the CJEU, which invalidated international agreements for noncompliance with EU law (cases *Schrems I*, C-362/14 and *Schrems II*, C-311/18) but also when the Court has expressed fear that the use of European data by third countries could have implied a violation of EU law (case *Digital Rights*, Cases C-293/12 and C-594/12 § 68).

The reflection on the global reach of EU law on cross-border data governance has been facilitated by the borderless constitutional status of rights to data protection and privacy as enshrined in the European Charter of Fundamental Rights (arts. 7 and 8 of the ECFR), but it does not appear to be a sufficient trajectory to reconfigure the relationship between space and information. Such an understanding is likely to converge with an attempt to frame the issue of extraterritoriality of privacy and data protection within the theory of states' positive and negative obligations. Even though this seems coherent with a broad interpretation of the protective principle that provides for universal jurisdiction based on the relevance of involved interests, extraterritoriality has been used as a way that extends better protection of fundamental rights within jurisdictions that do not ensure the same standard of protection. This has largely been done through the traction that EU fundamental obligations have on EU activities "implementing Union Law" (art. 51 ECFR) wherever they take pace. If a particular situation falls within the competence of EU law, the Charter applies automatically—even extraterritorially (Moreno Lax and Costello 2014). Although the Charter does not have any jurisdictional clause, such as the one included in the European Convention of Human Rights related to State Parties (art. 1, "within their jurisdiction") or in the International Covenant of Civil and Political Rights (art. 2) related to each State Party "within its territory and subject to its jurisdiction", it has been applied to expand the territorial remit of EU law.

In the field of law enforcement, the CJEU case law has also been proactive, pinpointing that the limitations on rights to privacy and data protection must constitute a necessary, appropriate and proportionate measure within a democratic society to safeguard national security, defense and public security, and the prevention, investigation, detection and prosecution of criminal offenses or of unauthorised use of the electronic communication system; must be provided for by law (meaning that the scope of limitation of the exercise of individual rights should be provided by the same legal basis which permits the interference; must respect the essence of those rights and comply be proportional (generally related to other potentially equal general interests recognised by the EU or the need to protect the rights and freedoms of others). This means that Member States shall lay down specific binding rules governing the scope and application of the limitation or restriction of individual rights and imposing minimum safeguards to ensure sufficient guarantees against the risk of abuse of data. In other words, what must be included in the provision of law authorising a limitation or restriction of data subjects' rights is the indication of what circumstances and under which conditions a measure providing for data processing that is not in compliance with data subjects' rights may be adopted.

The leading case, Digital Rights Ireland,[3] has declared Directive 2006/24/EC on data retained by providers of publicly available electronic communications services or of public communications networks invalid under EU law, affirming specific criteria to assess the legitimacy of data gathering: the presence of a serious crime; strictly necessary measures to combat serious crimes; judicial or independent administrative authorisation; information rights of data subjects; and data retention located in Europe.

In particular, the Court underlined the need to interpret the territorial scope of data protection and privacy in a broad manner, declaring the Data Retention Directive invalid as noncompliant with Arts 7 and 8 of the Charter of Fundamental Rights. Since the directive does not require data to be stored in the territory of the Union, the control by an independent authority, explicitly needed by Art 8, paragraph 3, of the Charter, cannot be considered fully guaranteed according to EU law (§ 68).

[3] Cases C-293/12 and C-594/12 Digital Rights Ireland Ltd. (CJEU, GC, 8 April 2014).

After the delivery of the judgement *Tele 2 Sverige/Watson*,[4] the compliance of Directive 2002/58 on the use of electronic communications by law enforcement authorities with Arts 7 and 8 of the Charter has determined in practice the obligation for Member States to adopt national laws that do not allow, as a preventive measure to combat only serious crimes, the storage of targeted traffic and location data, unless data storage is limited to what is strictly necessary, the categories of data, the media concerned, the data subjects and the storage time.

This means that national legislation cannot permit, for the purposes of the fight to crime, the general and indiscriminate retention of all traffic and location data of all subscribers and users.

In addition, the access by competent national authorities to the stored data for the purpose of fighting crime must be prohibited when it is not limited exclusively to the fight against serious crime, if access is not subject to prior judicial control by a court or by an independent administrative authority and there is no obligation to keep data within the European Union. In the field of data retention, the Court of Justice has reached important conclusions in the context of the algorithmic analysis of data collected through mass surveillance programs, leading up to Opinion 1/15 on the PNR Agreement EU-Canada.[5] Legislative measures must be subject to adequate safeguards. Therefore, they must establish clear and precise binding rules that indicate under what circumstances and under what conditions the service providers shall hand over data to public authorities on request. To ensure that access is limited to cases of strict necessity, national legislation must also establish substantive and procedural conditions governing access by competent national authorities to stored data.[6]

General access to all stored data cannot be regarded as limited to what is strictly necessary. Therefore, national legislation must be based on objective criteria to define the circumstances and conditions based on which national competent authorities should have access to the data. Access can only be granted to the data of persons suspected of having planned or having committed a serious crime or being implicated in one way or another in this crime. Access to data from other people can also be justified where there is objective evidence that the data could, in a specific case, effectively contribute to fighting against such activities. Access, as a rule, except in cases of verified emergency, is subject to preliminary review carried out by a court or by an administrative independent body (Aguinaldo and De Hert 2020, p. 157).

A person whose data have been accessed must be informed as soon as such notification is no longer likely to jeopardise any investigations. Such notification is needed to allow the persons concerned to exercise, among other things, their right to a legal remedy.

---

[4] Joined Cases C-203/15 and C-698/15 Tele 2 Sverige ab (CJEU, 21 December 2016).

[5] Opinion 1/15 of the Court (CJEU, 26 July 2017).

[6] See EDPB, Recommendations 02/2020 on the European Essential Guarantees for surveillance measures, adopted on 10 November 2020, https://edpb.europa.eu/sites/default/files/files/file1/edpb_recommendations_202002_europeanessentialguaranteessurveillance_en.pdf.

National legislation must provide for data to be retained within the EU and for the irreversible destruction of data at the end of the data retention period. Member states are also needed to ensure control by an independent authority on compliance with the level of protection guaranteed by EU law. In a following case, *Ministerio Fiscal*,[7] the CJEU ruled on a preliminary reference submitted by a Spanish court to obtain clarifications on the interpretation of the definition of "serious crime" in the case Tele 2. The Court of Justice found that public authorities' access to the data aimed at identifying holders of SIM cards activated with a telephone stolen mobile phone, through surname, first name and, if applicable, address of such subjects, represents an interference with fundamental rights of the latter, sanctioned by the aforementioned articles of the Charter of Rights fundamental, which is not sufficiently serious to limit the aforementioned access, given the purpose of prevention, investigation, detection and prosecution of crimes, to the fight against serious crime.

Recently, the Grand Chamber of the CJEU ruled again on data retention in four judgements concerning the Joined Cases C-511/18 (*La Quadrature du Net and Others*), C-512/18 (*French Data Network and Others*) and C-520/18 (Ordre des *barreaux francophones et germanophone and Others*), as well as in the case Privacy International, reaching disruptive conclusions.[8]

In all these cases, the Court excluded the national security exemption (Art 4(2) TEU),[9] based on the fact that the general and indiscriminate retention of traffic and location data relies on data processing by service providers and therefore falls under the scope of Directive 2002/58, which should be interpreted in a consistent manner with GDPR, regardless of the fact that it involves protecting national security and combating crime (Wahl 2020, p. 184). In fact, the exclusion of the scope of application of GDPR provided by Art 2 (according to which, GDPR does not apply to processing operations carried out "by competent authorities" for the purposes of, inter alia, the prevention and detection of criminal offences, including the safeguarding against and the prevention of threats to public security), in fact only applies to data processing carried out by competent authorities for the same purposes rather than by service providers. Consequently, national legislation that requires providers of electronic communications services to retain traffic and location data for the purposes of protecting national security and combating crime and national legislation enabling a State authority to require providers of electronic communications services to forward traffic data and location data to the security and intelligence agencies for the purpose of safeguarding national security fall within the scope of Directive 2002/58 (Tracol 2021). Moreover, the restriction of data subjects' rights provided by Art 23 GDPR in fields such as, for example, national security, defense, public security, law enforcement—cannot justify any indiscriminate and generalised data retention by providers of access to online public communication services

[7] Case C-207/16 Ministerio Fiscal (CJEU, GC, 2 October 2018).

[8] Joined Cases C-511/18, C-512/18 and C-520/18 La Quadrature du Net and Others (CJEU, GC, 6 October 2020); Case C-623/17 Privacy International (CJEU, 6 October 2020).

[9] See La Quadrature du Net and Others (n 20) § 99 and Privacy International (n 20) § 75.

and hosting service providers. Therefore, Directive 2002/58 must be interpreted in compliance with GDPR and Arts 7 and 8 of the European Charter of Fundamental Rights.

In la *Quadrature du Net and Others*, the Court develops its reasoning on the concept of procedural autonomy, equivalence and effectiveness (§ 223, 224, 225), holding that "procedural rules for actions intended to safeguard the rights that individuals derive from EU law", cannot be less favourable than the rules governing similar domestic actions (in light of the principle of equivalence) in order not to render "impossible in practice or excessively difficult the exercise of rights conferred by EU law (the principle of effectiveness)" (§ 223). This means that rights laid down by the directive on information rights do not prejudice data protection safeguards. In fact, based on the principle of equivalence, if information or evidence is gathered in contravention of Directive 2002/58, national law governing those proceedings cannot lay down "less favorable rules on the admissibility and use of such information and evidence than those governing information and evidence obtained in breach of domestic law" (§ 224). The third point developed by the Court deserves particular attention, as it focuses on the principle of effectiveness, by virtue of which "the objective of national rules on the admissibility and use of information and evidence is, in accordance with the choices made by national law, to prevent information and evidence obtained unlawfully from unduly prejudicing a person who is suspected of having committed criminal offences. That objective may be achieved under national law not only by prohibiting the use of such information and evidence but also by means of national rules and practices governing the assessment and weighting of such material, or by factoring in whether that material is unlawful when determining the sentence" (§ 225). These three principles are the core of the adversarial principle and of the right to a fair trial "entailed by the admissibility of such information and evidence" (§ 226). This may imply in fact that a court must disregard "information and evidence obtained by means of the general and indiscriminate retention of traffic and location data in breach of EU law, in the context of criminal proceedings against persons suspected of having committed criminal offences" (§ 227) on facts on which a party is not in a position to comment effectively on and that consequently on "evidence pertaining to a field of which the judges have no knowledge and is likely to have a preponderant influence on the findings of fact" (§ 226).[10] This lack of knowledge, impairing the right of defense, must entail the exclusion of the evidence from that proceeding to avoid the violation of the right to defense.

---

[10] See on this ECtHR case law on the right to understand fully the extent of the charges in order to prepare an adequate defence (Mattoccia v Italy App No 23969/94 (ECHR, 25 July 2000) § 60). This right may be exemplified if offences are sufficiently listed; the place and the date of the offence is stated; there is a reference to the relevant Articles of the Criminal Code, and the name of the victim is mentioned (Brozicek v Italy App No 10964/84 (ECHR, 19 December 1989) § 42). On the right to comment on the accusation, see Öcalan v Turkey App No 46221/99 (ECHR, GC, 12 May 2005) § 140; on the adversarial principle, see Rowe and Davis v the United Kingdom App No 28901/95 (ECHR, GC, 16 February 2000) § 59; Leas v Estonia App No 59577/08 (ECHR, 6 March 2012) § 76.

In conclusion, stating that "national criminal courts must disregard information and evidence obtained by means of the general and indiscriminate retention of traffic and location data in breach of EU law" (§ 229), this judgement upholds that data processed unlawfully cannot be used as information or evidence in criminal proceedings.

The La Quadrature du Net & Others case has been more recently coupled by another important judgement, *Prokuratuur*,[11] which has confirmed that the adversarial principle cannot be undermined by national rules on the admissibility and use of information and evidence that permit that information and evidence are obtained unlawfully and unduly prejudice a person who is suspected of having committed criminal offences (§ 43). This judgement not only joins the conclusions of *La Quadrature du Net & Others* in pointing out that national criminal courts cannot use information and evidence obtained by means of the general and indiscriminate retention of traffic and location data in breach of EU law but also extends to data access by competent authorities in breach of EU law. In this sense, it confirms the previous case law in limiting data access by public authorities only to procedures and proceedings to combat serious crime or prevent serious threats to public security (Greco 2021, p. 235). However, it specifies that access to electronic communication or regarding the location of the terminal equipment of individuals, for the purposes of the prevention, investigation, detection and prosecution of criminal offences, is prohibited regardless of the length of the data access period and of the quantity or nature of the data available (*La Quadrature du Net & Others*, § 45).

In extending the prohibition of a generalised and indiscriminate data access to data access by public authorities, this case does not consider the public prosecutor as an independent judicial authority enabled to carry out a preliminary review authorising access of a public authority to traffic and location data for the purposes of a criminal investigation. In fact, it holds that "national legislation that confers upon the public prosecutor's office, whose task is to direct the criminal pretrial procedure and to bring, where appropriate, the public prosecution in subsequent proceedings, the power to authorise access of a public authority to traffic and location data for the purposes of a criminal investigation" is in contrast with EU law (*La Quadrature du Net & Others,* § 59).

In the case of *Privacy International*, the Court applied the conclusions achieved in *La Quadrature du Net* not only to data retention but also to handovers and disclosures of traffic and location data in a generalised and indiscriminate way to the security and intelligence agencies (§§ 79, 82, 83). The fact that such a transmission is conducted in an indiscriminate way, meaning that it applies to all persons, does not provide any specific link with the objective of safeguarding national security (§ 80).

In the field of on-line content, the ECJ case law has also been inclined to extraterritoriality.

[11] Case C-746/18 Prokuratuur (CJEU, GC, 2 March 2021).

Dealing with content removal and freedom of expression under the umbrella of Directive 31/2000 on electronic commerce, in the case *Eva Glawischnig-Piesczek* v *Facebook Ireland Limited*,[12] the Court of Justice holds that EU law does not preclude a host provider such as Facebook from being ordered to remove identical and, in certain circumstances, equivalent comments previously declared to be illegal and, in particular, EU law does not preclude such an injunction from producing effects worldwide, within the framework of the relevant international law which is for Member States to take into account.[13]

The facts regarded the case of Mrs *Eva Glawischnig-Piesczek*, a member of the Nationalrat (National Council, Austria), chair of the parliamentary party Die Grünen (Greens) and federal spokesperson for that party who sued Facebook Ireland in the Austrian courts. She sought an order to compel Facebook Ireland to remove a comment published by a user on that social network that was harmful to her reputation and allegations that were identical and/or of an equivalent content.

Under EU law, it is possible to order a host provider to remove information that it stores, the content of which is identical to the content of information that was previously declared to be unlawful, or to block access to that information, irrespective of who requested the storage of that information. In addition, to order a host provider to remove information which it stores, the content of which is equivalent to the content of information which was previously declared to be unlawful, or to block access to that information, provided that the monitoring of and search for the information concerned in such an injunction are limited to information conveying a message the content of which remains essentially unchanged compared with the content which gave rise to the finding of illegality and containing the elements specified in the injunction, and provided that the differences in the wording of that equivalent content, compared with the wording characterising the information which was previously declared to be illegal, are not such as to require the host provider to carry out an independent assessment of that content. A host provider can also be ordered to remove information covered by the injunction or to block access to that information worldwide within the framework of the relevant international law.

The CJEU different approach towards freedom of expression in the *Eva Glawischnig-Piesczek* case and data protection in the CNIL case (where the right to dereferencing has been considered only to be limited within the EU) can be understood if we think that in the first case, we do not deal with harmonised law.

Two new pieces of legislation have now established some *ex ante* obligations for providers that also have an impact on the territorial reach of online content: the Digital Services Act (Regulation EU 2022/2065, DSA) and the Digital Market Act (Regulation EU 2022/1925, DMA). Digital services include a large category of online services, from simple websites to internet infrastructure services and online platforms. The applicable principle is the effective protection of persons according to European standards. Access controllers for the DMA and digital intermediaries

[12] (Case C-18/18, Judgement 3 October 2019).

[13] See https://curia.europa.eu/jcms/upload/docs/application/pdf/2019-10/cp190128en.pdf.

for the DSA have *ex ante* obligations of preventing unfair practices and infringements of competition law in the case of the DMA and limiting the dissemination of illegal content and the sale of illicit products in the case of the DSA. The DSA has an extraterritorial scope of application because any company that offers digital services to the EU market, such as social media platforms, online marketplaces, and search engines, will need to comply with the new rules and regulations set out in the DSA, facing otherwise the risk of receiving heavy fines.

While Article 2(1) of the DSA seems to mirror GDPR in its wording *("intermediary services offered to recipients of the service that have their place of establishment or are located in the Union, irrespective of where the providers of those intermediary services have their place of establishment"),* the definition of '*offering services*', provided by Article 3(d) of the DSA as "*enabling natural or legal persons in one or more Member States to use the services of a provider of intermediary services that has a substantial connection to the Union*", is different from the concept of main establishment under GDPR (De Hert and Czerniawski 2016, p. 234).

In the DSA, the concept of *'substantial connection to the Union'* is defined as *"a connection of a provider of intermediary services with the Union resulting either from its establishment in the Union or from specific factual criteria, such as: a significant number of recipients of the service in one or more Member States in relation to its or their population; or the targeting of activities towards one or more Member States".*

Recital 8 of the DSA outlines a number of factors that will be taken into account when determining whether an ISP's activities are 'targeted', such as the use by the ISP of a language or currency generally used in that Member State; the possibility of ordering products or services to that Member State; the use of a relevant top-level domain by that ISP; the availability of an ISP application in the relevant national application store; the provision of local advertising in that Member State or ISP advertising in a language used in that Member State; or the handling of customer relations, such as providing customer services in a language generally used in that Member State.

4.3.1 ECHR Case Law and Positive States Obligations

Functional jurisdiction is not a new concept in jurisdictional theories.

As correctly pointed out by a commentator, "When jurisdiction is understood in a functional sense, as an expression of public power that may combine legislative, executive and/or judicial action, there is no longer a need for unjustified distinctions between territorial and extraterritorial, and personal and spatial manifestations" (Moreno Lax 2020, p. 413). There are no references in the foundational treaties to the territory of the Union except for once (Moreno Lax and Costello 2014, p. 1663).

With respect to the regulation of data flows, several attempts have been made to conceptualise and systematise the duties of states to protect human rights universally.

The context of data protection has considerably expanded the field of action of states in relation to extraterritorial negative obligations, the basis of which has been the obligation to avoid that individuals could be harmed in the enjoyment of their rights.

The negative obligation to violate the right to data protection of individuals worldwide has been the trigger to apply international protection extraterritorially. Conversely, in many cases, the opposite position of states refusing extraterritorial actions of states undertaken according to the negative obligation to ensure respect for data protection has been presented as a legitimate prerogative of state territoriality.

The European Court of Human Rights has developed a model of extraterritoriality in the field of extradition or expulsion, when a consequence of military action implies effective control over an area outside a territory, in consular, diplomatic and flag jurisdiction cases, and where the acts of state authorities produce effects or were performed outside their own territory. This model is based on two schemes: the spatial model according to which extraterritorial jurisdiction requires a state's effective control over a territory (ECtHR, *Loizidou v. Turkey*, Appl. no. 15318/89) and the *personal model*, which ensures extraterritorial jurisdiction on the basis of the authority and control by a state or other actor over an individual outside the territory (ECtHR, *Al Skeini & Others v. UK*, Appl. no. 55721/0; *Al-Jedda v. UK*, Appl. no. 27021/08). The narrow and insufficient framework provided by the territoriality principle has led to the development of a third model based on positive and negative state obligations. The Court endorsed this model in the case *Issa v. Turkey* (App. no. 31821/96) by ruling that "art. 1 of the Convention cannot be interpreted to allow a State party to perpetrate violations of the Convention on the territory of another State which it could not perpetrate on its own territory". In a recent case on mass surveillance, *Big Brother Watch and Others v. UK* (Appl. nos. 58179/2013 and 58170/2013; Appl. no. 62322/2014; App. no. 24960/2015, Judgement 13 September 2018), the European Court of Human Rights was called on to rule on the applicability of the European Convention on Human Rights (ECHR) in the field of mass surveillance programs undertaken by the US and UK. However, the Court did not touch on the extraterritorial implications of the ECHR, taking for granted the universality of art. 8 ECHR (the right to private life) with regard to issues of bulk interception of communications and communications obtained by service providers, under which it found that there was a violation. In contrast, in the field of intelligence sharing, there is no violation of art. 8 was found. The Court did not engage with the issue of the effective control of fibre optic cables, which enable a state to access electronic traffic directed outside its territory.

In the field of digital human rights, the highest protection has been framed in the context of positive and negative obligations. However, positive obligations do not exclude complicity for violations of human rights by a territorial state or in qualified crimes by private actors, whereas negative obligations that do not actively violate human rights in other countries should be presumed in the sense that the state has jurisdiction to protect human rights online from wrongful acts that originate, occur or have effects outside a state's borders. The extraterritorial state has no permissive jurisdiction. Based on the debate in international human rights law and public international law, the approach to extraterritoriality depends upon human rights obligations enshrined in human rights treaties (Besson 2012; contra, Scheinin 2013) and can be summarised as follows: according to international human rights law, a state's human rights obligations may arise from the action of the state, irrespective of its territorial jurisdiction under public international law (Kanalan 2018, p. 44); according to public international law, states are considered sovereign insofar as they exercise exclusive jurisdiction in making and enforcing law in their own territories (Moreno Lax and Costello 2014). Despite this opposite approach, a new model is emerging relating to the factual conditions that mark the substance of human rights due diligence obligations with regards to the effective control of the sources that could be related to a violation for which a state may have obligations irrespective of the effective result of its conduct (Ollino 2022, p. 89; Besson 2012; Raible 2021, p. 7).

4.3.2 The EU Extraterritorial Reach for Digital Rights

The positioning of the EU as an international actor stabilises the extent of European values even in the external dimension. The aim to create a "rule-based international order" has been vehiculated even in the digital sphere by the use of the law as an instrument and goal of foreign policy (Cremona 2016, p. 371).

Even in the area of external activities, the EU deploys external power to extend its power beyond territory. What kind of international legal actor is the EU much depends on the way in which the EU mediates law, the way in which it uses law as an integration project and the way of conducting its policy (international agreements, bilateral agreements, economic and legal integration) as a regulatory actor.

However, the traditional problem arising from the application of the EU Charter in a global dimension is that art. 51 CFR applies to matters covered by EU law and to MS while implementing EU law (Spaventa 2016). In particular, the Charter applies to the acts of the EU institutions and to the acts of the Member States only in the presence of a connection with EU law, basically in two cases: when Member States are implementing EU law or should be compliant with the constitutional principles of the EU action regardless of taking place inside or outside territorial boundaries (Moreno Lax and Costello 2014, p. 1662).

Paragraph 2 of Art. 51 states that "The Charter does not extend the field of application of Union law beyond the powers of the Union or establish any new power or task for the Union, or modify powers and tasks as defined in the Treaties". This theoretically means that the Charter per se cannot be used as a gateway of fundamental rights protection and simply track EU activities but applies "whenever Member States act 'within the scope of EU law'" (Moreno Lax and Costello 2014, p. 1680).

Data governance has raised a polarisation between various dichotomies: data nationalism versus the universal reach of human rights (Chander and Lê 2015; Bignami and Resta 2018; Milanovic 2015, Besson 2012; *contra* Scheinin 2013); conflicts of law that can be solved through restraint, deference and joint sovereignty

(Woods 2018); and competition between different models of data governance, as for example Apple effect v. Bruxelles effect v. Beijing effect (Erie and Streinz 2021, p. 1).

However, irrespective of the extraterritorial reach of the European Charter of Fundamental Rights, with respect to the potential reach of some digital rights whose contents are not covered by fundamental rights protection, such as data protection and privacy or freedom of expression, one should distinguish the results of sectoral legislation.

For example, irrespective of whether the residence or the establishment of addressed companies is in the Union, the regulation on the free flow of nonpersonal data covers electronic nonpersonal data processing provided as a service to users residing or having an establishment in the Union (Art. 2. Reg (EU) 2018/1807); the Digital Services Act shall apply to intermediary services (mere conduit services, caching services or hosting services) offered to recipients of the service that have their place of establishment or are located in the Union; the AI Act applies to providers placing on the market or putting into service AI systems in the Union; users of AI systems located within the Union; providers and users located in third countries if the output is used in the Union.

The development of the territorial scope of the GDPR by the courts and DPAs will continue to be marked by tension between the protection of fundamental rights and the need to limit the extraterritorial reach of EU law.

4.3.3 Tallinn Manual and Public International Law of Cyberspace

Two definitions are important for the aims of this book: sovereignty and jurisdiction.

Sovereignty gives legal authority to exercise jurisdiction in a case. This principle also bars states from exercising jurisdiction beyond its borders, though with some possible exceptions, including the principle of nationality, passive personality principle, protective principle, and possibly universal jurisdiction in extreme cases of human rights violations.

As pointed out by Eichesener, data can be accessed everywhere and regardless of physical proximity (Eichensehr 2017, p. 145). The linkage with territory is then not excluded in principle; however, it is nonrelevant in the sense of ubiquity and continuity of data with respect to territories. This means that if data lies in territories, such territories should be continuous.

Different answers produce, however, different outcomes.

Rule 11 Tallinn Manual on "Extraterritorial enforcement jurisdiction" states that "enforcement jurisdiction over cyber infrastructure, cyber activities, and persons who engage in such cyber activities is generally limited to the territory of the State that is exercising the jurisdiction... but it recognises that a state may "exercise extraterritorial enforcement jurisdiction in relation to persons, objects, and cyber activities on the basis of: (a) a specific allocation of authority under international law; or (b) valid consent by a foreign government to exercise jurisdiction on its territory." Therefore, the alternatives are sovereign power recognised under international law or sovereign deference.

As the Tallinn Manual points out, "the physical, logical, and social layers of cyberspace are encompassed in the principle of sovereignty. The physical layer comprises the physical network components (i.e., hardware and other infrastructure, such as cables, routers, servers, and computers). The logical layer consists of the connections that exist between network devices. It includes applications, data, and protocols that allow the exchange of data across the physical layer. The social layer encompasses individuals and groups engaged in cyber activities".

Although the Tallinn Manual revised version is a non-legally binding instrument on international law and it aims at regulating cyber operations in the context of cyberwar, it is useful to explore the reasoning of international law in the field of data government. It starts by stating that the principle of sovereignty applies to cyberspace, although in international relations applied to cyberspace, the principle of sovereignty applies, for example, differently to diplomats from other state nationals and overlaps on many occasions with the idea of domestic law. Similarly, it deserves some specifications in the domains of the sea, air and space. In relation to sovereignty, jurisdiction can be defined as competence under national law.

This assumption is the precondition of any concept of sovereignty. According to Rule 2, a State enjoys internal sovereign authority with regard to the cyber infrastructure, persons, and cyber activities located within its territory, subject to its international legal obligations. To the premises of sovereign powers, both concepts of jurisdiction—territorial and extraterritorial—belong. According to Rule 8, for example, jurisdiction is subject to limitations set forth in international law, according to which a State may exercise territorial and extraterritorial jurisdiction over cyber activities. Extraterritorial claims, for example, allow states to exercise sovereign rights, including jurisdiction, over government data and that of their nationals stored or transmitted outside their territory, subject to specific restrictions that are imposed by international law.

One important principle—the due diligence principle—connected to the above mentioned principle is that every State has the obligation not to allow that its territory is used for acts that are contrary to the rights of other states.

4.3.4 GDPR and the Territorial Scope of Data Protection

Although the GDPR is a European Regulation, its territorial reach extends over European boundaries. This effect is not novel to privacy law (Svantesson 2014, p. 58) and has increasingly incentivized after GDPR. Nonetheless, contrary to some readings (Taylor 2023, p. 107), this book argues that territorial enlargement of the scope of application has nothing to do with the substantial connection enshrined in the Harvard Draft Principle.

The EU in fact solves the issue of replicating regulation over regulation. In fact, benefiting from its renowned experience as a global interlocutor and from its present and promising future role as a legal innovator, it first intended to build a highly successful piece of legislation, the GDPR, endowed it with extraterritorial effectiveness, and then shaped the regulation of data through the EU Data Strategy, such as the Data Governance Act, Data Act, Data Markets Act, Data Services Act, NIS Directive, AI Act, and Regulation on non-personal Data in its composite and heterogeneous fashion, based on the advantage of the "first mover" as a kind of positive spillover of regulatory know-how (Fahey 2022).

From a territorial perspective, the GDPR does not differentiate between controllers and processors and sets out the same territorial scope for both. The GDPR mainly applies in the following two situations: the processing of personal data takes place in the context of the activities of an establishment of the controller or processor within the EU; or the processing of the data of individuals within the EU is carried out by a controller or processor not established in the EU (Kuner 2023, p. 358).

Data protection represents the field of action where EU law has triggered mostly its global outreach. Many studies have already been devoted to the extensive case law of the European Court of Justice that oscillates between extraterritorial ambition of fundamental rights protection and self-restraint.

Emblematic in this sense has been the change of paradigm between *Google Spain* and *CNIL*, commented extensively as an example of the tensions between extraterritoriality and territorial extension under EU law.

Compared to Directive 95/46/EC, the GDPR seeks to extend the reach of EU data protection law under the material and territorial scope of application. In particular:

1. An EU-based data controller or processor comes under its scope where personal data are processed 'in the context of its activities';
2. Where no EU presence exists, the GDPR still applies whenever:
   (a) An EU resident's personal data are processed in connection with goods and services; or
   (b) The behaviour of individuals within the EU is 'monitored'.

If neither the controller nor the processor is established within the EU, the GDPR can nevertheless apply. According to this principle, the applicable law depends on where the relevant contractual performance is offered. Even the nationality of the customers is not relevant as long as they are located in the EU.

The GDPR sets up a cluster of core issues such as:

- establishment, as the effective and real exercise of activity through stable arrangements;[14] establishment principle, according to which the choice of law depends on where an entity is established;
- stable arrangement, which means that it does not matter whether the relevant body is a branch or a subsidiary company with legal personality;

[14] Recital 22: '[E]stablishment implies the effective and real exercise of activities through stable arrangements. The legal form of such arrangements, whether through a branch or a subsidiary with a legal personality, is not the determining factor in that respect.'

– stability, which must be determined in connection with the specific nature of the activity.

The GDPR applies under Article 3 in three circumstances:

- 'The processing of personal data in the context of the activities of an establishment of a controller or a processor in the Union, regardless of whether the processing takes place in the Union or not' (Article 3(1)); *or*
- 'The processing of personal data of data subjects who are in the Union by a controller or processor not established in the Union' where the processing is related to the offering of goods or services (regardless of payment) to data subjects in the Union or the monitoring of their behaviour as far as it takes place within the Union (Article 3(2)); *or*
- 'The processing of personal data by a controller not established in the Union, but in a place where Member State law applies by virtue of public international law' (Article 3(3)).

The first case is related to the processing 'in the context of the activities of an establishment of a controller or a processor in the Union, regardless of whether the processing takes place in the Union or not'.

The locution '*in the context of the activities*' must be interpreted in the sense that there has to be a connection between the economic activity of the establishment and the data processing, but it is not necessary that the establishment carries out any data processing itself (Azzi 2018, p. 126).

Moreover, it should be interpreted broadly (Case C-131/12, *Google Spain*, par. 53) and can apply if a non-EU controller/processor and an EU establishment are 'inextricably linked', such as if the EU establishment raises revenue that helps enable the processing (*Google Spain*, par. 56).

The locution 'Regardless of whether the processing takes place in the Union or not' can envisage different situations:

- A data processor with an EU establishment is subject to data processor obligations (Article 28) but not data controller obligations.
- When an EU controller uses a non-EU processor, the processor is not directly subject to the GDPR but may be indirectly subject by contract under Article 28 (e.g., the EU controller has to enter into a data processing agreement with a non-EU processor).
- An establishment of an EU data processor is not normally considered to be an establishment of the controller: i.e. a non-EU controller will not become subject to the GDPR by choosing a processor in the Union. This last case can leave a gap in protection (e.g., if the EU processor has a data breach, neither the controller nor the processor will have to notify this to DPAs or individuals).

Article 3 sets out the conditions under which the GDPR applies to data processing with connections beyond the EU.

It thus sets out the basis of the GDPR's relations with third countries and its place in the wider world.

There is enormous interest in third countries about the scope of Article 3 and the extent to which the GDPR can apply to them.

The predecessor to Article 3 was Article 4 of the EU Data Protection Directive 95/46/EC, which was both an applicable law and a jurisdictional provision (i.e., it determined both which Member State law applied and the territorial scope of the Directive). The Directive expressly referred to 'the context of the activities of an establishment of the controller on the territory of the Member State' whereas the change of focus of GDPR relies on offering goods or service or monitoring the behaviour in the relevant EU market (Taylor 2023, p. 100).

The evolution of the territorial scope of EU data protection law can be drawn through the most relevant CJC case law:

- In the *Bodil Lindqvist*, Case C-101/01 (2003) the Court found that the act of referring to and identifying people by names, telephone numbers, working conditions and hobbies on an internet page constituted 'the processing of personal data wholly or partly by automatic means' falls within the meaning of the European Data Protection Directive.
- *Digital Rights Ireland*, Joined Cases C-293/12 and C-594/12 (Grand Chamber) (2014), even if it does not deal with territorial scope per se, indicates that the retention of data outside the EU is subject to the respect of the principle of proportionality in the light of Articles 7, 8 and 52(1) of the Charter and that the control by an independent authority under article 8 shall apply also when data are not retained in the EU, as there is not a specific obligation in this sense.
- The *Google Spain*, Case 131-12 (Grand Chamber) (2014) applies the EU data protection law in light of the inextricable link between the activity of the search engine operated by Google Inc., the parent company, and the activity of Google Spain, the latter must be regarded as an establishment of the former and the processing of personal data is carried out in context of the activities of that establishment. The display of personal data on a search results page constitutes processing of such data if accompanied, on the same page, by the display of advertising linked to the search terms, because it is carried out in the context of the commercial and advertising activity of the controller's establishment on the territory of a Member State, that is the Spanish territory. The context of the activities of an establishment of the controller on the territory of a Member State relies on the activity of the operator of a search engine setting up in a Member State a branch or subsidiary which is intended to promote and sell advertising space offered by that engine and which orientates its activity towards the inhabitants of that Member State (Sartor and Viola De Azevedo Cuhna 2014, p. 657)
- *Weltimmo,* Case C-230/14 (2015): the case dealt with applicable data protection law of a Member State where the controller was located if the activities were 'mainly or entirely directed at that Member State', in so far as that controller exercises, through stable arrangements in the territory of that Member State, a real and effective activity in the context of which data processing is carried out. It also addresses the allocation of jurisdiction between Member State data pro-

tection authorities (DPAs) based on the effective powers of intervention only within the territory of their own Member State.

- *Schrems I*, Case C-362/14 (Grand Chamber) (2015): data transfer rules must comply with the standards enshrined in the application of the Charter of fundamental rights. In particular, the Court invalidated the EU-US Safe Harbour scheme because it did not ensure effective adequate protection against data access by US public authorities with regard to personal data that had been transferred to the United States;
- *Schrems II, Case C-311/18* (Grand Chamber) (2020): This case invalidated the adequacy decision issued by the European Commission on 12 July 2016 for European data transfers towards US on the basis of Privacy Shield (the act that replaced the Safe Harbor) for lack of compliance with the requirements "stemming from the GDPR read in the light of the Charter" (§ 161). This, on the one hand, means that EU data protection principles prevail in US security laws; on the other hand, it identifies the factors to be considered when assessing the limitation to fundamental rights pursuant to art. 52 CFR: legal provision; legal basis; proportionality regarding scope and application as well as minimum individual safeguards; effective and enforceable data subjects' rights;
- *EU-Canada PNR*, Opinion 1/15 (Grand Chamber) (2017): the Court evaluated the application of EU standards to data processing in Canada considering he EU-Canada Passenger Number Agreement incompatible with
- *Wirtschaftsakademie*, Case C-210/16 (Grand Chamber) (2018): the Court opined on applicable law and DPA competence in an intra-EU context.
- *Google* v *CNIL*, Case C-507/17, (Grand Chamber) (2019): under the DPD and the GDPR, the right to dereferencing of search engine results should only apply within the EU; the nature of the Internet means that the extraterritorial effects of EU law should not apply (note: the Court interprets the territorial scope of the right to erasure under Article 17 GDPR, which refers only to Member States and distinguishes it from the territorial scope of application of the GDPR under Article 3).

The second paragraph of Article 3 is related to the processing of personal data of data subjects in the Union by a controller or processor not established in the Union where the processing is related to the offering of goods or services to data subjects in the Union or the monitoring of their behaviour in as far as it takes place within the Union.

This situation requires the processing of the personal data of data subjects who are in the Union by a controller or processor not established in the Union *and* one of the two following factors: a) The processing is related to the offering of goods or services (regardless of payment) to data subjects in the Union, or b) The monitoring of their behaviour in as far as it takes place within the Union.

The processing of the personal data of data subjects who are in the Union applies only to individuals in the Union, regardless of nationality, residence, or legal status. Moreover, the processing of EU individuals in a third country is not covered unless related to the targeting of individuals in the Union or the monitoring of their behaviour.

Regarding the offering of goods or services (regardless of payment) to data subjects in the Union ('targeting'):

- CJEU judgments in other contexts are relevant (e.g., Joined Cases C-585/08 and C-144/09, *Pammer* and *Hotel Alpenhof*, where the Court of Justice ruled that in determining whether a trader is considered as *'directing'* its activity to a Member State, the trader must have manifested its intention to establish commercial relations with such consumers).[15]
- The EDPB has mentioned the following criteria that can indicate the offering of goods or services in the Union (EDPB, Guidelines 3/2018, pp. 15–16. In particular, regarding personal data of data subjects who are in the Union, GDPR does not apply if the processing is not related to the intentional targeting of individuals in the EU but relates to the targeting of individuals outside the EU, which will continue whether they remain outside the EU or whether they visit the Union.).[16]

The Guidelines drafted by the EDPB in 2018 state that *'The EDPB does not consider that any online collection or analysis of personal data of individuals in the*

[15] A non exhaustive list of examples for a trade who directs the activity is: the international nature of the activity; mention of itineraries from other Member States for going to the place where the trader is established; use of a language or a currency other than the language or currency generally used in the Member State in which the trader is established with the possibility of making and confirming the reservation in that other language; mention of telephone numbers with an international code; outlay of expenditure on an internet referencing service in order to facilitate access to the trader's site or that of its intermediary by consumers domiciled in other Member States, use of a top-level domain name other than that of the Member State in which the trader is established; mention of an international clientele composed of customers domiciled in various Member States. It is for the national courts to ascertain whether such evidence exists.

[16] (1) The EU or at least one Member State is designated by name with reference to the good or service offered; (2) the data controller or processor pays a search engine operator for an internet referencing service in order to facilitate access to its site by consumers in the Union; or the controller or processor has launched marketing and advertisement campaigns directed at an EU country audience; (3) the international nature of the activity at issue, such as certain tourist activities; (4) the mention of dedicated addresses or phone numbers to be reached from an EU country; (5) the use of a top-level domain name other than that of the third country in which the controller or processor is established, for example '.de', or the use of neutral top-level domain names such as '.eu'; (6) the description of travel instructions from one or more other EU Member States to the place where the service is provided; (7) the mention of an international clientele composed of customers domiciled in various EU Member States, in particular by presentation of accounts written by such customers; (8) the use of a language or a currency other than that generally used in the trader's country, especially a language or currency of one or more EU Member states; (9) the data controller offers the delivery of goods in EU Member States.

The monitoring of their behaviour as far as it takes place within the Union:

Recital 24: 'To determine whether a processing activity can be considered to monitor the behaviour of data subjects, it should be ascertained whether natural persons are tracked on the internet including potential subsequent use of personal data processing techniques which consist of profiling a natural person, particularly in order to take decisions concerning her or him or for analysing or predicting her or his personal preferences, behaviours and attitudes.'

EU would automatically count as 'monitoring'. It will be necessary to consider the controller's purpose for processing the data and, in particular, any subsequent behavioural analysis or profiling techniques involving that data.'

Potential examples of monitoring activities could be '*behavioural advertisement; geo-localisation activities, in particular for marketing purposes; online tracking through the use of cookies or other tracking techniques such as fingerprinting; personalised diet and health analytics services online; CCTV; market surveys and other behavioural studies based on individual profiles; monitoring or regular reporting on an individual's health status.*'[17]

The EU GDPR Guidelines also list a number of factors that may be taken into account when deciding whether services have been offered under the EU GDPR (which may also be relevant to the application of the DSA), such as (a) the company paying a search engine operator for an internet referencing service to facilitate access to its site by consumers within the EU; (b) the company has launched marketing and advertising campaigns directed at an EU country audience; or (c) the mention of dedicated addresses or phone numbers to be reached from an EU Member State.

The third case envisaged by Article 3 is 'the processing of personal data by a controller not established in the Union, but in a place where Member State law applies by virtue of public international law.'

The application of the GDPR to international organisations and the diplomatic missions of third countries is controversial. The EDPB gives examples of the GDPR applying in Member State embassies and on cruise ships.

However, Article 3(3) highlights the EU legislature's poor understanding of public international law, at least with regard to embassies. Member State law does not apply in an embassy or diplomatic representation 'by virtue of public international law' (Ryngaert 2015b).

In fact, public international law provides the opposite: under Article 41(1) of the Vienna Convention on Diplomatic Relations, a diplomatic representation must respect the law of the receiving State (without prejudice to its privileges and immunities).

Nothing prevents Member States from applying the GDPR in their embassies, but they have to reconcile it with application of the law of the receiving state; however, the receiving state law cannot be enforced against them because of their privileges and immunities.

Since *Digital Rights Ireland* in 2014, the CJEU has emphasised the need to expansively interpret the territorial scope of data protection law as a way to protect fundamental rights, also defining the essence of the right to privacy, which is represented by access to data contents (Tzanou 2021, p. 105).

The case *Google* v *CNIL* (Case C-507/17), against the backdrop of EDPB Guidelines 3/2018, indicates that the CJEU is restricted in the extraterritorial scope of the GDPR.

---

[17] EDPB, Guidelines 3/2108, available at https://edpb.europa.eu/our-work-tools/public-consultations/2018/guidelines-32018-territorial-scope-gdpr-article-3en, at 18.

The right to dereferencing of search engine results should only apply within the EU. As a data subject has the right to obtain from the controller the erasure of personal data concerning him or her without undue delay and the controller has the obligation to erase personal data without undue delay where one of the grounds listed in that provision applies, the fact that the search engine is operated by an undertaking that has its seat in a third State cannot result in the processing of personal data carried out for the purposes of the operation of that search engine in the context of the advertising and commercial activity of an establishment of the controller on the territory of a Member State escaping the obligations of EU law. The supervisory or judicial authorities of Member States are competent to weigh up a data subject's right to privacy and the protection of personal data concerning him or her, on the one hand, and the right to freedom of information, on the other hand, and, after weighing those rights against each other, to order, where appropriate, the operator of that search engine to carry out a dereferencing concerning all versions of that search engine. Nonetheless, numerous third States do not recognise the right to dereferencing. Therefore, while the EU legislature has, in Article 17(3) GDPR, struck a balance between that right and that freedom so far as the Union is concerned, it must be found that, by contrast, it has not struck such a balance as regards the scope of a dereferencing outside the Union. Article 17 GDPR should be interpreted in the sense that it does not confer a scope on the rights enshrined in it that would go beyond the territory of the Member States and it does not impose on an operator which, like Google, falls within the scope of that Directive or that regulation a dereferencing obligation which also concerns the national versions of its search engine that do not correspond to the Member States.

4.3.5 *Mutual Legal Assistance Treaties and the Exemption of the Cloud Act*

The adoption of the CLOUD Act (Clarifying Lawful Overseas Use of Data Act)[18] in the US—an Act that enables public authorities to compel private intermediaries to hand over data regardless its location—might be read as a reaction to European activism towards the expansion of the scope of the European Charter of Fundamental Rights and the GDPR beyond the Atlantic. The CLOUD Act created a conflict of jurisdiction with Art. 48 GDPR (Kuner 2019, p. 112). In fact, this provision provides that any judgment of a court or tribunal and any decision by an administrative authority of a third country requiring a controller or processor to transfer or disclose personal data may only be recognised or enforceable in any manner if based on an international agreement, such as a mutual legal assistance treaty, in force between the requesting third country and the Union or a member state. However, this provision applies neither to data used for fighting crimes under the Law Enforcement

[18] H.R. 4943, Cloud Act (Clarifying Lawful Overseas Use of Data Act), introduced in House 02/06/2018.

Directive (Dir. EU 2016/680), nor can it block the extraterritorial requests for data located in Europe that are lawful under foreign law. The CLOUD Act, on the contrary, overreaches every foreign country signing CLOUD Act agreements (or so-called executive agreements), allowing direct requests of data from US-based companies based on executive agreements with partner governments where US companies conduct activities (Daskal 2020, p. 319).

Executive agreements carry out cross-border data sharing through rogatory and mutual legal assistance treaties (MLATs). Whereas MLATs create treaty-based obligations between governments resulting in diplomatic requests that often conflict with some restrictions in data disclosures (Osula 2015; Woods 2016), executive agreements quickly and directly bind service providers to release the contents of electronic communications to the foreign government with whom the US has signed them. This is done via a system of certification that is not subject to judicial or administrative oversight (Mullighan 2018). In the case of MLAT and rogatory letters, a federal court reviews and approves a foreign government's request for information before issuing a warrant or a court order; under CLOUD Act agreements, foreign governments can submit orders directly to service providers.

The CLOUD Act enables the Executive branch to permit certain foreign countries to request data from American providers without the need to resort to Mutual Legal Assistance Treaties (MLAts agreements). As correctly pointed out by Daskal "The CLOUD Act thus represents an effort by the United States to set international standards, but via domestic regulation rather than a global meeting of governments" (Daskal 2018, p. 15). The lack of technological autonomy in the EU—with respect to data storage in the cloud—has generated extraterritorial claims over data in reaction to extraterritorial violations of EU rights by third countries. This was exemplified by the *NSA* scandal. Consequently, the EU has tried to reappropriate territorial shares through different degrees of extraterritorial reach: the enlargement of the territorial scope of application, strengthening the requirements for data transfers to third countries (*Schrems I* and *II*), and a defensive approach to standards setting against extraterritorial interferences (Bradford 2012, 2020).

The failure to recognise this, in terms of regulatory responses, is that cloud providers cannot obey two sovereign powers at the same time, as jurisdiction is the result of exclusive power. This creates a chain reaction: the state with more technological and economic power will exercise the strongest extraterritorial claim, as exemplified by the adoption of the US CLOUD Act, which has allowed an overreaching extraterritorial use of sovereign powers (police orders) all over the world, while EU law has limited itself to prohibit recognition or enforcement of any judgment and administrative decisions of a third country requiring data transfers or data disclosures, if not based on an international agreement under its law (Art. 48 GDPR). This example shows how asymmetrical the use of extraterritoriality can be. Moreover, the extraterritorial reach of EU data protection law always preserves the right of non-EU citizens to access legal remedies within the EU, as is granted to any individual (Rec. 1 GDPR, Art. 3 GDPR, Art. 8 CFEU, Art. 16TFEU). Conversely, outside the EU, individuals generally do not have the right to redress before a state issuing an extraterritorial order regarding the data of individuals who are stored on clouds subject to the jurisdiction of a non-EU state.

Legal Sources

GDPR: Regulation (EU) 2016/679 of the European Parliament and of the Council of 27 April 2016 on the protection of natural persons with regard to the processing of personal data and on the free movement of such data, and repealing Directive 95/46/EC (General Data Protection Regulation), *OJ L 119*

H.R. 4943, Cloud Act (Clarifying Lawful Overseas Use of Data Act), introduced in House 02/06/2018.

EDPB, Guidelines 3/2018 on the territorial scope of the GDPR (Article 3) (12 November 2019)

CJEU

Case C-101/01 *Bodil Lindqvist* [2003], ECLI:EU:C:2003:596

Digital Rights Ireland, Joined Cases C-293/12 and C-594/12 (Grand Chamber) [2014] ECLI:EU:C:2014:238

Case C-131/12 Google Spain v AEPD and Mario Costeja Gonzalez [2014] ECLI:EU:C: 2014:317.

Case C-362/14 Maximillian Schrems v Data Protection Commissioner [2015] ECLI: EU:C: 2015:650.

Case C-230/14 Weltimmo s. r. o. v Nemzeti Adatvédelmi és Információszabadság Hatóság [2015] ECLI:EU:C: 2015:639

Case C-18/18 Eva Glawischnig-Piesczek v Facebook Ireland Limited ECLI:EU:C:2019:821

Case C-507/17 Google LLC v. Commission nationale de l'informatique et des libertés (CNIL), ECLI:EU:C:2019:772

Joined Cases C-511/18, C-512/18 and C-520/18 La Quadrature du Net and Others (Grand Chamber) [2020] ECLI:EU:C:2020:791

Case C-207/16 Ministerio Fiscal (Grand Chamber) [2018] ECLI:EU:C:2018:788

Joined Cases C-585/08 and C-144/09, Pammer and Hotel Alpenhof (Grand Chamber) [2010]. ECLI:EU:C:2010:740

EU-Canada PNR, Opinion 1/15 (Grand Chamber) [2017] ECLI:EU:C:2017:592

Case C-623/17 Privacy International (Grand Chamber) [2020] ECLI:EU:C:2020:790

Case C-746/18 Prokuratuur (Grand Chamber) [2021] ECLI:EU:C:2021:152

Case C-210/16 Wirtschaftsakademie (Grand Chamber) [2018] OJ C 48, 8.2.2016

ECtHR

Al Skeini & Others v. UK, Appl. no. 55721/0;

Al-Jedda v. UK, Appl. no. 27021/08

Big Brother Watch and Others v. UK (Appl. nos. 58179/2013 and. 58170/2013; Appl. no. 62322/2014; App. no. 24960/2015
Brozicek v Italy App No 10964/84 (ECHR, 19 December 1989
Issa v. Turkey App. no. 31821/96
Loizidou v. Turkey, Appl. no. 15318/89
Mattoccia v Italy App No 23969/94
Rowe and Davis v the United Kingdom App No 28901/95
Leas v Estonia App No 59577/08

References

Aguinaldo A, De Hert P (2020) European law enforcement and US data companies. In: Celeste E, Fabbrini F, Quinn J (eds) Data protection beyond borders, and EU-US discussions regarding Lae enforcement access to data across borders. Hart, pp 157-172

Altwicker T (2020) Justice beyond borders. Extraterritorial obligations from Thucydides to Grotius. Rechtsphilosophie - Zeitschrift für die Grunlagen des Rechts, pp 234–248

Azzi A (2018) The challenges faced by the extraterritorial scope of the General Data Protection Regulation. JIPITEC 9:126, para 1

Beale J (1935) A treatise on the conflict of laws. Baker

Becker A, Teubner G (2022) Three liability regimes for artificial intelligence. Algorithmic actants, hybrids, crowds. Bloomsbury

Berman PS (2005) Towards a cosmopolitan vision of conflict of laws: redefining governmental interests in a global era. Univ Pa Law Rev

Berman PS (2012) Global legal pluralism. A jurisprudence of law beyond borders. Cambridge University Press

Besson S (2012) The extraterritoriality of the European Convention on Human Rights: why human rights depend on jurisdiction and what jurisdiction amounts to. Leiden J Int Law 25(4):857–884, 869

Bignami F, Resta G (2018) Transatlantic privacy regulation: conflict and cooperation. Law Contemp Probl 78:231–266

Bradford A (2020) The Brussels effect: how the European Union rules the world. Oxford University Press

Bradford, A. (2012) The Brussels Effect, 107 Nw. U. L. Rev. 1.

Bradford A (2023) Digital empires. The global battle to regulate technology. Oxford University Press

Celeste E (2021) Digital sovereignty in the EU: challenges and future perspectives. In: Fabbrini F, Celeste E, Quinn J (eds) Data protection beyond borders: transatlantic perspectives on extraterritoriality and sovereignty. Hart, pp 211–228

Chander A, Lê U (2015) Data nationalism. Emory Law J 64(3):677

Crawford K (2021) The atlas of AI. Yale University Press

Cremona M (2016) EU external relations and the law. In: Patterson D, Södersten A (eds) A companion to European Union law and international law. Wiley, Hoboken, NJ, pp 371–393

Daskal J (2018) *Microsoft Ireland*, the CLOUD Act, and International Lawmaking 2.0. Stanford Law Review Online, p 9

Daskal K (2020) The opening salvo. The CLOUD Act, e-evidence proposals, and EU–US discussions regarding law enforcement access to data across borders. In: Bignami F (ed) EU law in populist times. Crisis and prospects Cambridge University Press, pp 319–341

De Hert P, Czerniawski M (2016) Expanding the European Data Protection scope beyond territory: Article 3 of the General Data Protection Regulation in its wider context. Int Data Privacy Law 6(3):230, 234
Eichensehr K (2017) Data extraterritoriality. Tex Law Rev 95:145–160
Erie M, Streinz T (2021) The Beijing effect: China's 'Digital Silk Road' as transnational data governance. N Y Univ J Int Law Polit 54:1
Fahey E (2022) The EU as a global digital actor: institutionalizing global data protection, trade, and cybersecurity. Hart
Ferrajoli L (2022) Il futuro del costituzionalismo. costituzionalismo.it, 2/2022, p 185
Goldsmith G and Posner E (2007) The limits of international law. Oxford University Press
Greco C (2021) Quest'acquisizione non s'ha da fare: ennesimo 'no' della Corte di Giustizia alla data retention indiscriminata in campo penale. Nota a CGUE 2 marzo 2021, Prokuratuur. Diritto dell'Informazione e dell'Informatica 2, p 235
Haskell JD (2019) Ways of doing extraterritoriality in scholarship. In: Margolies DS, Özsu U, Päl M, Tzouvala N (eds) The extraterritoriality of law. History, theory, politics. Routledge, pp 13–29
Hörnle J (2021) Internet jurisdiction: law and practice. Oxford University Press
Huo Z, Yip M (2021) Extraterritoriality of *Chinese Law*: myths, realities and the future. Chin J Comp Law 9(3):328–358
Kanalan I (2018) Extraterritorial state obligations beyond the concept of jurisdiction. German Law J 19(1):44
Kuner C (2019) The internet and the global reach of EU law. In: Cramona M, Scott J (eds) EU law beyond EU borders: the extraterritorial reach of EU law. Oxford University Press, pp 112–145
Kuner C (2023) Data and extraterritoriality. In: Parrish A, Ryngaert C (eds) Research handbook on extraterritoriality in international law. Edward Elgar, p 358
Milanovic M (2015) Human rights treaties and foreign surveillance: privacy in the digital age. Harv Int Law J 56:81
Moreno Lax V (2020) The architecture of functional jurisdiction: unpacking contactless control—on public powers, S.S. And others v. Italy, and the "operational model". Ger Law J 21:385–416
Moreno Lax V, Costello C (2014) The extraterritorial application of the charter: from territoriality to facticity, the effectiveness model. In: Peers S et al (eds) Commentary on the EU Charter of Fundamental Rights, pp 1657–1683
Mullighan SP (2018) Cross-border data sharing under the Cloud Act. Congressional Research Service. https://sgp.fas.org/crs/misc/R45173.pdf
Nicolini M (2022) Legal geography. Comparative law and the production of space. Springer
Ollino A (2022) The 'capacity-impact' model of jurisdiction and its implications for states' positive human rights obligations. QIL, Zoom-in 82, pp 81–100
Osula AM (2015) Accessing extraterritorially located data: options for states. NATO Cooperative Cyber Defence Center of Excellence. https://ccdcoe.org/uploads/2018/10/Accessing-extraterritorially-located-data-options-for-States_Anna-Maria_Osula.pdf
Päl M (2021) Jurisdictional accumulation. An early modern history of law, empires and capital. Cambridge University Press
Pariotti E (2004) La giustizia oltre lo Stato: forme e problemi. Giappichelli
Pollicino O (2023) Di cosa parliamo quando parliamo di costituzionalismo digitale? Quaderni Costituzionali 3:569–594
Raible L (2021) Extraterritoriality between a rock and a hard place. QIL Questions Int Law 82:7
Rodotà S (2004, or.ed. 1997) Tecnopolitica. La democrazia e le nuove tecnologie della comunicazione. Laterza
Rodotà S (2012) Il diritto di avere diritti. Laterza
Ryngaert C (2015a) Unilateral jurisdiction and global values. Eleven
Ryngaert C (2015b) Jurisdiction in international law. Oxford University Press
Ryngaert C (2020) Selfless intervention: the exercise of jurisdiction in the common interest. OUP
Ryngaert C, Taylor MSC (2020) The GDPR as global data protection regulation? Am J Int Law 114, pp 5–9

Saluzzo S (2019) The principle of territoriality in EU data protection law. In: Natoli T, Riccardi A (eds) Borders, legal spaces and territories in contemporary international law. Within and beyond. Springer, pp 121–141
Sartor G, Viola De Azevedo Cuhna M (2014) Il caso Google e i rapporti regolatori USA/EU. Diritto dell'Informazione e dell'Informatica:657–680
Scheinin M (2013) Just another word?: jurisdiction in the roadmaps of state responsibilities and human rights. In: Langford M, Vandenhole W, Scheinin M, Van Genugten W (eds) Global justice, state duties: the extraterritorial scope of economic, social, and cultural rights in international law. Cambridge University Press, pp. 212–232
Scott J (2014a) Extraterritoriality and territorial extension in EU law. AJCL 62, pp. 87–126
Scott J (2014b) The new EU "extraterritoriality". Common Mark Law Rev 51:1343–1380
Spaventa E (2016) The interpretation of Article 51 of the EU Charter of Fundamental Rights: the dilemma of stricter or broader application of the Charter to national measures, European Parliament, Directorate General for Internal Policies. https://www.europarl.europa.eu/RegData/etudes/STUD/2016/556930/IPOL_STU%282016%29556930_EN.pdf
Svantesson DJ (2014) The extraterritoriality of EU data privacy law – its theoretical justification and its practical effect on U.S. businesses. Stanf J Int Law, pp. 50, 53
Svantesson DJ (2015) A jurisprudential justification for extraterritoriality in (private) international law. Santa Clara J Int Law 13(2):518–571
Svantesson DJ (2017) Solving the internet jurisdictional puzzle. Oxford University Press
Szigeti PD (2019) In the middle of nowhere: the futile quest to distinguish territoriality from extraterritoriality. In: Margolies DS, Özsu U, Päl M, Tzouvala N (eds) The extraterritoriality of law. History, theory, politics. Routledge, pp 30–48
Taylor M (2023) Transatlantic jurisdictional conflicts in data protection law: fundamental rights, privacy and extraterritoriality. Cambridge University Press
Tracol X (2021) The two judgments of the European court of justice in the four cases of privacy international, La quadrature du net and others, French data network and others and ordre des Barreaux francophones et germanophone and others: the grand chamber is trying hard to square the circle of data retention. Comp Law Sec Rev 41. https://www.sciencedirect.com/journal/computer-law-and-security-review, accessed 25 Jan 2022
Tzanou M (2021) Schrems I and Schrems II: Assessing the Case for the Extraterritoriality of EU Fundamental Rights. In: Fabbrini. F, Celeste E, Quinn J Data Protection Beyond Borders: Transatlantic Perspectives on Extraterritoriality and Sovereignty, Hart, pp 99–116
Wahl, T. (2020) CJEU: data Retention allowed in Exceptional Cases, eucrim, 3, p 184
Woods AK (2016) Against data exceptionalism. Stanf Law Rev 68:729
Woods AK (2018) Litigating data sovereignty. Yale Law J 128:328
Velasco C, Hörnle J, Osula AM (2016) Global views on internet jurisdiction and trans-border access. In: Gutwirth S, Leenes R, De Hert P (eds) Data protection on the move: current developments in ICT and privacy/data protection. Springer, pp 465–476
Yildiz E (2019) Extraterritoriality reconsidered. Functional boundaries as repositories of jurisdiction. In: Margolies DS, Özsu U, Päl M, Tzouvala N (eds) The extraterritoriality of law. History, theory, politics. Routledge, p 215
Zeno Zencovich V (2021) Free-flow of data. Is international trade law the appropriate answer. In: Fabbrini F, Celeste E, Quinn J (eds) Data protection beyond Borders. Transatlantic perspectives on extraterritoriality and sovereignty. Hart, pp 173-188

Chapter 5
Digital Jurisdiction and Data Sovereignty

5.1 Avoiding Conflicts of Law Through the Law of Conflict

The European space is the space where the benchmark of territorialization/deterritorialization of data is playing a major role (Scaccia 2017, pp. 14 and 19). First, it is a derivative concept from the one of national territories, as European foundational treaties do not speak out the term territory as associated with the European space (Ciolli 2020).

The law of the war has always been the *extrema ratio* of the post second world war international order (for another conceptualization of extrema ratio of international law see Margiotta 2005). Resorting to it has been presented as the lawmaking process of *ius publicum europaeum* that has identified territory with the concept of *imperium* rather than with the one of *dominium* (Ciolli 2010, pp. 28 and 71).

The politics of borders has magnified the territorial reasons in such a way that territory has been used as a parameter of equality among peers and as a physical warning of the principle of nonintervention. For instance, in the digital context, the idea of a data-driven war is potentially devastating, as it is borderless by definition. The very aim of the law to limit the war is then completely questioned, as it is disconnected from the territorial state. However, during the time, using territory to limit war and conflicts has also been applied to digital phenomena.

Nonetheless, while territory in the law of the war had the precise meaning of limiting war as far as all states recognize each other as peers, this has not been the case in the data architecture because the territory does not play the same role as in terrestrial war. This has been completely ignored in legal and political actions emerging from the practice of data governance that continued to perpetrate the logic of territorial expansion over a space that is incommensurable with territory.

With the emergence of data flows and fifth generation technologies for communication, space travelled by data has been transformed into functional shares, depending on the relevant subject matter.

M. Catanzariti, *Disconnecting Sovereignty*, Law, Governance and Technology Series 65, https://doi.org/10.1007/978-3-031-60734-9_5

If we focus on the reasons that lead to conflicts of law, we can realize that they mainly relate to the fact that the same subject is obliged to different duties prescribed by different jurisdictions that may conflict or that a subject is obliged to stick to jurisdictional requirements of all states with whom it came into contact.

One proposal has been technical interoperability that, instead of jurisdictional interoperability, preserves state jurisdiction. This is possible because of the assumption that technical standards' application is not conflated with jurisdictional claims. State jurisdiction is an indispensable priority for the state's stability and for the geopolitical order (Kapczynski 2020, p. 1460).

In fact, international customary law hardly supplements the state of the art. All the extraterritorial claims in the field of data government are based on rough ideas of effects doctrine, according to which a state exerts legitimate jurisdiction as far as it applies to persons located over a territory where a state exerts its jurisdiction.

5.1.1 *From* ius gentium *to Space Laws*

From classical studies, we always heard that ius gentium is a system of rules that the natural reason establishes for all men and which opposes to civil law that is referred to as one state or person.

Data flows crossing territories need both to regulate relationships between states and within states. However, data have recently expanded the horizon of applicable laws depending on the place in which they are stored. It is not fiction to deal with space laws while having to do with data transfers.

Outerspace belongs to all humanity as *ius gentium*. However, to whom is it applicable?

There are five UN Space Treaties on the outer space, the most well-known of which the Outer Space Treaty (Treaty on Principles Governing the Activities of States in the Exploration and Use of Outer Space, including the Moon and Other Celestial Bodies) is providing some indications that exclude sovereignty. First, the exploration and use of outer space shall be carried out for the benefit and in the interests of all countries and shall be the province of all mankind; second, outer space shall be free for exploration and use by all States; third, outer space is not subject to national appropriation by claim of sovereignty, by means of use or occupation, or by any other means (Article II) (Zolea 2020, p. 1)

However, international space law entitles nation states and not international bodies to manage space activities. Moreover, when data flow throughout the use of space technology, such as space cloud computing or satellites, they flow through near space and airspace, which are governed under the territoriality principle. It is then not clear enough how international treaties and customary law can supply the lack of consistency in dealing with possible conflicts of law. One possible answer, even in the field of data regulation, has been sovereign deference through two different forms: one via comity, which encourages sovereign deference by courts to avoid national governments moving from regulation by compulsion to regulation by control (Woods 2018, p. 328), and the other via courts' interpretation, which is contrary to the preference of legislatures (Goldsmith 2019; Canale 2022).

Currently, there are a variety of geospatial technologies that are based on the acquisition of data on precise locations on the surface of the Earth, hence the term 'geospatial'is mostly used. The most developed technologies in this field are (a) remote sensing, which develops data collected from space or airborne cameras and sensor platforms; (b) geographical information systems, which are based on software that maps and detects all data that are georeferenced (assigned a specific location on the surface of the Earth, otherwise known as geospatial data); (c) a global positioning system, which is a network of U.S. Department of Defense satellites that can give precise coordinate locations to civilian and military users with proper receiving equipment; and (d) Internet Mapping Technologies, in which software programs such as Google Earth and web features such as Microsoft Virtual Earth are changing the way geospatial data are viewed and shared. The developments in user interfaces are also making such technologies available to a wider audience, whereas traditional GIS has been reserved for specialists and those who invest time in learning complex software programs.

5.1.2 Mutual Exclusivity: One Jurisdiction, One Sovereignty

Jurisdiction is a "one-or-nothing concept", as correctly asserted by Besson, in the sense that "once jurisdiction is assessed, duties and rights arise" (Besson 2012, p. 878).

The problem is that it is not always possible to differentiate a defensive concept of sovereignty from an assertive one. Sovereignty has two faces that cannot be separated or used alternatively. Sovereignty is such if it means the capacity to exert jurisdictional claims over issues that are not the object of any other sovereign powers (Grimm 2023).

The issue here is that the linkage between sovereignty and data necessarily needs to be framed within the rising of certain rights that are functionally linked to data. Data are then located within the right that it represents, not on the territory where the state exerts its own jurisdiction.

In the field of data regulation, Svantesson's theories seem to be very convincing. Although they mainly refer to personal data, we believe that their rationales can be applied in different fields of data regulation. According to his hypothesis, the European model of extraterritorial jurisdiction over data has not been revealed to be optimal and talks about the tyranny of territoriality principle. He argues that the tension between territoriality and extraterritoriality has been a way over time to expand the legitimate authority of territorial states (Svantesson 2017, p. 15).[1]

[1] For internet intermediaries for example Svantesson proposes the theory of selective legal compliance.

He then tries to reconceptualize and update the applicability of the Harvard draft principle. It was drafted in the context of law enforcement to highlight the substantial connection factors (defendant's or plaintiff's connection factors with forum jurisdictions), the legitimate interest of the state that claims jurisdiction and the reasonableness of the exercise of jurisdiction sometimes sought as balance of interests (defendant's or plaintiff's or third parties' or contacts with other jurisdictions). Svantesson points out that if it is not easy to assess data when an activity takes place in the territory of a state, then the use of the territoriality principle risks not reflecting reality and being illegitimate (Svantesson 2017, p. 79).

An issue that increasingly gets relevance is that all has a virtual side, but not all can be considered within the data realm to justify a jurisdictional claim exceeding nation states' prerogatives.

Conflicts of law stemming from data regulation may involve different kinds of conflicts that have nothing to do with territoriality.

From a theoretical perspective, the process of juridification went through the decolonization of words. For instance, dominium has been transformed into sovereignty, with all limitations deriving from legal definitions, and property has been translated into jurisdiction.

In cyberlaw, prescriptive jurisdiction is competing with other jurisdictional claims (Schmitt 2017, p. 52 & Rule 10), whereas enforcement jurisdiction is generally exclusive (only upon consent of receiving States or pursuant to international law) (Tallin Manual 2017, Rule 11).

Three are the cases for the exercise of territorial jurisdiction: (a) cyber infrastructure and persons engaged in cyber activities in its territory; (b) cyber activities originating in, or completed on, its territory; or (c) cyber activities having a substantial effect in its territory.

Kristen Eichensehr, for example, proposes a double test consisting of the location of data and the location where data are accessed (Eichensehr 2017, p. 145).

Prescriptive jurisdiction over persons engaged in cyber activities abroad, cyber infrastructure located abroad, or cyber-related conduct taking place or having effects beyond a State's territory must be grounded upon one of the generally recognized bases for extraterritorial jurisdiction. The jurisdictional relation is traditionally conceived as one-to-one. The sovereign deference does not preclude extraterritorial production orders, global injunctions, or international agreements (Woods 2018, p. 386). In any event, there could be several reasons to better justify the connection between jurisdiction and the object of regulation, such as the structure of global governance through which some states govern transboundary markets. This requires considering territory as a political technology rather than a naturally limited state: the fact that a created space is not natural may also imply its nonexistence. On such a radical, although Krisch builds on the concept of "unbound jurisdiction", which is based on alternative connections to the state nexus, "the various points of contact are seen as an expression not only of a broader principle but also of a new general rule according to which the exercise of jurisdiction is permissible if there is a 'genuine connection' between the state and the object of regulation" (Krisch 2022, p. 485). The traditional function of jurisdiction summarized in Ryngaert's formulation, consisting of 'delimiting States' spheres of action and thus reducing conflicts between States' (Ryngaert 2015a; Krisch 2022, p. 486), increasingly needs to recenter itself.

The option is twofold: continuing to follow traditional categories reterritorializing global phenomena, as for example "Ralf Michaels' call for domestic courts to act as 'global courts' in order to tackle global problems is a good example of this approach […] to advocate for a broader jurisdictional reach of national courts when faced with globalized markets, transboundary human rights violations and other problems of a global character" (Krisch 2022, p. 487) or structuring an assemblage of competing claims. In the first case, following traditional categories represents a risk for states because "jurisdiction operates less as a principle of demarcation than as 'a diverse array of strategies used by national regulators to exert regulatory authority over often mobile market participants'" (Krisch 2022, p. 512).

5.1.3 Relinquishing Sovereignty

Digital sovereignty means acting independently in the digital world. However, this definition is far from precise. It draws a vague and indefinite trajectory: the new European strategy seeks to put together sovereignty and ethics, where sovereignty is used to revenge autonomy and independence, while ethics represents a tool to harmonize different legal frameworks.

In recent years, Europe has adopted a buzzy regulatory methodology to proceed in uncovered areas that uses different tools to ascertain the European leading role in the values' architecture.

On the one hand, this choice is because different approaches encompass a real strategy of a polity that tries to find its own leeway to see what is the most suitable modality to gain regulatory traction towards global interlocutors (Foucault 2023, p. 81).

The perplexity arises from the fact that applied principles and values risk showing their weakness if they are not contextualized within an industrial strategy that supports possible choices.

Information tries to follow the states' routes of control, although not coinciding with those.

Nonetheless, territory is not included in Hobbes's definition of sovereignty. They are assumed to be the outer limit of authority (Glenn 2013).

In light of users, digital sovereignty has to do with the power to grant or deny access to data generated by users. Translated into functionalities, this means storing data where users consider it useful to do so, considering the respective data classification. This means that users can retain command over particularly sensitive data while simultaneously sharing other data with partners for joint use.

The enormous debate on the incompatibility between the internet and sovereign powers has been revealed to be vague and non-effective. Sovereignty is a powerful concept in addition to being a legal construction. For this reason, it can be filled in with contingent needs that turn relevant depending on the context. There are evocative narratives surrounding the concept of digital sovereignty, such as the economic narrative, the modern state narrative, the security narrative and the European way of life narrative, that contribute to what Lambach and Oppermann call "rethorical performativity" (Lambach and Oppermann 2022, p. 14).

As correctly commented by Julie Cohen, "networked digital media technologies and infrastructures are not—and never could be—simply instrumentalities of liberation, and law is not—and never could be—simply an instrumentality for the promotion of just outcomes, a neutral arbiter of disputes, or a disinterested agent of modernization" (Cohen 2021, p. 5). This thesis complements the famous Lessig's theory of "code is law" in which however, as Lessig warns, unregulability is also a function of the code that should be controlled (Lessig 1999).

5.2 Data Nationalism Through Data Location

The securitization of borders has imposed a new narrative of places and spaces (Chander and Lê 2015, p. 677). Protecting borders gives the impression of making territories safer, enhancing sovereign powers or reducing the risk of threats. The different declinations of security clearly represent the stakes of civilization and at the same time the threat of its sinking. Such a trend is generalized and overarching and works regardless of democratic institutions. The use of territorial mechanisms is traditionally a way to assert power with respect to different situations, individuals and places.

The objective of the EU data strategy is to overcome sector data spaces throughout data sharing. While the Data Governance Act sets up rules for data sharing across sectors and EU countries, the Data Act lays down harmonised rules on making data generated by the use of a product or related service available to the user of that product or service. If data is personal, data holders are considered controllers. Nonpersonal data, on the contrary, can use any data generated by the products on the basis of contractual agreements. At the same time, upon request by a user or by a party acting on behalf of a user, data holders shall make available the data generated by the use of a product or related service. Data should be made available for exceptional needs to public sector bodies or Union agencies where the data requested are necessary to respond to a public emergency:

1. where the data request is limited in time and scope and necessary to prevent a public emergency or to assist the recovery from a public emergency;
2. where the lack of available data prevents the public sector body or Union institution, agency or body from fulfilling a specific task in the public interest.

Switching between cloud and edge computing should be ensured in relation to the possibility of stipulating contracts with minimum content. Cloud computing services are rarely offered in one member state only. The cross-border processing of data within the Union is essential for conducting business in the internal market. It is therefore crucial that provisions on switching data processing services are applied at the union level to avoid harmful fragmentation in an otherwise unified market for data processing services.

The impulse to securitization has been exponentially accelerated by computational power to handle enormous quantities of data. Identity checks happen at border controls, which is why the bodies of foreigners are conceptualized as borders themselves and checked through sophisticated scans. However, the construction of autonomous borders clashes with the concept of contingency in the use of territory, as it aims at predetermining the rights of entry and stay of individuals through algorithmic profiling and facial recognition. Some policies have been sharpened throughout the use of advanced technologies aimed at targeted and capillary techniques of control. Recent reforms in security, migration and border management across the EU show this trend very well.

5.2.1 *Jeopardizing Sovereign Powers Through Borderless Governance*

The Data Act establishes a set of rules on the use of data. The Data Governance Act instead aims to create a safe space for data sharing between public actors and private sector data.

However, the EU Digital Strategy, although being very structured through the flourishing of many legal instruments, is still limited to a reaction towards big techs. The EU compass for innovation is based on rules that act in a defensive way with respect to informational asymmetries and the commercial power of private sector data. Information technologies reflect and reproduce economic and political power (Costabile 2002; Casadei and Pietropaoli 2024). It is the inherent non-materiality of data that creates confusion.

The problem is not the ownership of data but rather the ownership of servers through which transactions are made: an enormous power to collect, craft and extract value.

As Cohen describes, "[r]ealizing the profit potential of commercial surveillance activity requires practices that mark data flows with indicia of ownership" (Cohen 2021, p. 62).

Public domain data management works alongside other legal rules that protect platforms—so the fact that there are no property rights is true under the law but false in reality.

Law is a complex system that works all together. The problem of territoriality is increasingly emerging with digital law, but it has since been the benchmark of the law.

In Carl Schmitt's theorization, the equality of sovereign powers is something that only happened during the interstate period. Maritime war is the representation of a war that does not respect the principle of equality, either against private parties. It is the equivalent of something that may happen with data governance and power relationships (Schmitt 1991, p. 413).

The blurring of private parties belonging to the territorial state determines a blurring in the concept of the war. Metaphors of war have been very powerful in describing jurisdictional claims exceeding territory. The post-11/9 has represented an excuse for an extraterritorial policy regarding the judicial authority of the US (Putnam 2016, p. 28).

As far as territoriality is preserved, we can ensure that a community of enemies and repeated players performs its duties. The idea of an oriented law, i.e., a contingent international law, bears the memory of its origin.

The relationship between order and orientation is not called a decision; it is called a nomos in Schmittian theorization.

Nomos is both *Ordnung* und *Ortung*, order and orientation, concrete historical orders, which arise from something, are for someone and against someone.

Liberalism believes that politics is the realm of the private sphere. Technique is the typical tool of liberal-capitalist democracies. The ius publicum europaeum is the counterhistory of the state—anti-universalism. However, contingency being a constant variable of politics means not being able not to be. This implies deconstructing modernity, that the principle of equality can be twisted. Schmitt is a great enemy of the concept of the liberal democratic West.

Common sense, even scientific common sense, follows the winners. The history of the Western hemisphere is the history of the shifting of a line. The West is indeterminate because it provides no orientation.

The state is a concrete detail; it can never be the universal political form extended across the planet.

In Schmittian view, the universal character of human rights is inconceivable because it should mean that the world is a smooth space. The only form of order is division, in the form of large spaces. Universality produces uncontrolled effects. Schmitt believes that the unconditioned character is a conditional character that ignores itself for which the necessary contingency of reason exists.

Applying Schmitt's idea of nomos to the governance of data distorts the principle of free movement and the division of space. Data amplify spaces by connecting them, but they are not connected by their nature to any space, and for this, they realize universality.

Autonomy means the absence of any technological interdependency from other countries, namely, from the US and China. The issue at stake is that in Europe, the law comes first, as cultural factor, instead of technological infrastructures. Digital innovation is then constructed across digital law. However, the factual character of nomos has historically preceded the positioning of the law in the sense that the act of sharing is itself implicitly an appropriation of land.

In legal terms, the essence of state sovereignty is the monopoly of decision-making (Schmitt 1972b, p. 40; Preterossi 1996). The exception makes it visible the essence of the state authority. Here, decision-making is different from legal rules; in fact, the authority shows that it does not need the law to create/make the law.

Carl Schmitt warns about the fact that among all legal concepts, sovereignty is the one that is more subject to the influence of actual interests (Schmitt 1972a, p. 43).

Max Weber elaborated three concepts of legal form. The first is the conceptual clarification of legal content as normative content. The second is the function of decision-making that specializes and rationalizes as the need for communication grows: modern rationalization of law in a specialized legal sense and construction of the formal qualities or of the transcendental conditioning of legal knowledge and always equal regularity. The third one, most relevant, is the concept of legal form that does not have the aprioristic emptiness of the transcendental form, since it arises precisely from legal concreteness. The problem of the legal form lies in the contrast between the subject and the content of the decision and in the autonomous meaning of the subject (Weber 1990, pp. 59–60; Viola 1990; Pennisi 1997).

Once we acknowledge that territory is not adequate for data, then it would be foolish to think that sovereignty is dead because of the lack of territorial connection. The legal notion of territory allows reconfiguring the space as the place of action for sovereignty. What is misleading is to think in terms of overuse of territory to save sovereignty. Sovereignty finds its own way. The problem is to exert a power that is totally opposite with regard to another issue at the same time.

Digital sovereignty is defined as "the possibility of independent self-determination by the state and by organizations with regard to the use and structuring of digital systems themselves, the data produced and stored in them, and the process depicted as a result".[2] Complete control over stored and processed data and the independent decision on who is permitted to have access to it. Differently from data sovereignty which only refers to access, disclosure and control of data, digital sovereignty also encompasses infrastructures.

Digital sovereignty denotes a form of control over digital assets, which can be material and immaterial entities, thus potentially 'located' in a space that transcends physical boundaries.

It is substantial to country-specific requirements that data must be kept within the borders where they originate (collected or processed). Data are subject to the geographic location where data are collected and processed. The divarication between the geographical location of data and the place where it is processed. Together with data, even encryption keys are stored.

---

[2] Federal Ministry of Foreign Affairs and Energy, Project GAIA-X A Federated Data Infrastructure as a Cradle of a Vibrant European Ecosystem, p. 7, quoting the Digital Summit Focus Group "Digital Sovereignty in a Connected Economy" (2018).

Disconnecting sovereignty from territory does not stop the logic of accumulation, which means that sovereignty in any event accomplishes its mission. When territory becomes a space of production, then sovereignty reconfigures its rules towards a historical geography of capitalism (Blomley 1994; Blomley et al. 2001). Capitalistic accumulation is a matter of geography. In fact, Harvey argues that without the possibilities associated with geographical expansion, spatial organization and geographical development, capitalism would long since have ceased to function as a political economic system (Harvey 2018, p. 100; Celata 2009). This reasoning also fits a conscious model of digital regulation. If we embrace a functional approach, we may agree that territorial space does not necessarily coincide with the geography of power. In the field of data sovereignty, it is hard to conceptualize to what subjects the idea of effective and legitimate control may apply (Roberts et al. 2021).

5.2.2 *Jurisdictional Trends of Shifting Paradigms: Digital Sovereignty*

In the field of data protection, however, there is a lively debate that aims to extend the concept of informational self-determination (Scwhartz and Peifer 2017, p. 115) to the prerogatives of states that should be autonomous in terms of technological self-determination. This led to appraising the option of keeping data domestically stored to prevent third countries' onwards use of data previously shared and to avoid conflicts of law arising from data requests. Against this backdrop, this book wonders whether a model of digital sovereignty that fosters sustainable forms of data sharing may reject data localization as the operational tool of the EU cloud.

Digital sovereignty means that data is subject to the rules of the country where it is processed and/or stored (Peuker 2020). This approach is functional to use and access. In fact, two milestones of the concept of digital sovereignty are residency and locality. While residency refers to the physical location where data is stored, locality refers to the geographical and physical location of data and infrastructures (networks, storage, servers, and other hardware and software components). Companies can be considered data residents in a specific country, if their servers are located in that country. Data instead can be stored in a data centre located within a country also using self-hosted servers on the premises of the organizations.

According to Hobbes, jurisdictional authority could be the object of a natural personal proprietary right. "The sovereign owns sovereignty in the precise sense that it can control it, use it, lends its use or exercise to others, and even sell it or transfer it as he sees fit" (Abizadeh 2016, p. 411). However, modern theories clearly state that sovereignty is not the object of property (Abizadeh 2016, p. 405).

Sometimes the aspiration to exert national power over digital entities has different facets.

European digital protectionism, for example, acts as a moral leader of the digital revolution (Bertola 2022; Naef 2023, p. 205), whereas Chinese policies on data localization requirements require cloud service providers not only to locate the relevant physical infrastructures within national borders but also that ownership and control belong to Chinese entities (Erie and Streinz 2021, p. 32).

Data localization is the only way to make data governance compelling, transforming the concept of digital sovereignty into a principle of digital policy-making (Pohle and Thiel 2020, p. 6). However, mechanisms of mutual trust would enable cross-border data access to work without impeding data flows and avoiding the creation of nation-based clouds.

Data localization is assumed, asalready anticipated, as the functional equivalent of the territoriality principle for an EU cloud. I question this option of a cloud based on data localization by rethinking the legal foundations of digital sovereignty. In addition to the practical effect that data localization may produce on market isolation and the rise of market protectionism (Herr 2020), data localization in fact represents the territorial metaphor of an obsolete model of data governance I advocate for a different way to build the legal and technological operational space for Europe based on the potential of the law as a binding form that ensures that the interests of all parties are equally protected. Legal expertise is used to find equivalent binding alternatives to local storage requirements. In other words, territorial jurisdiction does not need data localization to cover data in movement or to avoid any impact outside borders on international trade, individual rights or national security.

There are many reasons to reject data localization for the EU cloud: data localization undermines the free flow of personal and nonpersonal data and hampers competitiveness among markets. It also produces excessive costs for users and companies that want to have the flexibility to use different cloud providers and access the most advanced technological solutions (Christakis 2020, p. 64). Data localization also reduces the incentive to invest more in updating products and offering services (Herr 2020).

Additionally, data localization would make it impossible to differentiate between personal and nonpersonal data in the sense that it should be applicable to all data or none in the cloud.

In terms of data security concerns, if governments mandate local storage of data, in practice, what they are doing is requiring that companies split the data they possess and store it in multiple versions to comply with the local requirements of different jurisdictions (Christakis 2020, p. 80).

From a technological standpoint, data localization implies making web services technically unviable because of the technical obstacles to providing online services. In a situation in which companies are subject to several data localization regimes, they cannot fully ensure data localization in many jurisdictions. Data might be stored in edge caches across borders and replicated to supply the restrictions of data location; they might be "sharded" across multiple machines in multiple data centres; and they might be backed up to multiple locations in case of failure and made accessible in many places for maintenance and debugging (Reisman 2017).

5.3 Old and New Territories for Data Flows

Borrowing a conceptualization of territoriality from geography, Atzili and Kaderkan are right in observing that "territory is conceived as being shaped by territoriality" (Atzili and Kaderkan 2019, p. 120). Territoriality has historically been a technique that has connected space and society.

Besson insists on the fundamental relation between states and individuals who needs to be realized through a sharable connection (Besson 2011).

Constructing territorial design implies a double action: the construction of space inside boundaries (constitution of territory) and the construction of proper boundaries (delineation of territory). Each of these tasks has a domestic and an external dimension. The first consists of designing domestic identities while sticking compliance to external standards (as in the case of the EU); the second consists of defining borders while drafting internal constitutions.

European data spaces represent legal ecosystems that bring together relevant data infrastructures and governance frameworks to facilitate data pooling and sharing.

In particular, this formulation refers to various kinds of actions:

1. deployment of data-sharing tools and services for the pooling, processing and sharing of data by an open number of organizations, as well as federate energy-efficient and trustworthy cloud capacities and related services;
2. inclusion of data governance structures, compatible with relevant EU legislation, which determine, in a transparent and fair way, the rights concerning access to and processing of the data;
3. improvement of the availability, quality and interoperability of data—both in domain-specific settings and across sectors.

Around the concepts of data spaces, the entire project of European digital sovereignty plays its game: a project of sovereignty without territory or with a fictitious one. The four pillars of digital sovereignty are the following:

1. To ensure the European Union's role as a protective power, Europe must strengthen the security of citizens, public services and businesses in cyberspace and set down an industrial data strategy that can stand as a bulwark against extraterritorial laws.
2. To hold the European Union's role as a standard-setting power over the globe, Europe must maintain democratic institutions in the long run, promote the return to a fair playing field for businesses in the digital single market and put forward new rules and regulations to increase accountability among tech firms;

3. To foster the European Union's role as a power for innovation, Europe must attract foreign investors and foreign talent and foster an environment in which world-class tech firms are created.
4. To promote the European Union's role as a power for openness, Europe must encourage free and open standards, support building physical and software infrastructure that is open and shared in the global digital commons, and back such efforts from a technological and financial perspective.

There is not a good or a bad concept of sovereignty in the official programmes. However, what is odd is the lack of reference to the term sovereignty. It is clear that there is a mismatch between the institutional language and the reality of the problem.

There is a conceptual misunderstanding: Europe uses the idea of digital sovereignty to vehiculate individual and state instances, but it may be misleading and weak. On the one hand, Europe does not have its own territory to claim sovereignty; on the other hand, if digital sovereignty only means technological autonomy, what is the reason to use such a term? To evocate something that is meaningful unless something else happens. It is a totally vague idea because it applies interchangeably on an individual basis or toward nations. The absence of a European cyberspace opens the door to foreign influence; however, it is not feasible to abuse territoriality with regard to data.

Many emblematic examples are enshrined in the CJEU's case law.

In *Google v. CNIL*,[3] the CJEU stated that even though EU law does not require search engine operators to automatically delist links globally, national courts and DPAs can order, when appropriate, a dereferencing at a global level.

There is no obligation under EU law for search engines to apply GDPR extraterritorially, e.g., to remove all links from all search engine's domain names worldwide. The referencing obligation does not include non-EU national versions of their search engines. The Court then privileges an EU-wide approach requiring the removal of links on versions corresponding to all Member States and not only on the version corresponding to the Member State of residence of the person requesting it (Samonte 2019, p. 839).

This schizophrenic trend of the CJEU can be understood in the framework of EU Digital Sovereignty. In a regulatory modality to which the EU is familiar, the EU has therefore sought to gain more control over third country-based digital intermediaries through legislative solutions regulating its internal market and judicial case law. This also shows, despite the specific cultural choice to follow regulatory routes, the weakness in facing the tech industry.

On the one hand, should states only have to deal with their territorial space, it would be not ideal but for sure equal in a sense. What Europe is doing is avoiding extraterritorial claims by restricting its digital influence within its borders.

[3] CJEU, case C-507/17, 24 September 2019, ECLI:EU:C:2019:772.

5.3.1 Analogies Between Data Spaces and Other Non-territorial Spheres

Paradoxically, in the context of digital sovereignty, some initiatives shall run in parallel: the creation of digital infrastructures, such as a wide cloud infrastructure, coupled with the EU regulatory framework, support investment in frontier technologies, public and private partnerships in AI, common EU standards for 5G networks and smart connectivity systems (Renda, 2014, p. 24).

The European Strategy for Data provides that data can freely flow within the EU across sectors. Data spaces include at the moment 14 sectors, and they are meant to be made interoperable: cultural heritage, industry, language, green deal, health, mobility, finance, energy, agriculture, media, skills, tourism, public administration, and research and innovation. To implement these fields of policy, Europe has adopted legislative measures on data governance, access and reuse.[4]

Data spaces need to be assumed for their potential as a relationship, as spaces of data sharing without connection with location factors.

They are rather functional spaces where the actors who have access to data define the features of those spaces. These spaces are then not characterized by territorial connection but rather by the powers and capacities of actors who interact within them and are based on certain rules.

Differently from data integration, which is based on semantic integration as a requirement to provide services, data spaces support a data coexistence approach that makes all data sources functional.

Europe is made of functional spaces, and the data strategy seems to continue on this conceptual pathway. The initiatives supported by the Data Governance Act (now adopted as Regulation 868/2022), and more generally by the European Data Strategy: the reuse of data held by the public administration (Government-to-Business, G2B), the sharing of data between companies under remuneration (Business-to-Business, B2B), the introduction of an "intermediary for the sharing of personal data" in order to assist individuals in the exercise of their rights of protection, and the sharing of data on a voluntary basis for research projects (data altruism).

The idea of data spaces represents an example of this trend, where the connection with the physical space is replaced by the subject matter related to each data space.

Europe has tried to design its own relationships with territoriality by creating a space of rights and freedoms applicable as much as possible broadly, ending up to a programme of data sharing based on reciprocal interests that overcomes all possible concepts of powers based on the exercise of jurisdiction. The scheme is tailored on the global reach of fundamental rights—on which the deployment of communication and information technologies has one of the agreements rather than the unilateral jurisdictional claim.

---

[4] https://digital-strategy.ec.europa.eu/en/policies/strategy-data.

If from a mere legal perspective, it is quite unusual to put on the same layer jurisdiction and agreements, it is, however, interesting to observe the opportunities that data offers to face the elephant in the room, sovereignty in fact.

Europe is operating a conceptual transformation that aims to achieve the objective of controlling data flows and favoring data circulation based on safeguards and rights protection.

It is certainly not easy for a political and economic supranational union to artificially construct its common field of integration, regulation, policy and legitimacy.

The project of the EU towards a data strategy is ambitious, although it deserves certain critiques.

All tools adopted in the field of data regulation include a territorial scope of application that is far-reaching and potentially conflicting with foreign laws. Although EU law takes for granted being based upon a territory that overlaps with that of Member States, the idea of a European territory does not exist. Europe does not have its own territory as legitimising legal action. Its competence is a subject-matter competence based on the areas that are covered by EU law.

This factor cannot be underestimated because—if it is true that often the relevance of territory has been filtered through the use of legal categories into the scope of application of the law—it is also true that one thing is transforming a territory that exists in reality and one thing is transforming a territory that is only fictitious.

In the digital field, the operation of Europe now—as well as of the United States over the last decade—is to deploy the notion of territory quite instrumentally, also when territory in fact does not mean anything substantially to data flows nor exists to limit a sovereign power over a physical space.

As we know, sovereignty means that an established authority exerts power over a territory and over the persons who are based on that territory. Individual perspectives in reaching technological autonomy predominantly involve individual consumer protection, whereas individual sovereignty regarding control over data flows is a useless concept. The emerging quest for digital sovereignty requires taking the issue seriously to avoid misunderstandings.

As Besson pinpoints, sovereignty is a pivotal concept. How can the enormous potential of data-driven innovation be unleashed? Sovereignty is a concept that allows states to be equal in reciprocal relationships. As far as digital sovereignty does not undermine this principle, it could be a helpful concept. However, are we sure that digital sovereignty is a useful concept?

Internal sovereignty can be defined as the supreme authority over a territory. What does data have to do with territory? External sovereignty means absolute independence. However, are we sure that we can use a concept that only has relevance in its external dimension?

Besson correctly observes that "The paradox or dilemma of sovereignty implies indeed that States must be capable of binding themselves if international law is to exist, and incapable of binding themselves through international law if they are to be absolutely independent" (Besson 2011, § 97).

If States are deemed as officials either from law-makers and proxy-subjects of authority in the international legal order, their independence cannot simply be equated with that of any of their domestic legal subjects. It is the product of those subjects' autonomy as a political entity and the value of that autonomy, which itself depends on that of the individuals of which it is constituted.

Independence should correspond to reciprocal rights, e.g., the right not to be subject to external influence, the absence of subordination, plenary territorial and personal jurisdiction within one's territorial boundaries, the presumption of legality of one's sovereign acts, constitutional and organizational autonomy including self-determination, and the protection of one's *domaine résérve*. Those main sovereignty rights are listed, among others, in Art. 2 UN Charter (sovereign equality, territorial integrity and political independence) and in the 1970 Friendly Relations Declaration (nonintervention, international peace and security, international boundaries, international lines of demarcation). The concept of reciprocity is of utmost importance because it is a rationale commonly used by international actors: compliance with minimal international standards of human rights protection makes it possible for international sovereignty and human rights protection to coexist. "International sovereignty objectively limited in this way became, in other words, a direct way to secure domestic sovereignty in a legitimate fashion" (Besson 2011, § 131).

In the case of the EU, there is a significant divide between EU competencies and the scope of EU law (Weinzierl 2021, pp. 654 and 657). This would make it possible to unify state territories to create a normative European territory.

Edge computing in AI and blockchain, for example, replaces states' sovereignty. The logic of edges is the real opposite to territoriality. Territory is based on an idea of sovereignty that is profoundly linked to defense.

In Europe, a weird relation with the lack of territory has led to first adopting regulations and then building infrastructures. In other words, the EU has occupied territory with the law rather than with physical appraisal.

Data is an elastic regulatory target leveraging technique, either legal systems or technologies. For example, the model of data sovereignty creates a form of legitimacy for governmental control over data flows (the Beijing Effect). Its spillover effect consists of territorial data localization requirements for companies (national jurisdiction over the internet). Metaphorically, in relation to the state's prerogatives, this means expanding the rationale of citizenship to market players.

While examining the disruptive revolution that the law undergoes in relation to information technologies, one should think of possible shifting boundaries. It is misleading to think that sovereignty is only dependent upon its linkage with territory, and without it, it can disappear. Sovereignty has been historically based on territoriality because the connection of a legitimate authority with a territory has been useful to produce some effects: typically, the control over persons who are present in that territory is the legitimizing factor.

Once they are created, sovereign powers have the ability to refer and rely on any other basis. Sometimes the linkage with territory is only an excuse to develop a model of sovereignty that is predatory in fact, supporting all possible linkages between established powers with persons and things.

The legal appropriation of space goes beyond territory. It does not solve the issue of territoriality because it overcomes the territory in the sense of exceeding it or adding parts to existing spheres of influence to confirm its relevance as an ordering concept.

When sovereignty lacks the link with contingency, it may become a dangerous issue. This means, for instance, that sovereignty can be justified in the name of itself without any reference to a particular situation. This risk has been experienced many times during totalitarian regimes that have enhanced the role of the law regardless of any rational justification.

This would be by the way the first time in history. Pistor argues that the rise of a global money system means a new definition of sovereignty: the control of money (Pistor 2017).

Seemingly, the relevance of territory without any justification may create conflicts into an order that is based on the sovereign equality of states (Ryngaert 2015b) whose power is limited by precise material boundaries.

Nonetheless, forcing the linkage between sovereignty and territory may create issues because the visible limits of sovereignty do not correspond to the real limits.

If sovereignty has been progressively expanded or reduced according to its function and in the name of its relationship with the person who has the power to be exerted over a limited space, its disconnection from territory does not appear a novelty. What should be clear is its foundation.

The problem of data regulation is its catalyst grid. The enormous amount of data that is processed all over the world raises the issue of technological capacity. This is mostly in the hands of large providers established in the US and China. Being digitally sovereign means being independent from other countries as well as from the technological solutions imposed by private sector data.

Andromède, Bundescloud, Trusted Cloud Cloudwatt, G-Cloud and Numergy were the first examples of European clouds designed to compete with US clouds, but they failed to be competitive (Autolitano and Pawlowska 2021).

This means that data must regain the function of representing reality—not then in their aggregated form—otherwise what they represent remains obscure and can be represented as any other thing. The problem is that when the space is not the visible factor of a conquest, sovereignty does not mean anything and becomes a misleading concept.

Sovereignty overlaps with representative concepts of a given space. In short, one can say that the issue of data space is the mimetic nature of data on the space.

References

Abizadeh A (2016) Sovereign jurisdiction, territorial rights, and membership in Hobbes. In: Martinich AP, Hoekstra K (eds) The Oxford Handbook of Hobbes, pp 397–431

Atzili B, Kaderkan B (2019) Territorial designs and international politics inside-out and outside-in. Routledge

Autolitano S, Pawlowska A (2021) Europe's quest for digital sovereignty: GAIA-X as a case study. IAI. https://www.iai.it/sites/default/files/iaip2114.pdf

Bertola V (2022) La sovranità digitale e il future di internet. Rivista italiana di informatica e diritto. 1. https://doi.org/10.32091/RIID0050
Besson S (2011) Sovereignty. Max Planck Encyclopedias of International Law. Oxford University Press. https://opil.ouplaw.com/display/10.1093/law:epil/9780199231690/law-9780199231690-e1472?prd=EPIL
Besson S (2012) The extraterritoriality of the European Convention on Human Rights: why human rights depend on jurisdiction and what jurisdiction amounts to. Leiden J Int Law 25(4):857–884, 869.
Blomley NK (1994) Law, space, and the geographies of power. Guilford Press
Blomley NK, Delaney D, Ford RT (eds) (2001) The legal geographies reader: law, power, and space. Blackwell
Canale D (2022) Per una filosofia inferenziale del diritto.I. Ragionamento e interpretazione giuridica. Giappichelli
Casadei T, Pietroapoli S (2024) Diritto e tecnologie informatiche. Wolters Kluwer
Celata F (2009) Spazi di produzione. Una prospettiva relazionale. Giappichelli
Chander A, Lê U (2015) Data nationalism. Emory Law J 64(3):677
Christakis T (2020) “European Digital Sovereignty”: successfully navigating between the “Brussels Effect” and Europe’s quest for strategic autonomy. Multidisciplinary Institute on Artificial Intelligence/Grenoble Alpes Data Institute: Studies on Digital Governance
Ciolli I (2010) Il territorio rappresentato. Profili costituzionali. Jovene
Ciolli I (2020) Il territorio europeo tra processi federali e spinte neofeudali. federalismi.it
Cohen J (2021) Between truth and power. The legal constructions of informational capitalism. OUP
Costabile A (2002) Il potere politico. Carocci
De Vitoria F (2005, or.ed. 1539). In: Galli C (ed) De iure belli, Laterza
Eichensehr K (2017) Data extraterritoriality. Tex Law Rev 95:145–160
Erie M, Streinz T (2021) The Beijing effect: China’s ‘Digital Silk Road’ as transnational data governance. N Y Univ J Int Law Polit 54:1
Glenn P (2013) The cosmopolitan state. Oxford University Press
Goldsmith J (2019) Sovereign deference and sovereign difference on the internet. The Yale Law Journal Forum, 18 March 2019. https://www.yalelawjournal.org/pdf/Goldsmith1mjtvg2i.pdf
Grimm D (2023, tr. it Malatesta O) Sovranità. Origine e futuro di un concetto chiave. Laterza
Harvey D (2018) Geografia del dominio. Capitalismo e produzione dello spazio. Ombre corte
Herr T (2020) Four myths about the cloud: the geopolitics of cloud computing. https://www.strategicstudyindia.com/2020/09/four-myths-about-cloud-geopolitics-of.html
Kapczynski A (2020) The law of informational capitalism. Yale Law J 129(5):1460–1515
Krisch N (2022) Jurisdiction unbound: (extra)territorial regulation as global governance. EJIL 33(2):481–514
Lambach D, Oppermann K (2022) Narratives of digital sovereignty in German political discourse. Governance 36(3)
Lessig L (1999) Code and other laws of cyberspace. Basic Books
Margiotta C (2005) L’ultimo diritto. Profili storici e teorici della secessione. Il Mulino
Naef T (2023) Data protection without data protectionism. The right to protection of personal data and data transfers in EU Law and International Trade Law. Springer
Pennisi C (1997) Istituzioni e cultura giuridica. I procedimenti come strutture di comunicazione. Giappichelli
Peuker E (2020) Verfassungswandel durch Digitalisierung. Digitale Souveranität als verfassungsrechtliches Leitbild. Mohr Siebek
Pistor K (2017) From territorial to monetary sovereignty. J Theor Inq Law 18(2):491–517
Preterossi G (1996) Carl Schmitt e la tradizione moderna. Laterza
Pohle J, Thiel T (2020) Digital sovereignty. Internet Policy Rev 9(4):47
Putnam TL (2016) Court without borders. Law, politics, and US extraterritoriality. Cambridge University Press

Reisman D (2017) Where is your data, really? The technical case against data localization. 22 May 2017. https://www.lawfareblog.com/where-your-data-really-technical-case-against-data-localization

Renda A (2014) The digital infrastructure as the next "EU Grand Project". IAI, January 2014, p 24. https://www.iai.it/sites/default/files/ImaginingEurope_03.pdf

Roberts H, Cowls J, Casolari F, Morley J, Taddeo M, Floridi L (2021) Safeguarding European values with digital sovereignty: an analysis of statements and policies. Internet Policy Rev 10(3). https://doi.org/10.14763/2021.3.1575

Ryngaert C (2015a) Jurisdiction in international law. Oxford University Press

Ryngaert C (2015b) Unilateral jurisdiction and global values. Eleven

Samonte M (2019) Google vs CNIL: the territorial scope of the right to be forgotten under EU law. European Papers 4(3), European Forum, pp 839–851. https://www.europeanpapers.eu/en/europeanforum/google-v-cnil-territorial-scope-of-right-to-be-forgotten-under-eu-law

Scaccia G (2017) Il territorio fra sovranità statale e globalizzazione dello spazio economico. 3, rivistaaic.it

Schmitt C (1972a) Il problema della sovranità come problema della forma giuridica e della decisione. In: Le categorie del politico, Il Mulino, p 44

Schmitt C (1972b) Definizione di sovranità. In: Le categorie del politico, Il Mulino, p 40

Schmitt C (1991, or. ed. Der nomos der erde im Völkerrecht des Jus Publicum Europaeum 1950), Il nomos della terra nel diritto internazionale dello "ius publicum europaeum". Il Mulino

Schmitt MN (2017) Tallin Manual 2.0 on the international law applicable to cyber warfare. Cambridge University Press

Scwhartz PM, Peifer KN (2017) Transatlantic data privacy law. Georgetown Law J 106:115

Svantesson DJ (2017) Solving the internet jurisdictional puzzle. Oxford University Press

Viola F (1990) Il diritto come pratica sociale. Jaca Book

Weber M (1990) Economia e società. Edizioni di Comunità

Weinzierl J (2021) Territoriality beyond the state: the EU's territorial claims and the search for their legitimacy. German Law J 22:650–672

Woods AK (2018) Litigating data sovereignty. Yale Law J 128:328

Zolea S (2020) Esplorazione spaziale e nuove forme di appartenenza: spunti comparativi. Cardozo Electronic Law Bulletin, Vol. 26, 1.

Chapter 6
How Technology Replaces Territory

6.1 Territory as a Digital Border: Discrimination and Geoblocking

In configuring a territory as a digital border, one of the main issues to be addressed is possible territorial discrimination by means of access restriction (Reg EU 302/2018). Ban of access to goods and services, payment means and conditions and access to online platforms can be differentiated according to the actors involved. This produces different treatment for market players. The market artificially fragments users' habits along internal frontiers and hampers the free movement of goods and services. This may affect the rights of customers producing discriminatory practices and reducing cross-border transactions.

The issue of borders is the fact that the external borders of the EU overlap with the internal borders of some of the Member States. However, what remains at the end? Is territory an ontological concept to be replaced by borders? If yes, then better taking territoriality seriously, advocating for a limited territory rather than for an over-territory.

The platformization of society has gone hand in hand with forms of seclusion of market shares that have been realised through specific technologies (Marotta 2008). One of these is geo-blocking, *a* technology that restricts access to Internet content based upon the user's geographical location. It represents an example of ownership of exclusive territorial rights to contents of which providers can be entitled. In fact, property rights often include territorial limitations aimed at operating price discrimination or at coping with specific bans. The risks of these practices consist of the fact that customers cannot buy goods and services from sellers located in another Member State for reasons related to their citizenship, place of residence or location.

In 2018, the European Union approved the Regulation on Measures to Combat Unjustified Geoblocking and Other Forms of Discrimination Based on Citizenship,

M. Catanzariti, *Disconnecting Sovereignty*, Law, Governance and Technology Series 65, https://doi.org/10.1007/978-3-031-60734-9_6

Place of Residence or Location of a Person in the Internal Market (Reg EU 302/2018).

The geo-blocking regulation defines three specific situations of unjustified geo-blocking through the denial of online customers' access and ability to purchase products or services on a website that is located in another EU: the sale of goods without physical delivery, the sale of electronically supplied services and the sale of services provided in a specific physical location. In substance, traders cannot block or redirect the access of users to website interfaces based on their location or redirect them to another online interface without express consent. Ending unjustified geo-blocking, however, does not cover transport services, retail financial services and audiovisual services for which the cross-border portability of online content applies.

Europe has been never conceived as a sovereign territory but rather as a legal construction whose action is subsidiary to that of sovereign Member States (Streinz 2021, p. 902).

The global reach of EU law in digital matters is a synonym of legal imperialism that, however, does not reflect corresponding technological strength.

Many are initiatives representing this trend specifically related to the territorial scope of application:

- In the field of data protection, EU law applies to all data subjects in Europe as well as to all companies that from outside Europe offer goods and services to the European market (Article 3 GDPR);
- The *AI Act*, making EU law applicable to providers placing on the market or putting into service AI systems in the Union, irrespective of the place of their establishment, to users of AI systems located within the Union, and also to all companies established in a foreign country whose output is used in Europe (Art. 2);
- *Data Governance Act* (Regulation EU 2022/868) provides conditions for the reuse of data held by public sector bodies across Member States;
- The *Digital Services Act* provides that EU law applies to intermediary services provided to recipients of the service that have their place of establishment or residence in the Union, irrespective of the place of establishment of the providers of those services (Article 1 (3)).
- The *Data Act* (Regulation EU 2023/2854) applies to manufacturers of products and suppliers of services placed on the market in the Union or offering services to the Union market as well as to data holders who share data with data recipients in the EU and public sector bodies and Union institutions, agencies or bodies that request data holders to make data available.
- The *Digital Market Act*, in the field of exemption from liability of platforms, applies EU law to all gatekeepers that under certain requirements provide core platform services in at least three Member States (Art 3. a);
- *The NIS2 Directive* (Directive EU 2022/2555 repealing Directive Nis 1) provided that jurisdiction with respect to digital service providers should be attributed to the member state in which the digital service provider - such as DNS service providers, TLD name registries, entities providing domain name registra-

tion services, cloud computing service providers, data centre service providers, content delivery network providers, managed service providers, managed security service providers, as well as providers of online marketplaces, of online search engines or of social networking services platforms - concerned has its main establishment in the Union, which in principle corresponds to the place where the provider has its head office in the Union. The "main establishment" is the criterion to attribute jurisdiction also for public administrations. Providers of public electronic communications networks or providers of publicly available electronic communications services shall instead be considered to fall under the jurisdiction of the Member State in which they provide their services (Art. 26).

In the case of the EU, it is the will to be an independent international interlocutor and actor to be taken seriously by the others. However all the territorial scopes related to legislative pieces of Data Strategy are quite broad regardless of the fact that European Union is a legitimate disconnector from territory. But misteriously, territory comes back.

6.1.1 Data Localisation as Reterritorialization

The relationship between the EU strategy for data and territoriality regards the most comprehensive problems. Data localisation requirements are the most common means used by states to achieve the quest for digital sovereignty.

In principle, a digital infrastructure encompasses three architecture levels (functions): data transfers, data storage, data processing and use level.

The major risks identified by Riesman are the following: data might be stored in edge caches across borders depending on changing demands to include certain data in edge caches; data might be replicated for load balancing if there are troubles in meeting the demand; data might be "sharded" across multiple machines in multiple data centers because the network, for reasons of efficiency and performance, might choose which "shards" of data need to be copied and distributed based on demand; data might be backed up to multiple locations in case of failure; data might be made accessible to engineers in different countries for maintenance and debugging; data might be processed in batches at a central location to add features, such as search or artificial intelligence; and data might be processed to generate "derived data" (Reisman 2017).

However, issues arise in the field of data transfers since the compatibility of safeguards provided by third countries with the European level of protection[1] is always to be ascertained. For example, countries differ greatly from each other. Whereas there is generally a ban of data transfers in China and Russia, countries such as India

[1] Interesting are EDPB Recommendations 02/2020 on the European Essential Guarantees for surveillance measures and on measures that supplement transfer tools to ensure compliance with the EU level of protection of personal data.

require data copy; Europe and Brazil instead make data transfers conditional to the fulfilment of certain requirements, e.g., usually an adequate level of protection. Specialists usually distinguish between data residency, data sovereignty and data localisation. Data residency refers to the geographical location of data that is achieved, for example, through a requirement to use certain infrastructures. Data sovereignty refers to the fact that data is stored within a designated location and that data are also subject to the laws of the country where they reside. Data localisation finally requires that data be stored within a country or, better, that data cannot be stored in foreign countries. It requires businesses to store and process data locally. The soft form of this requirement usually needs that only a copy is stored within the country.

6.1.2 Interoperable Standards for Data Sharing in the Cloud: The Case of Gaia-X

Interoperability is one of the central milestones of federated data infrastructure. Three infrastructure levels are considered: technical and semantic interconnectivity at the network, data and service levels. This means, in practice, data sharing (Nissen and Eggeling 2024).

According to the Gaia-X project, data infrastructure is defined as "a federated technical infrastructure, consisting of components and services that make it possible to access data and to store, exchange and use it according to predefined rules. We understand a digital ecosystem as the network of developers, providers and users of digital products and services, connected with transparency, wide-based access and a vibrant process of interchange. Such a system thus serves as a crucial foundation for European growth, digital innovation and new business models".[2]

The issue at stake is that technological independence draws legal sovereignty, but the contrary is not true. Data infrastructure solves three fundamental issues: data transfer, data storage, access to services and data processing. The ambition is to pool together edge computing and cloud computing.

For example, in principle, edge computing interacts with the principle of territoriality in a functional way—as it is a form of computing that is done on site or near a particular data source, minimising the need for data to be processed in a remote data centre.

How does the federated data infrastructure work? A software repository makes components available that, depending on the categorisation, must or can be used by all providers, especially identification services and authorisation services, interface components, or certificates. In technical terms, these components could be made

[2] Federal Ministry for Economic Affairs and Energy, 2019, https://www.bmwk.de/Redaktion/EN/Dossier/gaia-x.html p. 2.

available on a centralised basis via a 'peer-to-peer' approach or distributed across several nodes.

The individual services within a node and for the exchange between different nodes are implemented as functions ('Function as a Service'). This makes the following possible: a high level of interoperability between different nodes; exchangeability among different service providers (to avoid a lock-in effect); and efficient use and charging of services. The interfaces, services and products needed for this are to be harmonised through standards; they must also be able to be identified simply and used easily in a central directory for all participants. Through this, we develop an infrastructure that is the basis for a vigorous and growing digital data ecosystem.

The Gaia-X project defines data infrastructure as a federated technical infrastructure consisting of components and services that make it possible to access data and to store, exchange and use it according to predefined rules, whereas a digital ecosystem can be defined as the network of developers, providers and users of digital products and services connected with transparency, wide-based access and a vibrant process of interchange.

The test implementation involves three core areas: 1) Data storage, by creating a system similar to a dropbox for storage and exchange of files whose objective is a first evaluation of the architecture as a whole, with a limited scope of functions. First test of mechanisms for authorization and security. 2) Edge Cloud Industry scenario using edge computer centers and machine data with the objective of assessing the interplay between cloud and edge and providing a test of real-time capability as well as the interplay with 5G (Campus network). 3) Machine Learning High-performance scenario with Machine Learning and an instance of Big Data. The objective is evaluating a larger cloud scenario, with demanding requirements in terms of data volume, data-transfer and computing performance.

However, as pointed out by Renda, "Europe is trapped in an innovation emergency" and "cannot count on a world class broadband infrastructure today" (Renda 2014, p. 24).

The European approach is value- and human rights-based and focuses on ethics and privacy (Punzi 2003), whereas the American tradition leans more toward liberty (Whitman 2004, p. 1151). The US model is a mix of a technology- and commercially driven approach. The Chinese model promotes its own tech giants—for instance, Baidu, Tencent and Alibaba—which work under close governmental control.[3]

Edge computing combined with cloud computing gives the possibility to process data not solely in a cloud but also where it is generated, worldwide, i.e., close to the production processes. This is a clear example of how many places are relevant for a digital phenomenon that heavily questions the idea of exclusive jurisdiction. In this sense, we can reasonably discuss fragmentation effects arising from data flows.

[3] European Digital Infrastructure and Data Sovereignty. A Policy Perspective. Full Report, EIT Digital, 2022, https://eit.europa.eu/sites/default/files/eit-digital-data-sovereignty-full-report.pdf, p. 12.

However, the fragmentation here refers to different as well as differentiated legal effects that data flows may generate, with respect to applicable law, with respect to potential produced harm, with respect to liability regimes.

Types of data relationship between trusted partners (data providers, users and intermediaries) are encourages by the application of the same high standards for processing and storage and tools for data pooling and sharing. The software is cloud/edge cloud infrastructures. They are divided based on subject matters. The interest in sharing connects territories, people, administrations and business. Data is absorbing space. For instance, Starlink is the constellation of satellites programmed by SpaceX, currently in the launch state (with a beta released in some states), which aims to access ultrabroadband globally. Kuiper is Amazon's project for a constellation of low-orbit satellites to provide broadband connectivity.

When someone argues that the connection of sovereignty and territory is nonupdated, this is not a good reason to reject it. Why would territory no longer be valid for sovereignty? In other words, territory is a container of phenomena such as digital phenomena that are irrelevant to it. Territory continues to perform as it is related to physical phenomena. Therefore, Europe cannot risk undertaking an approach such as soft infrastructure control and strong data protection.[4]

The framework's conditions are architecture, interfaces, data classification, processes between those involved, interoperability and interconnectivity.

Coordinating operations are ensured throughout necessary central services such as repositories, directories of service providers and nodes, identity management and quality monitoring (Woods 2018). Svantesson envisages for now jurisdictional interoperability as the path for solving the Internet jurisdiction puzzle. However, I do not think that jurisdiction is a sharable concept because it is inherently exclusive. As argued by Svantesson, "our conundrum is associated with the choice of forum" (Svantesson 2017, p. 114). However, it is not only this. The aim is not only that from the perspective of international law, "there are no norms that contradict other norms" but also that logically digital jurisdiction cannot be grounded in territory.

Interoperability is a fancy word compared with an old-fashion term such as jurisdiction. However, the point is that we should know what interoperability means in practice. Interoperability does not automatically imply data sharing nor interoperable jurisdiction in the sense of having to authorities that decide on the same controversies.

Interoperability can involve common standards that become applicable as far as an interest in agreeing in certain regulating activities is permitted. This does not mean exerting sovereign powers on the same areas but rather agreeing that one exerts some sovereign powers on something and the other exerts other sovereign powers on the other.

The point is that mechanisms of interoperability should lead to solutions of agreed deference according to a substantial interest. Interoperability can only have

---

[4] Ibidem, p. 32.

a technical feature. Standards of interoperability that technically allow jurisdictions to set up rules that do not conflict with each other in regulating data flows' aftermath in different countries?

6.1.3 Reconnecting IoT

The opportunities offered by the Data Act, in addition to others, consist of the possibility of switching between data processing services by eliminating all the obstacles that impede providers of data processing services to remove commercial, technical, contractual and organisational obstacles. Moreover, this should be made possible by ensuring functional equivalence in the use of the new service.

The rationale of connecting the dots by data sharing is that the use and disposal of data should be a natural consequence of IoT data access rights.

The Internet of Things data access rights address this situation by further empowering consumers using products or related services to meaningfully control how the data generated by their use of the product or related service are used and enabling innovation by more market players, regardless of the geographical place where data transactions take place.

Untying the operational functioning of digital jurisdiction from the geographical location of data has a fundamental impact on the model of digital sovereignty for Europe. First, storing data on EU servers requires an enormous investment in infrastructure, but it can only be done on a voluntary basis. This entails offering users and private actors incentives to choose to locate data on EU servers rather than with other services. Second, ensuring Europe and the Member States maintain jurisdictional power on the basis of operational functional criteria that are alternatives to data location creates a valuable network of partners that voluntarily decide to share data on a cloud that guarantees better standards. These standards can be, for example, interoperability adequacy standards, technological security standards and/or rights protection standards. The operational functioning of the EU cloud strongly depends on the type of data that are shared: if they are user data (the data stored in the cloud), derived data (data learned by cloud providers about behaviours on the cloud) or system data (data learned by cloud providers about system functioning). My idea favours the integration of all these data through a transparent mechanism notifying users that would allow full control of data that are processed through decentralised edge mechanisms that are independent of localisation requirements. This implies the possibility of enlarging the number of actors who can operate on the cloud, the purposes of data sharing among the users of the cloud, and the capacity to exert jurisdictional claims based on compliance with interoperability adequacy standards and not based on the territorial connecting factors of data and infrastructure.

6.1.4 5G Technology and "Golden Power" Rules

The state veto power to prohibit the adoption of corporate resolutions or impose restrictions/conditions on an investment by foreign persons in certain industries is deemed strategic for states. In this sense, the physical borders of state act as a limitation.

The establishment of 5G networks has created several issues because the level of security has an impact on essential State functions. Moreover, these networks may favor national security if national companies want to use the 5G technology of non-EU suppliers of 5G infrastructures, components and services. Avoiding an approach that is based on the geographical origin parameter of suppliers has needed setting alternative rules—stricter requirements and conditions included in contracts that may undermine essential state interests, such as state veto power in regard to purchasing shareholdings by foreign subjects in many industrial sectors, such as communication, media, data processing and storage, cybersecurity, and access to sensitive information (the so-called Golden Power Rule). To supplement national measures, the EU has recently implemented screening procedures for new foreign direct investments that aim to help Member States assess potential cross-border threats to security.

According to Art. 28 Italian D.L. 21 March 2022, n. 21 special powers are exercised in the form of the imposition of specific prescriptions or conditions whenever this is sufficient to ensure the protection of the essential interests of defense and national security. To this end, the elements indicating the presence of vulnerability factors that could compromise the integrity and security of the networks and data passing through them are also subject to evaluation, including those identified on the basis of the principles and guidelines developed. internationally and by the European Union. If the requirements or conditions are not sufficient to ensure the protection of the aforementioned interests, the Government, taking into account the contents of the notified plan, the obsolescence, the cost and timing of replacement of the equipment and the need not to slow down the development of the 5G technology or other technologies in the country, in compliance with the principles of proportionality and adequacy, approves, in whole or in part, the plan for a period of time, even limited, indicating a deadline for the possible replacement of certain goods or services or does not approve the plan by exercising the power of veto.

6.2 The Promise of the Data Governance Act: An Input of Legitimacy

The promise of the Data Governance Act is to achieve more trust in data sharing, abandoning the perception that the public sector may overuse data to increase its control in an undue way. The way is data sharing through facilitating access and use of data; enabling public authorities, Union institutions, agencies and bodies in the use of data held by private sector data; and facilitating switch between cloud and edge services.

Facing the challenge of competing with the uncomparable capacities of the private sector to access data, this instrument has institutionalised the right to reuse data granted.

While the EU has traditionally built itself on the architecture of personal data protection as a primary pillar of its policy, drawing from European legal traditions, the other pieces of legislation have developed around a similar logic. The rationales of the Data Governance Act visibly show this tendency. For example, the importance given to the data itself, regardless of its personal or nonpersonal character, is a specific feature. Even certain types of nonpersonal data "may be identified as highly sensitive in future specific Union legislative acts, with regard to the transfer to third countries, if such transfer could jeopardise Union public policy objectives, in line with international commitments" (Rec. 24, DGA).

The borderless Europe has realised that leverages that are stronger than territorial borders—namely, regulatory sectors based on data clusters, e.g., normative spaces, such as health, transport, energy, environment and finance—should be developed together with harmonised practices to protect highly sensitive nonpersonal public data.

Sharing harmonised rules is basically the key issue of a regenerated Europe that wants to compete with other global powers. However, it is undeniable that developing an infrastructure on data sharing together with reterritorialization of borders, for example, in the area of migration and control as well as scattered projects on digital sovereignty, appears somehow contradictory (Rigo 2007). In other words, the new pathway beaten by Europe appears more as a cumbersome multipronged mode of regulation than a conscious model of digital regulation.

Data sharing is intuitively based on the overcoming of a proprietary logic related to data that consists, for obvious reasons related to the structure of legal regimes involved, of the transformation of the originator control principle - according to which only data originators can decide to grant access to data - into rules of sharing. These rules could in fact include "terms applicable for the transfer or technical arrangements, such as the requirement to use a secure processing environment, limitations with regard to the reuse of data in third countries or categories of persons entitled to transfer such data to third countries or to access the data in the third country. In exceptional cases such conditions could also include restrictions to the transfer of the data to third countries to protect the public interest" (Rec. 24, DGA).

6.2.1 The Forum of Algorithms

Along the composite strategy for data, what is at stake is that technology aims to create a uniformized global market through the parcellation of normative spaces.

The EU finds itself now prompt to this attempt in which data are the fuel of a "composite area of contemporary regulation" (Fahey 2022, p. 3).

Artificial intelligence, however, is much more based on concepts related to legal subjectivity and civil liability (Anat 2020; Teubner 2018; Sartor 2022). Prominent scholars have identified three forms of liability regimes for AI systems: vicarious liability for autonomous software agents (actants); enterprise liability for inseparable human-AI interactions (hybrids); and collective fund liability for interconnected AI systems (crowds) (Becker and Teubner 2022). This makes the territorial dimension almost irrelevant to address conduct to an agent.

Inspired by the 1979 Berne Convention, the *lex loci protection* principle generally may apply to the outputs of artificial intelligence as an alternative to the law of origin. AI software is generally protected by intellectual property rights according to which "the law of the country in which legal protection for the intellectual property is claimed" applies. According to the Kyoto Guidelines, "the law applicable to determine the existence, validity, registration, duration, transferability, and scope of an intellectual property right, and all other matters concerning the right as such, is the law of the State for which protection is sought".

In the European framework, this seems to be the scenario only for European companies.

AI operates without geographical limits, but in fact, its use depends on the way by which it is commercialised. AI systems do not have territory, although their outputs relate to a relevant market.

EU law applies all over the world, depending on whether the outputs are produced in Europe.

The AI Act's territorial scope relates in fact to providers placing on the market or putting into service AI systems in the Union, irrespective of whether those providers are established within the Union or in a third country; users of AI systems located within the Union; providers and users of AI systems that are located in a third country, where the output produced by the system is used in the Union.

The letter of the proposal seems to keep out of the scope of application on the one hand AI systems used by physical persons, on the other hand the use of AI for scientific research.

This basically means that AI should be regulated according to the EU law of EU companies address whatever market or if foreign companies address the EU. As correctly pointed out by Ruschemeier, "any state or corporation can theoretically be impacted by the AIA", but foundation models of AI systems remain out of the scope of application as the proposal only addresses specific uses (Ruschemeier 2023, pp. 368–370).

6.2.2 *Transitioning Rights for Data in Transition*

The fleeting nature of data generally sets up rules that refer to stabilised effects related to typified situations requiring protection. However, because of the changing nature of data as well as of the changing usage that can be done of data, rights arising from them can also be mutable in many cases. This relies on the correspondence between what data stand for and situational aspects that are relevant for the law.

Sharing data often represents an intermediate activity generated by data flows for rights in evolution. Rules on data sharing reflect the necessity to prompt rules in advance to regulate data flows aiming at producing certain effects but not necessarily generating rights.

In light of data sharing through interoperability standards, the Data Act sets out some requirements for operators of data spaces that regard certain requirements: the dataset content, use restrictions, licences, data collection methodology, data quality and uncertainty shall be sufficiently described to allow the recipient to find, access and use the data; the data structures, data formats, vocabularies, classification schemes, taxonomies and code lists shall be described in a publicly available and consistent manner; the technical means to access the data, such as application programming interfaces, and their terms of use and quality of service; the means to enable the interoperability of smart contracts within their services and activities shall be provided.

Sharing these standards is also aimed at achieving interoperability, enhancing the portability of digital assets and guaranteeing, where technically feasible, functional equivalence between different data processing services that cover the same service type. Interoperability based on shared rules for data access may enable users to easily access data. To achieve interoperable data sharing, uniformity of essential requirements is needed and provided by the new Data Act. These requirements include dataset contents, use restrictions, licences, data collection methodology, data structures, data formats, vocabularies, classification schemes, taxonomies and code lists as well as data structures, data formats, vocabularies, classification schemes, taxonomies and code lists.

The Data Act applies to a wide range of subjects: manufacturers of products and suppliers of related services placed on the market in the Union and the users of such products or services; data holders that make data available to data recipients in the Union; data recipients in the Union to whom data are made available; public sector bodies and Union institutions, agencies or bodies that request data holders to make data available where there is an exceptional need to that data for the performance of a task carried out in the public interest and the data holders that provide those data in response to such request; and providers of data processing services offering such services to customers in the Union. Three are the essential functions of interoperability for data processing services: being performance oriented towards achieving interoperability between different data processing services that cover the same service type and enhancing the portability of digital assets between different data processing services that cover the same service type. Performance orientation, the portability of digital assets and functional equivalence are the objectives of data sharing. Among the main purposes of the "Data-sharing" Act are the contribution of research organisations or statistical bodies in the context of exceptional needs, mutual assistance and cross-border cooperation.

The emancipatory function of the law is to avoid dependencies on market leaders. Data sovereignty does not identify a political concept, but it relies on a plurality of functionalities: security, control, freedom of choices, and technological neutrality. The mimetic power towards GDPR is the first building block of data sovereignty. The European cloud, which culminated in the Gaia-X project, is the result of cooperation between the French National Cybersecurity Agency and the German Federal Office of Information Security.

In such a project, the state dimension depends on national IT security technologies. The European digital strategy aims to represent a trust framework of highest security and privacy standards that benefit users. In other words, the vendor's option is equal to a sovereign claim for users as a common ecosystem for public administrations, the health sector, enterprises and scientific institutions.

Standards for data sharing consist of standardised interfaces and suitable semantics to link up data that ensure forms of integration of cloud-based storage sensitive data over Europe. However, the spread of standards creates a tension between cyber exceptionalism/cyber libertarianism and regulation.

State independence (external sovereignty) should coincide with control over territory (internal sovereignty); however, challenges to sovereignty in the digital realm mainly consist of the power of private actors who share control and operate technological interference while affecting the security of national infrastructures (Celeste 2021, p. 211).

What emerges in the competition of powers is that a state overuse of territory determines the reaction of digital imperialism through the erection of digital barriers. We maintain that an idea that reconciles the digital sovereignty of states and individuals is misleading. Sovereignty is not the correct word to identify phenomena such as informational self-determination or control over data flows.

Why then bothering legal and political categories that have a precise meaning? Is the word "digital" something that radically changes the meaning of "sovereignty"?[5]

6.2.3 *Sharing Data for Sharing Power or for Monopolising Access?*

Behind the idea of data sharing, there is the issue of the division of powers and tasks among different actors. In data management, actors' powers are mostly related to their capacity to access data and to their discretion in sharing the data they intend to. Confidentiality and integrity are the keys to ensuring that data sharing complies with the basic requirements of safe data circulation.

[5] See the conceptualisation of the term "State" in the planetary order offered by Schiera. Among the possible scenarios the one related to the adaptation of state to emerging conflicts has dominated many historical transformations (Schiera 2004, p. 115).

One of the most problematic issues related to data sharing is the power of data originators in designing the legal regime related to data usage. The Originator Control (ORCON) principle, which is a principle mostly used in the security field, according to which the subject who generates data has the power to grant or to deny access to them, cannot be considered as an example of data ownership, as the right of disposal in the two cases is different: while in the first case, it essentially relies on the control over the information sharing chain and on the power to deny access to third parties, in the second case, it may encompass all single defensive rights that allow originators to set up rules of data usage/data access without exceeding the limits of their rights (such as injunction against further exploitation, exclusion from commercialisation of services and products built on the basis of misused data, compensation for damages for unauthorised use of data, and denied access to third parties[6]) included under the general notion of the right of disposal.

Sometimes originators freely decide to share data, but once they share data, it is unclear whether they enjoy a certain degree of discretion to impose their own rules and limits on sharing. This inevitably affects the access and onwards use by others because originators may have the power to decide which kind of use their 'original' data should be subject to.

Recent steps in EU data governance show awareness of the need for data sharing despite the inability to depict a clear normative framework. If data sharing is considered for its potential capability to avoid transaction costs and speed up various processes related to business and well-functioning administration, then it is revealed to be a frontier that may overcome the barrier of territoriality. There is in particular a provision included in the Data Governance Act that traces the aim of this project to set up the conditions for its reuse: "Public sector bodies which are competent under national law to grant or refuse access for the reuse of certain categories of data shall make publicly available the conditions for allowing such reuse and the procedure to request reuse" (Art. 5, DGA). This potentially means that sharing data while sharing rules on data sharing is a way to accommodate different interests, those of data holders and those of recipients who can find a way to cooperate understanding each other their reciprocal interest in sharing. The Data Governance Act defines data sharing as "the provision of data by a data subject or a data holder to a data user for the purpose of the joint or individual use of such data, based on voluntary agreements or Union or national law, directly or through an intermediary, for example under open or commercial licences subject to a fee or free of charge" (Art. 2, n. 10). The creation of a harmonised framework for data exchanges as well as of basic requirements for data governance aims at facilitating cooperation between Member States. The minor emphasis posed on territorial constraints makes it easy

[6] On basis of rights *in rem* that include the right to licence data usage (a set of rights enforceable against any party independent of contractual relations thus preventing further use of data by third parties who have no right to use the data, including the right to claim damages for unauthorised access to and use of data) or a set of purely defensive rights, the general opinion is that the right should be only protected at the syntactic level (code and data) and not at the semantic one (information incorporated in the code).

to understand how data fragmentation may represent an opportunity to connect different spatial and temporal dimensions without having nothing to do with physical territories.

Sharing draws a new modality to carry out business, take better care of interests maximising benefits and reducing costs, and reuse data against any exclusive logic. New fictitious spaces are needed for data sharing to take place, however nonphysical but normative.

6.3 Legal Alternatives to Territoriality: Towards Functional Criteria

Territorial control (effective control over an area) is internationally lawful if on domestic territory and on foreign territory by invitation; it is internationally unlawful if on foreign territory by unlawful occupation. Personal control (state agent control and authority) is internationally lawful if made through diplomats and consuls, through other state agents including the military by invitation, through other state agents, including the military, on ships, aircrafts or buildings (these two cases can also be internationally unlawful). That recalled, the ongoing strategy to establish a model of EU cloud computing may overcome the territoriality/extraterritoriality dichotomy. The function of a European cloud would primarily be to store, share and reuse personal and nonpersonal data in the European data infrastructure to achieve technological autonomy. Based on the institutional French-German Gaia-X Initiative (Federated Data Infrastructure for Europe), the European trend toward a model of digital sovereignty has great potential if it is based on the technical interoperability of adequacy standards instead of on a model of digital borders. Being digitally sovereign means Europe being independent from other countries and from technological solutions imposed by the private sector. The Digital Summit Focus Group defines digital sovereignty as the "possibility of independent self-determination by the state and by organisations with regard to the use and structuring of digital systems themselves, the data produced and stored in them, and the process depicted as a result" to gain "complete control over stored and processed data and the independent decision on who is permitted to have access to it."[7]

Overcoming territoriality in cloud computing, for example, implies using functional criteria for the EU cloud that make control over data possible through interoperable standards. I rely in particular on a novel functional perspective that considers what data stand for: underlying interests at stake in sharing data as jurisdictional connecting factors. Functional criteria promise to better address the nonterritorial nature of data according to (a) a substantial connection between data access and use and the protection of underlying interests; (b) the interest in sharing data in case of conflicts of law; (c) the compatibility of purposes of data sharing with multiple

[7] Project Gaia-X, 2019, https://www.data-infrastructure.eu/GAIAX/Redaktion/EN/Publications/project-gaia-x.pdf?__blob=publicationFile&v=5, p. 7.

jurisdictional claims; and (d) high standards of protection for data users (Svantesson 2015, p. 74).

The functional perspective recognises jurisdiction over physical space in an attempt to balance state interests with other equal sovereign powers when data flow beyond territorial borders. This has important practical implications for regulating data sharing in a European cloud. From a legal point of view, this may be done by means of regulation or contracts. From a technological point of view, a model of digital sovereignty is only sustainable if it is constructed on a voluntary basis with common security standards and trustworthy interoperable mechanisms rather than on the basis of unilateral territorial action. Creating a theoretical regulatory model for data sharing in the EU cloud has the advantage of focusing on the interaction between specific jurisdictional powers and operational technological solutions. Based on a theoretical functional reframing of territoriality as applied to data, a cutting-edge project of cloud computing should reject data localisation as a prerequisite to build a European data cloud infrastructure. This certainly does not mean to pretend that infrastructures do not count in terms of regulation but to recognise a legal status for data that is nondepending on physical premises. This could be a way toward a model of digital sovereignty, and it only has great potential if it is based on the technical interoperability of adequacy standards instead of on a model of digital borders based on data localisation requirements. My point is that moving away from location-based approaches to data will reduce the tension caused by the global overreach of many data regulation schemes adopted by countries. To date, the EU's extraterritorial claims have been determined by the increasing dependence of state-critical digital infrastructure on a limited number of foreign market players. Conversely, functional criteria can better address the ubiquitous and nonphysical nature of data than territorial connection factors can. In particular, functional criteria can attribute jurisdictional powers over data to states based on (1) the relevant interests in data sharing and (2) the prevalence of the advantages of data sharing and agreed common rules in potential conflicts of law. Data localisation is assumed to be the functional equivalent of the territoriality principle for an EU cloud. The functional perspective questions the territorial connection as a relevant factor in data disputes and investigates how other factors better address what data stand for and what the underlying interests at stake behind data flows are.

A European cloud might compete with major cloud computing services such as Alibaba, Microsoft and Amazon. A cloud that combines public cloud services with locally managed infrastructure would allow sensitive data to be located in specific jurisdictions while being linked to public cloud services. Cloud providers have much influence on data governance not only in terms of intellectual property rights regarding data and the operational functioning of physical infrastructure but also in terms of their impact on the marketplace where they deploy their technology. From the functional perspective, the project of a European cloud should be based on legal and technical standards of data sharing that move from the necessary idea of jurisdictional claim over data. Data sharing is in fact more oriented to Svantesson's theorization of a substantial interest in data that may legitimate access and use of data irrespective of a stable jurisdictional justification (Svantesson 2017, pp. 113, 139,

146) that can be contingent, produce joint entitlements to access and use and not use any reference to territorial sovereignty.

6.3.1 Post-Territorial Technologies

Some years ago, Svantesson precognised that "the Internet will inevitably be transformed from a relatively borderless dimension into a medium that recognises geographical and legal borders" (Svantesson 2017, p. 214).

It is easy to understand that we inevitably assist in an ineliminable conflict between over-territorialization and territorial anarchy simply cannot exist as technologies that only work with respect to a special delimitation.

Territory has received its technological confirmation through the deployment of geo-location technologies (Svantesson 2017, p. 203).

Geo-blocking technologies parcel the Internet, but geolocation serves to avoid the side effects of geo-blocking technologies. This is a virtuous circle by which territorial strategies apply to limit territorial claims achieved through technologies (Svantesson 2017, p. 211).

One of the most promising technologies for postterritories is the cloud, either based on centralised technology or ledger technology. The application of territoriality in the context of data flows gives rise to various operational issues. The Cloud Evidence Group has highlighted the difficulties of applying a territorial framework based on the location of data and instead suggested the need for a "common international solution" centered on "the location of the person in possession or control of the data" or "[t]he location of the victim at the time of the crime.[8]

A technology that may be developed regardless of a territorial logic is in fact the cloud. The European cloud's project represents an opportunity in this sense. The strategy beyond its construction, however, raises several issues. First, to be effective, 75% of European countries should adhere (Meyers 2023). Second, a cloud could be based on standards that are different from localisation requirements. Third, the creation of cloud infrastructure does not necessarily imply data storage if specific standards of data sharing are deployed. Fourth, cloud infrastructure cannot be based on foreign laws, which may produce immunity for the data included in it. Data included in a cloud infrastructure can then be subtracted from the application of foreign laws without the necessity of a territorial linkage to the local jurisdiction where the infrastructure is established.

The whole architecture for an EU cloud requires a legal analysis in which functional criteria for data sharing rather than data location act as jurisdictional triggers. This reconceptualisation is not merely theoretical. It has immediate consequences both in terms of the limits of extraterritorial claims in digital matters and the legal architecture for the establishment of an EU cloud infrastructure. Deterritorializing data aims to provide a legal alternative to the territoriality principle for an EU cloud.

[8] Cybercrime Convention Committee (T-CY), Final report of the T-CY Cloud Evidence Group, https://rm.coe.int/16806a495e, p. 58.

It focuses on the relevant factors in this model: (a) openness to actors, including foreign cloud-hosting providers from third countries; and (b) the inapplicability of foreign laws to EU cloud capacities. These two requirements can be used differently depending on the degree to which users share data and the choice of legal basis for the application of foreign laws to clouds. The technological autonomy of cloud infrastructure allows the use and exchange of data among EU and non-EU actors on the basis of shared security protocols and common legal standards.

There are different models for building clouds: (1) a model that imposes local data storage by European companies and public actors limiting data movement; (2) data sharing in an EU cloud among European and non-European companies based upon dedicated protocols (enhancement of the encryption measures and data security); and (3) a transparent system of notifications of use and measures taken with data. A functional model of an EU cloud can be based on the feasibility of compatible interests in data sharing among different actors. In a case in which cloud providers are subject to the jurisdiction of foreign countries—countries the laws of which conflict with EU law in relation to some specific piece of sensitive data—they should make it clear in such a way that it allows other interoperable actors to avoid the risk or adopt technical measures to prevent themselves from violating EU law. Cloud providers should otherwise certify that there is a conflict and verify whether any access, request for data or reuse of data by foreign countries violates EU law.

6.3.2 *Substantial Connection*

Svantesson embraces the theory based on legitimate interests to justify a more realistic linkage between the state's jurisdictional claims and concrete situations that need to be regulated. Ryngaert to a certain extent reinforced this theory resorting to the principle of subsidiarity according to which sovereignty can be modelled on the substantial interest provided that states agree on sharing responsibilities (Ryngaert 2015, p. 90) towards the ideal model of self-less unilateral jurisdiction (Ryngaert 2020, p. 1).

Elaborating on this implies finding common grounds to anchor data sharing to relevant interests that may justify jurisdictional claims. If this option apparently appears as an alternative between regulation and negotiation, this in practice is certainly problematic.

Interoperability, enhanced by advanced technologies such as 5G, may represent, for instance, a way that replaces jurisdictional claims in a technologically sustainable way. The Data Act defines interoperability as 'interoperability' as "the ability of two or more data spaces or communication networks, systems, products, applications or components to exchange and use data in order to perform their functions" (Art. 2, n. 19). By digital sustainability, I essentially refer to the following parameters: intergenerational justice, regenerative capacity, economic use of resources, risk reduction, absorptive capacity, and ecological and economic added value.

All technologies whose output is produced in Europe are subject to European standards and values. The idea of data sharing is something that unifies territories and harmonises laws. However, this book has pointed out that territory shall be helpful in achieving a goal, and if this is not the case, it needs to be dismissed.

We should give up borrowing territory to data as a means of power that concentrates capital, labor and infrastructures (Crawford 2021, p. 18). The illusion of abstraction for the industry of data extraction has revealed to be a fallacy thus far, as it has been always based on "abstracting away the material conditions of production while extracting more information and resources" (Crawford 2021, p. 217; Zuboff 2019).

The Data Services Act displays at the moment a very salient example of substantial connection to the Union, defining it, differently from GDPR, as "a connection of a provider of intermediary services with the Union resulting either from its establishment in the Union or from specific factual criteria, such as: a significant number of recipients of the service in one or more Member States in relation to its or their population; or the targeting of activities towards one or more Member States" (Art. 3 Definitions).

This may represent a step forward in the awareness of a complex jurisdictional model that cannot be based on territoriality but needs to discover an alternative basis for the exercise of authority, although it is presented as regulatory power.

6.3.3 What's Territory in the End?

These pages have tried to show that disconnection of sovereignty from territory is not disruptive as it may appear. The various challenges to territoriality experienced by history represent a common problem to which answers in terms of territorial elasticity have been several and different. Recentering the problem of territoriality is not a trivial operation. Territory represents a place where things are made visible and it is possible to pursue limited objectives, although there could be other alternatives to achieve the same objectives in several situations. Data governance makes the use of territoriality to cover the territorial scope for data regulation increasingly problematic. In recent decades, this challenge has been apparently addressed throughout the use of extraterritoriality as a form of influence of a territorial order over another.[9]

The challenge presented by data to territoriality can be solved by overcoming territoriality in different ways. One thing is to anchor data regulation into alternative

[9] As pointly observed by Nicolini, "In politico-legal terms, context supplies a 'cognitive mode of gaining control. Over the. world', which makes. It. also possible to synthesise 'cultural and geographical. information'. Again, comparative law shares this way of 'ordering the world and. Rendering it meaningful for the particular audience'. This was evident in the nineteenth century, when both geography and comparative law furnished the 'knowledge production' useful for manufacturing and establishing Western legal geopolitics around the world" (Nicolini 2022, p. 5).

factors to territoriality. One thing is to overuse territoriality in a way that may create frictions among powers. Territory substantially resists as a criterion. throughout its legitimacy. Its legitimacy derives from the fact that it should be useful to divide portions and to measure them. Disconnection from territoriality does not constitute an issue itself for data governance but rather the natural order of the digital world that connects the dots by creating a disconnection from physical realities.

Neither the concept of land, as contended by Otto Brunner (Brunner 1983), has always been in the history synonym of sovereign power as opposed to private subjects. Sovereignty is an absolute concept by definition. This means that it can be disconnected, and more is disconnected more is stronger, being it an example of what Niklas Luhmann calls the operative closure of the legal system.[10] Disconnection from territory means that it is possible to limit sovereignty in ways other than with territorial limitations. The issue at stake is whether data are capable of sparing that linkage between territory and the state in such a way that it preserves the international order.

Disconnecting sovereignty is not a heresy. It has to do with the normal functioning of the law, which disconnects itself from other structures as far as it roots itself into something else (Luhmann 2004; Pennisi 2024). Disconnecting sovereignty is the only way to allow territoriality to be disconnected from jurisdiction. This is not the way to achieve self-regulation of data clusters but rather to anchor legitimate jurisdictional claims on data on factual circumstances that may change depending on the legal status of data.

Whether data represents an asset for a company or for individuals who are located in the territory of a state is of course something that enormously affects the linkage between data and jurisdictions.

Territory historically functioned to measure recognizable and limited portions of power, all equal the one with the other, and became very widespread because of its functional character. It is not said that with respect to data, territory's function should be the same as in the physical world. This observation does not imply rejecting a model of state jurisdiction that is naturally and obviously based on territoriality. This means instead to selectively use territoriality for what it is right to use it.

The fallacy of technologies replicating territory can be stopped anytime, according to the idea of the world a society has in mind. The territorialization of data can hardly resist as a rationale in the lack of its legitimised foundation.

[10] Luhmann defines operative systems those systems operatively closed that rely on their own networks of operations for the production of their own operations and which, in this sense, reproduce themselves. Luhmann (2004), p. 80.

Legal Sources

AI Act: European Parliament legislative resolution of 13 March 2024 on the proposal for a regulation of the European Parliament and of the Council on laying down harmonised rules on Artificial Intelligence (Artificial Intelligence Act) and amending certain Union Legislative Acts (COM(2021)0206 – C9-0146/2021 – 2021/0106(COD))

Data Act: Regulation (EU) 2023/2854 of the European Parliament and the Council of 13 December 2023 on harmonised rules on fair access to and use of data and amending Regulation (EU) 2017/2394 and Directive (EU) 2020/1828, 27 November 2023

Data Governance Act: Regulation (EU) 2022/868 of the European Parliament and of the Council of 30 May 2022 on European data governance and amending Regulation (EU) 2018/1724, PE/85/2021/REV/1, *OJ L 152, 3.6.2022*

Digital Market Act: Regulation (EU) 2022/1925 of the European Parliament and of the Council of 14 September 2022 on contestable and fair markets in the digital sector and amending Directives (EU) 2019/1937 and (EU) 2020/1828

Digital Services Act: Regulation (EU) 2022/2065 of the European Parliament and of the Council of 19 October 2022 on a Single Market For Digital Services and amending Directive 2000/31/EC, PE/30/2022/REV/1, *OJ L 277*

Regulation (EU) 2018/302 of the European Parliament and of the Council of 28 February 2018 on addressing unjustified geo-blocking and other forms of discrimination based on customers' nationality, place of residence or place of establishment within the internal market and amending Regulations (EC) No 2006/2004 and (EU) 2017/2394 and Directive 2009/22/EC, *OJ L 60I, 2.3.2018*

GDPR: Regulation (EU) 2016/679 of the European Parliament and of the Council of 27 April 2016 on the protection of natural persons with regard to the processing of personal data and on the free movement of such data, and repealing Directive 95/46/EC, *OJ L 119*

Guidelines on Intellectual Property and Private International Law ILA Committee on Intellectual Property and Private International Law, RESOLUTION 6/2020 ILA COMMITTEE ON INTELLECTUAL PROPERTY AND PRIVATE INTERNATIONAL LAW

NIS Directive: Directive (EU) 2022/2555 of the European Parliament and of the Council of 14 December 2022 on measures for a high common level of cybersecurity across the Union, amending Regulation (EU) No 910/2014 and Directive (EU) 2018/1972, and repealing Directive (EU) 2016/1148 (NIS 2 Directive) (Text with EEA relevance), PE/32/2022/REV/2, *OJ L 333*

References

Anat L (2020) AI entities as AI agents: artificial intelligence liability and the AI respondeat superior analogy. Mitchell Hamline Law Rev 46(5), Article 2

Becker A, Teubner G (2022) Three liability regimes for artificial intelligence. Algorithmic actants, hybrids, crowds. Bloomsbury
Brunner O (1983, or.ed. Land und Herrschaft: Grundfragen der territorialen Verfassungsgeschichte Österreichs im Mittelalter, Rohrer, 1939), Terra e potere: strutture prestatuali e premoderne nella storia costituzionale dell'Austria. Giuffrè, 1983
Celeste E (2021) Digital sovereignty in the EU: challenges and future perspectives. In: Fabbrini F, Celeste E, Quinn J (eds) Data protection beyond borders: transatlantic perspectives on extraterritoriality and sovereignty. Hart Publishing, pp 211–228
Crawford K (2021) The atlas of AI. Yale University Press
Fahey E (2022) The EU as a global digital actor: institutionalizing global data protection, trade, and cybersecurity. Hart, Oxford
Luhmann N (2004) Law as a social system. Oxford University Press
Marotta S (2008) L'individuo senza stato. Globalizzazione e sfera pubblica. Editoriale Scientifica
Meyers Z (2023) Can the EU afford to drive out American cloud services? 2 March 2023, https://www.cer.eu/sites/default/files/insight_ZM_cloud_2.3.23.pdf
Nicolini M (2022) Legal geography. Comparative law and the production of space. Springer
Nissen RA, Eggeling KA (2024) The discursive struggle for digital sovereignty: security, economy, rights and the cloud project Gaia-X. J Common Mark Stud
Pennisi C (2024) Il diritto come rappresentazione del sistema giuridico. Spunti di sociologia del diritto, Maggioli
Punzi A (2003) L'ordine giuridico delle macchine: la Mettrie, Helvétius, d'Holbach: l'uomo-macchina verso l'intelligenza collettiva, Giappichelli
Reisman D (2017) Where is your data, really? The technical case against data localization. 22 May 2017. https://www.lawfareblog.com/where-your-data-really-technical-case-against-data-localization
Renda A (2014) The digital infrastructure as the next "EU grand project". IAI., January 2014. https://www.iai.it/sites/default/files/ImaginingEurope_03.pdf, p 24
Rigo E (2007) Europa di Confine. Trasformazioni della cittadinanza nell'Unione allargata. Meltemi
Ruschemeier A (2023) AI as a challenge for legal regulation—the scope of application of the artificial intelligence act proposal. ERA Forum 23:361–376
Ryngaert C (2015) Unilateral jurisdiction and global values. Eleven
Ryngaert C (2020) Selfless intervention: the exercise of jurisdiction in the common interest. Oxford University Press
Sartor G (2022) L'intelligenza artificiale e il diritto. Giappichelli
Schiera P (2004) Lo Stato moderno. Origini e degenerazioni. Clueb
Streinz T (2021) The evolution of EU data law. In: De Burca G, Craig P (eds) The evolution of EU law. Oxford University Press, pp 902–936
Svantesson DJ (2015) A jurisprudential justification for extraterritoriality in (private) international law. Santa Clara J Int Law 13(2):518–571
Svantesson, D. J. (2017), Solving the internet jurisdictional puzzle, Oxford University Press
Teubner G (2018) Digital personhood? The status of autonomous software agents in private law, Ancilla Iuris, https://www.anci.ch
Whitman JQ (2004) The two Western cultures of privacy: dignity versus liberty. Yale Law J 113:1151
Woods AK (2018) Litigating Data Sovereignty. Yale Law J 128:328
Zuboff S (2019) The age of surveillance capitalism: the fight for a human future at the new frontier of power. Public Affairs

Chapter 7
Conclusions

This book stemmed from the awareness of the difficulty of betraying territoriality in the global order of data. It started from the binary vision of the world nestled between the Schmittian need for concrete sovereignty over space, and the Kelsenian quest for universal jurisdiction for which sovereignty can be denied, but it remained stuck between back and forth.

Conceptually, although this book is profoundly inspired by this opposition, it has attempted to overcome it by moving from assumptions that depart from the two theories examined.

On the one hand, data pursues its own operational logic of fragmentation, use and circulation. On the other, sovereignty is proper to the instrument used for regulatory purposes, law, and not necessarily to the territorial state. Tying jurisdiction over data to territorial limits does not do justice to the nature of data, which is not a mere hypostasis of physical reality. The surplus of data over physical and material space lies precisely in the fragmentation in a broad sense—both spatial and conceptual—which is all the more productive the more it has the capacity to modify existing reality. The uncritical applicability of the principle of territoriality to data offers a distorted view of the 'physiological' potential of data by flattening it to a statist logic that forces the fictio iuris of territory in often unacceptable manners. This happens for two reasons. The first depends on competition between global players who are inclined to force the boundaries of regulatory spaces to apply proprietary logics to data. The second is related to the potentially infinite creativity of law in creating regulatory solutions that succeed even without regard to the substance of the facts.

This is a book that I originally wrote embracing the Schmittian idea of the necessity of territory to accomplish contingent sovereign purposes as opposed to the Kelsenian thesis of normative international peace substantiated in the denial of state sovereignty. During its writing, the deepness of views and conceptualizations of territoriality as a necessary order of state sovereignty and, conversely, the primacy of international law to overcome the problem of state sovereignty, literally tore at me to the point that I felt, especially toward the end of the journey, much closer to

M. Catanzariti, *Disconnecting Sovereignty*, Law, Governance and Technology Series 65, https://doi.org/10.1007/978-3-031-60734-9_7

Kelsen's thesis on the necessity to reconceptualize the shortcomings of state sovereignty.

According to Schmitt, the effort to realize sovereignty automatically makes the result infallible as long as one acts within the horizon of law. From this perspective, if for Schmitt territory is the only concrete form that represents abstract law in a unity, it is also true that the identification of sovereignty with its concrete form is the problem.

This is taken fully into account in the theorisation of this book, which, however, departs from what is for Schmitt the concrete form of the law, that is territory.

In fact, neither of these theses appears to be conclusive and entirely applicable to the data case because of the overlapping and conflicting nature of the problems at stake. Both theses imply a complementarity of views that is unthinkable in the physical world in the aftermath of the two World Wars but necessary in the liquid world of global data flows. On the one hand, sovereignty cannot be denied contrary to what Kelsen argues. Sovereignty survives adopting a mimetic approach to its object and being able to substantiate territoriality technically or to substitute it with other criteria of jurisdiction. However, if it is true that sovereignty uses territoriality, it should not be true the contrary. On the other hand, Schmitt's powerful insight has been to identify the contingent extent of territoriality: territoriality is good insofar as it serves an objective and can be justified on the basis of the categories of spatiality. Clearly, in Schmitt's theory, on balance, territory and physical spatiality have been the only concrete possibility to which opposing the logic of the sea as an example of a non-physical world. Non-physicality for Schmitt means that the sea cannot be occupied yet according terrestrial rules and in fact it is free because it is not yet occupied.

Currently, territory is still considered the save path: the most helpful solution to address many phenomena, but not digital phenomena. However, what emerges from this book is the impossibility of either erasing the logic of territoriality or applying territoriality to unterritorial entities such as data. What's the way ahead in the end?

In this complex dialectic between data and borders, the book has traced in Spinoza's theory of the vital interest in preserving within one's own being not only the principle of mutual resistance of two orders that are otherwise destined to prevail one over the other, the proliferation of data activated by technology and state sovereignty, but also the theoretical deus ex machina to make the two orders truly coexistent.

We saw that the issue at stake is not the rising of conflict of laws, rather the incapability to give institutional answers to certain applicative issues respecting the rationality of different orders. This in the long run affects the geopolitical balance, increasingly empowering the strongest states to the detriment of weaker ones. The result of the misuse of territoriality for situations that do not logically justify it (such as the lack of substantial connection between data flows and jurisdictional claims) undermines the same rationale that grounds the principle of territoriality—the equality among states, the territorial delimitation of nation states and the principle of non intervention.

In the end, neither Schmitt nor Kelsen but Spinoza wins in this book, however ex post thanks to Schmitt and Kelsen.

Every order should persevere according to their rules of functioning without limiting the other but not prevailing in areas that are naturally non-compatible with its rules. This means that if it is technically possible to exert territorial or extraterritorial claims over data, what should be instead relevant is the way by which a concept of jurisdiction would be substantially connected to its object.

It is self-evident that the use of advanced technologies in different legal areas has completely replaced certain procedures to that extent that they can basically provide whatever possible linkage with a predetermined territory. This in practice means either the use of extraterritorial powers or, in any event, an overproduction of effects related to localization requirements for foreign countries.

As an alternative to this backdrop, this book has tried to conceptualize the Spinozian principle of status maintenance. This means that these two antithetical orders have over time needed to talk each other, sometimes colliding and sometimes complementing each other. The reality principle has then often reversed them. What to take away from Carl Schmitt and what to take away from Hans Kelsen?

From both groundbreaking theories, the necessity of territory and the impossibility of it at the same time in the data government emerge. It is quite counterintuitive that both, although reaching opposite conclusions, motivate their thesis because of the primacy of the principle of territoriality.

The same reasons led me to embrace a different conclusion consisting in which sovereignty no longer actually needs territory to survive, but it continues to use it. This jarring caesura between historical necessity and the reality produced by data regulation opens up a horizon that is new and unusual. Making use of an instrument that was conceived for appropriating physical shares is logically unthinkable.

What this book does not take from either Schmitt or Kelsen is the total divarication between law and fact, because data law cannot treat data as mere form but must necessarily draws on its capacity to represent concrete factual situations. Concreteness, therefore, crucial in Schmitt's elaboration in the sense of a visible form of the will to power, and absent in Kelsen's except in the negative—in the sense that the solution is to deny concrete legal orders in order to affirm the primacy of international law—is in this book understood as the recognition of a different order, that of data. This order has its own internal logic, pursues its own purposes and carries them out in the maximum capacity of circulation, representation and modification of facts.

Territory has traditionally been a harbinger of exclusionary law to preserve certain subjects. In the global world, territory loses its connotations, but this does not mean that sovereignty vanishes. Sovereignty simply no longer necessarily needs territory because it has exhausted many of its effects or almost all of them in the digital sphere.

This book has carried out a journey throughout various dimensions of data regulation. While investigating the tensions underlying the use of territoriality in the framework of data regulation, this book sought to explore the potential of a reconfiguration of sovereignty as applied to data flows. If sovereignty manages to disconnect itself from territory, then territory practically loses its weight in pursuing a concrete objective of effective and overall control.

Territoriality has historically been a way to achieve concrete results in terms of appropriation and exertion of power over a physical space. This possibility depended upon the linkage between territory and the goals of its use. It cannot be the opposite—that sovereignty instead predetermined its scope throughout a fixed use of a term—as territoriality needs a concrete use to justify itself.

If data has nothing to do with the logic of territory in its ontology—not in its use—then the application of a territorial logic of regulation to govern data does not have any reason to persist. In addition, the transformation of a nonphysical space into a physical one creates a constriction that in the long run alters the capacity to legitimate and justify power.

Territoriality works with limited territories and to limit the use of space not to overuse territory. As it is a very multitasking concept, it also accomplishes its objectives if it applies to data by reterritorializing them or by reaching them extraterritorially. This is a wrong perspective on both facets: while extraterritorial overuse undermines the international equality of states, securitization of borders implies an indefinite notion of territorial borders that may amplify from the inside to have traction power.

If notwithstanding this, territory is modelled over the metaphorical capacity of data to represent physical assets; in this very simple sense, it only seeks to reterritorialize data, producing a distortion in the regulatory capacity of the law.

Contrary to this tendency that has been reflected in global regulatory digital models across the world over the last decades, an alternative modality that aims to preserve the inherent and natural order of objects needs to be developed. This alternative philosophically builds on the Spinozian theory of natural law to self-preservation of all entities.

We have seen how exactly disconnection from territory in the digital realm may contribute to reshaping the law, e.g. preserving the linkages between data and prerogatives of control over it.

Can it be argued that data flows determine the end of territoriality? It seems that territoriality and data naturally follow different logics and rules. Additionally, extraterritoriality cannot be considered a solution for nonterritorial entities because it reflects upon an overuse of territoriality. Territoriality cannot justify an inherently a-territorial logic, the logic of data, which works precisely to share and circulate data. Geopolitical balance, also encompassing the principle of equality among state actors, is not compatible with the uncontrolled expansion of territorial limits that aim to reterritorialize data. It is in fact the law itself that is sovereign over the very factor that justifies it, namely, territory. If the law is able to create normative spaces why then the obsession of territory?

The attempt of this book has been to show how data and the law interact parallelly, trying to follow their own rules of functioning and how the same effect that is apparently negative for the law—data fragmentation—may contribute to building legal conditions of coexistence between the logic of data and the logic of the law. This requires practicing realism with respect to the relation between ruling and factual situations that cannot be overlooked. Data does not stand to the overuse of territoriality because it does not fulfil all the conditions needed by legal fiction. The overuse of territoriality in data ruling is in fact also accompanied by a hybrid use of logics: if data function according to the rules of technology that are barely covered by the legal design of a territorial scope (if not fictitiously), its regulation cannot be based instead on false spatial conditions.

The effort to persevere in its own being is the natural right of data in Spinoza's words.

Data and the law may continue to autonomously preserve themselves if territory is not overused; otherwise, territory only becomes a technique to manage data flows. Digital flows, as all other entities, shall follow their nature, which consists of being disconnected from a limited space.

Although the law strives to treat data as physical objects to more easily anchor them to the territorial and material purpose of applying a rule, data follow their own nature, which is fluctuating.

If it is true that the highest purpose of the state is, according to Spinoza, to ensure the freedom of individuals, this freedom must necessarily also apply to the entities of which individual identity is composed.

This, contrary to any neo-liberal logic that places expectations in the servant function of states with respect to a market-driven model, has the advantage of emancipating states with respect to territoriality, which cannot be used to enforce data regulation.

In fact, the clash between territoriality and data is visible at various latitudes: either in the presence of digital territories or of an extended notion of legal territories,

Both Leviathans and data can continue to pursue their natural effort to maintain the purpose for which they are existing, states to produce order and data to free flow, discovering new criteria under which data regulation can be grounded. Digitalizing territories or unleashing the territorial scope of application of law is a twofold risky operation: in the first case, states, under the illusion that they can 'technologize' territory, which has been conceived as an eminently terrestrial and spatial instrument of the exercise of power and based on the logic of jurisdiction, actually cede their prerogatives to big techs that create omnivorous territories capable of exceeding the legitimate limits of physical territoriality. In the second case, the extraterritorial exercise of state prerogatives in relation to data located in other spaces produces a regulatory and economic struggle between weaker and stronger states in which the latter prevail over the former in contrast to the principle of state equality.

It is obvious that both paths are doomed to failure in digital regulation, which instead must identify certain forms of coexistence starting from the type of object being regulated and not ex post facto from the purpose of regulation.

Disconnecting sovereignty from territory can be the way for digital law to preserve its rationality and for digital rights to flourish as well in a way that could be more consistent with the modalities of digital interaction and digital phenomena.

The fear of the reproducibility of reality is ultimately the real dilemma to be overcome. In the face of this fear, which is highly problematic to manage through institutions and rules, however, naive solutions are the ones that are farthest removed from solving theoretical and practical problems.

The apparent solution to a problem is what instead determines the 'shipwreck with spectator'.

This book would like to generate awareness about what is not to be renounced from an old world and what is to be taken from a new one. Not all in both worlds, but not nothing in one and all in the other. The issue at stake is very urgent and has to do with the very concept of democracy, which encompasses both democratic liberties and democratic institutions. We have seen over the book how the overuse of territory undermines both aspects in different and conflicting ways.

The hope is instead to build a digital environment that asks the law what to do not only to be compliant with existing requirements but also to create room for emancipation and freedom without undergoing unjustified tradeoffs. It is no longer time to legitimize understandings such as 'innovation at the cost of rights' or 'more rights for less innovation' because they are both ruinous paths. The law should reappropriate its functions, which are not based on technicalities per se but to better accommodate the needs of conflicting players in a peaceful cohexistence.

Applying the principle of territoriality to data basically translates into making the operational law of data flows, i.e. the regulatory models, coincide with the legitimizing rationale of data law. In fact, there is a tendency to flatten what in fact gives rise to the interests at stake in deciding the rules to be applied to data flows with the rules on jurisdiction, assuming that just as for things and persons, also for data, spatiality delimits operational possibilities. Conversely, the operability of data is completely independent from spatial limitation and may even be undermined by space, certainly not emphasized.

Translated into practical terms, the conceptualisation proposed by this book offers insights into alternative functional applications of the territoriality principle in data governance. This implies, let it be understood, that sometimes the jurisdictional solution may coincide with the application of a territorial model, where there is a specific justification in relation to the activity performed by the data flow and the precise function that the data fulfil in a given case. Functional criteria thus represent justifications of regulatory models to be provided on a case-by-case basis, not instead normative metaphors for the scope of application of a given regulation. In this context, the application of functional criteria to cross-border data flows would operate as lex specialis vis-à-vis the general rule of the territorial scope of application, due to the peculiar nature of the data. In fact, the representative capacity of the data is clearly more stringent than any criterion of territorial connection, which would therefore have to completely disappear as the normative rationale of digital legal instruments as well as of digital rights themselves.

This book ultimately implies an optimistic view of law that opens up to factuality by taking shape from it and being strongly inspired by it. The disruptive factuality of data multiplies the real both through representative capacity and through the selection of the possibilities of the real that data are able to formalise. In the face of such an excess of living material, the capacity of law to orient by localising, to stabilise while triggering expansive processes, does not fail if it dispenses with territoriality. On the contrary, the artificial use of a concrete form that has no longer a substantive connection with data flows except in the domain of infrastructures, risks to be counterproductive even on the effects of regulatory capacity: insofar it does not legitimise itself through stable recognition of a inherent capacity of data to freely circulate. Such a freedom shall reconfigure normative spaces, individual relationships and legal subjectivity in a creative way that is respectful of its nature.

Bibliography

Abizadeh A (2016) Sovereign jurisdiction, territorial rights, and membership in Hobbes. In: Martinich A, Hoekstra K (eds) The Oxford handbook of Hobbes. Oxford University Press, pp 397–431

Aguinaldo A, De Hert P (2021) European law enforcement and US data companies. In: Celeste E, Fabbrini F, Quinn J (eds) Data protection beyond borders, and EU-US discussions regarding Lae enforcement access to data across borders. Hart, pp 157–172

Altwicker T (2020) Justice beyond borders—extraterritorial obligations from Thucydides to Grotius. Rechtsphilosophie - Zeitschrift für die Grundlagen des Rechts (RphZ) 6(3):234–248

Amato G (2012) Il costituzionalismo oltre i confini dello Stato. In: Costituzionalismo e Globalizzazione, Annuario AIC 2012:9

Anat L (2020) AI entities as AI agents: artificial intelligence liability and the AI Respondeat superior analogy. Mitchell Hamline L Rev 46(5) Article 2

Andreucci F, Pescarolo A (1989) Gli spazi del potere. Aree, regioni, Stati: coordinate territoriali della storia contemporanea. La Casa Usher

Andronico A (2002) La decostruzione come metodo. Riflessi di Derrida nella teoria del diritto, Giuffrè

Atzili B, Kaderkan B (2019) Territorial designs and international politics inside-out and outside-in. Routledge

Autolitano S, Pawlowska A (2021) Europe's quest for digital sovereignty: GAIA-X as a case study. IAI. https://www.iai.it/sites/default/files/iaip2114.pdf

Barbero M (2017) Study on emerging issues of data ownership, interoperability, (re-)usability and access to data, and liability. European Union

Bathelt H, Feldman MP, Kogler DF (2011) Beyond territory. Dynamic geographies of knowledge creation, diffusion, and innovation. Routledge

Beale J (1935) A treatise on the conflict of Laws. Baker

Becker A, Teubner G (2022) Three liability regimes for artificial intelligence. Algorithmic actants, hybrids, crowds. Bloomsbury

Benda-Beckmann F, Benda-Beckmann K, Griffiths AMO (2009) Spatializing law: an anthropological geography of law in society. Ashgate

Benkler Y (2007) The wealth of networks: how social production transforms markets and freedom. Yale University Press

Benton L (2010) A Search for sovereignty. Law and geography in European empires, 1400-1900. Cambridge University Press

Bergelson V (2003) It's personal, but is it mine? Toward property rights in personal information. UC Davis L Rev 37:379

M. Catanzariti, *Disconnecting Sovereignty*, Law, Governance and Technology Series 65, https://doi.org/10.1007/978-3-031-60734-9

Berman PS (2012) Global legal pluralism. A jurisprudence of law beyond Borders. Cambridge University Press

Bertola V (2022) La sovranità digitale e il future di internet. Rivista italiana di informatica e diritto 1. https://doi.org/10.32091/RIID0050

Besson S (2011) Sovereignty, max Planck encyclopedias of international law. Oxford University Press. https://opil.ouplaw.com/display/10.1093/law:epil/9780199231690/law-9780199231690-e1472?prd=EPIL

Besson S (2012) The extraterritoriality of the European convention on human rights: why human rights depend on jurisdiction and what jurisdiction amounts to. Leiden J Int Law 25(4):857–884. 869

Besson S (2019) Why and what (state) jurisdiction. Legal plurality, individual equality and territorial legitimacy. In: Klabbers J, Palombella G (eds) The challenge of inter-legality. Cambridge University Press, pp 91–132

Besson S (2020) Due diligence and extraterritorial human rights obligations—mind the gap! ESIL Reflections 9:1. https://esil-sedi.eu/wp-content/uploads/2020/04/ESIL-Reflection-Besson-S.-3.pdf

Bignami F, Resta G (2015) Transatlantic privacy regulation: conflict and cooperation. Law Contemp Probl 78:231–266

Blomley NK (1994) Law, space, and the geographies of power. Guilford Press

Blomley NK, Delaney D, Ford RT (eds) (2001) The legal geographies reader: law, power, and space. Blackwell

Boaz A, Burak K (2017) Territorial designs and international politics: the diverging constitution of space and boundaries. Territ Politics Gov 5(2):115–130

Bodin J (2014) The six books of a Commonweale. Richard Knolles (Trans). Impensis G. Bishop 1606, Harvard University Press

Bradford, A. (2020) The Brussels effect: how the European Union rules the world. Oxford University Press

Bradford A (2023) Digital empires. The global Battle to regulate technology. Oxford University Press

Braverman I, Blomley NK, Delaney D, Kedar A (eds) (2015) The expanding spaces of law: a timely legal geography. Stanford University Press

Brenner N (1999) Beyond state-centrism? Space, territoriality, and geographical scale in globalization studies. Theory Soc 28(1):39–78

Brunner O (1983, or.ed. *Land und Herrschaft: Grundfragen der territorialen Verfassungsgeschichte Österreichs im Mittelalter*, Rohrer, 1939), *Terra e potere: strutture prestatuali e premoderne nella storia costituzionale dell'Austria*. Giuffrè

Calabresi G, Melamed AD (1972) Property rules, liability rules, and inalienability: one view of the cathedral. Harv Law Rev 85:1092

Canale D (2022) Per una filosofia inferenziale del diritto.I. Ragionamento e interpretazione giuridica. Giappichelli

Cannizzaro E (2020) La sovranità oltre lo stato. Il Mulino

Casadei T, Pietroapoli S (2024) Diritto e tecnologie informatiche. Wolters Kluwer

Cassano F (2005) Il pensiero meridiano, 2nd edn. Laterza

Catanzariti M, Curtin D (2023) Beyond originator control of personal data in EU interoperable information systems: towards data originalism. In: Curtin D, Catanzariti M (eds) Data at the boundaries of law. Oxford University Press, pp 133–174

Celata F (2009) Spazi di produzione. Una prospettiva relazionale. Giappichelli

Celeste E (2021) Digital sovereignty in the EU: challenges and future perspectives. In: Fabbrini F, Celeste E, Quinn J (eds) Data protection beyond borders: transatlantic perspectives on extraterritoriality and sovereignty. Hart, pp 211–228

Chander A, Lê U (2015) Data Nationalism. Emory Law J 64(3):677

Christakis T (2020) "European digital sovereignty": successfully navigating between the "Brussels effect" and Europe's quest for strategic autonomy. Multidisciplinary Institute on Artificial Intelligence/Grenoble Alpes Data Institute: Studies on Digital Governance

Ciolli I (2010) Il territorio rappresentato. Profili costituzionali. Jovene

Ciolli I (2020) Il territorio europeo tra processi federali e spinte neofeudali. federalismi.it
Clopton ZD (2016) Data institutionalism: a reply to Andrew Woods. Stanford L Rev Online 69
Cohen MR (1927) Property and sovereignty. Cornell Law Q:8–30
Cohen J (2019) Between truth and power. The legal constructions of informational capitalism. Oxford University Press
Corso L (2019) 'Vulnerabilità e concetto di diritto', in Corso L - Talamo (eds), *Vulnerabilità di fronte alle istituzioni. Vulnerabilità delle istituzioni*, Giappichelli, pp 3–14
Costa P (2013) Riflessioni su alcuni aspetti teorici della territorialitá», 1, costituzionalismo.it
Costabile A (2002) Il potere politico. Carocci
Costabile A, Coco A (2018) Power relationships and social practices within contemporary democracies. The manipulation of institutional- normative processes. In: Saccà F (ed) Democracy, power and territories. Franco Angeli, pp 13–29
Couture S, Toupin S (2019) What does the notion of "sovereignty" mean when referring to the digital? New Media Soc 21(10):2305–2322
Crawford K (2021) The atlas of AI. Yale University Press
Cremona M (2016) EU external relations and the law. In: Patterson D, Södersten A (eds) A companion to European Union law and international law. Wiley, pp 371–393
Cremona M (ed) (2018) Structural principles and their role in EU external relations law. Hart
Curtin D (2009) Executive power in the European Union. Law, Practices and the living constitution. Oxford University Press
Daskal J (2015) The un-territoriality of data. Yale Law J 125:326
Daskal J (2016) Law enforcement access to data across Borders: the evolving security and right issues. J Natl Sec L & Pol'y 8:473
Daskal J (2018) Borders and bits. Vanderbilt Law Rev 71:179
Daskal J (2020) The opening Salvo. The CLOUD act, e-evidence proposals, and EU–US discussions regarding law enforcement access to data across Borders. In: Bignami F (ed) EU law in populist times. Cambridge University Press, pp 319–341
De Filippi P, Mannan M, Reijers W (2022) The alegality of blockchain technology. Polic Soc 41(3):358–372
De Franceschi A (2021) Personal data as counter-performance. In: Senigaglia R, Irti C, Bernes A (eds) Data protection in software services. Giuffrè, pp 153–176
De Gregorio G, Ranchordas S (2020) Breaking down information silos with big data: a legal analysis of data sharing. In: Cannataci J, Falce V, Pollicino O (eds) New legal challenges of big data. Edward Elgar, pp 174–203
De Hert P (2023) Post-GDPR lawmaking in the digital data society: mimesis without integration. Topological understandings of twisted boundary setting in EU data protection law. In: Catanzariti M, Curtin D (eds) Data at the boundaries of European law. Oxford University Press, pp 95–132
Del Vecchio A (2021) La legge nell'Oceano. Ugo Grozio e le origini dello spazio politico moderno. Il Mulino, Bologna
De Vitoria, F (2005) De iure belli (Galli C ed.). Laterza
Deleuze G, Guattari F (1997) *Millepiani. Capitalismo e schizofrenia*, sez. I. Rizoma, Castelvecchi
Della Morte G (2018) Big data e protezione internazionale dei diritti umani. Regole e conflitti. Editoriale Scientifica
Drexl J (2017a) Designing competitive Markets for Industrial Data. Between Propertisation and access. JIPITEC 8:257–267
Drexl J (2017b) On the future EU legal framework for the digital economy: a competition-based response to the 'ownership and access' debate. In: Lohsse S, Schulze R, Staudenmayer D (eds) Trading data in the digital economy: legal concepts and tools. Nomos, pp 223–244
Duch-Brown N, Martens B, Mueller-Langer F (2017) The economics of ownership, access and trade in digital data. European Commission, Joint Research Centre. https://www.econstor.eu/bitstream/10419/202223/1/jrc-dewp201701.pdf
Elden S (2013) The Birth of territory. The University of Chicago Press

Efroni Z (2020) Location data as contractual counter-performance: a consumer perspective on recent EU legislation. In: Finck M et al (eds) Smart urban mobility, MPI studies on intellectual property and competition law. Springer, p 29. https://doi.org/10.1007/978-3-662-61920-9_13

Eichensehr K (2017) Data Extraterritoriality. Texas Law Rev 95:145–160

Elden S (2013) The birth of territory. The University of Chicago Press

Erie M, Streinz T (2021) The Beijing effect: China's 'digital silk road' as transnational data governance. NYU J Int L Polit 54:1

Esposito R (2023) Vitam instituere. Geneaologia dell'istituzione. Einaudi

Fahey E (2017) The global reach of EU law. Routledge

Fahey E (2022) The EU as a global digital actor: institutionalizing global data protection, trade, and cybersecurity. Hart

Ferrajoli L (1997) La sovranità nel mondo moderno, Laterza

Ferrajoli L (2022) Il futuro del costituzionalismo, costituzionalismo.it, 2, p 185

Ferrarese MR (2006) Diritto sconfinato: inventiva giuridica e spazi nel mondo globale. Laterza

Figg R (2019) The application of data protection laws in (Outer) space, www.iclg.com

Floridi L (2020) The fight for digital sovereignty: what it is, and why it matters, especially for the EU. Philo Technol 33:369–378

Floridi L, Taddeo M (2014) The ethics of information warfare. Springer

Foucault M (2023) "Lo spazio è sempre strategico", included into M. Foucault, Metafisica del potere, Torino, 1977, re-published in Limes, Il Bluff Globale, 4/2023, pp. 81–91

Fricker KV (1901) Gebiet und Gebietshoheit. Mit einem Anhang: Vom Staatsgebiet. Verlag der H. Laupp'schen Buchhandlung Tübingen

Galli C (2001) Spazi politici. L'età moderna e l'età globale. Il Mulino

Galli C (2017) Introduzione. Schmitt e Hobbes: una strana coppia?, in Carl Schmitt. Sul Leviatano. Il Mulino

Galli C (2019) Sovranità. Il Mulino

Gaudino U (2017) Carl Schmitt e la critica geografica contemporanea. Geopolitica Rivista semestrale dell'Isag 7(2)

Giuffré M (2021) A functional-impact model of jurisdiction: extraterritoriality before the European court of human rights. QIL - Questions of International Law 82:53

Glenn P (2013) The cosmopolitan state. Oxford University Press

Goldsmith JL (1998) The internet and the abiding significance of territorial sovereignty. Glob Leg Stud J 79:476

Goldsmith J (1999) Against cyberanarchy. Univ Chic. Law Rev 65:1250

Goldsmith J (2019) Sovereign deference and sovereign difference on the internet. The Yale Law Journal Forum. March 18, 2019, https://www.yalelawjournal.org/pdf/Goldsmith1mjtvg2i.pdf

Goldsmith JL, Posner EA (2005) The limits of international law. Oxford University Press

Goldsmith J, Wu T (2006) Who controls the internet?: illusions of a borderless world, vol 2006. Oxford University Press

Greco C (2021) Quest'acquisizione non s'ha da fare: ennesimo 'no' della Corte di Giustizia alla data retention indiscriminata in campo penale. Nota a CGUE 2 marzo 2021, Prokuratuur. Diritto dell'Informazione e dell'Informatica 2:235

Greco T (2012) Diritto e legame sociale. Giappichelli

Grimm D (2023, tr. it Malatesta O) Sovranità. Origine e futuro di un concetto chiave, Laterza

Grotius H (2012) In: Neff SC (ed) Hugo Grotius on the law of war and peace. Cambridge University Press

Harvey D (2018) Geografia del dominio. Capitalismo e produzione dello spazio. Ombre corte

Haskell JD (2019) Ways of doing extraterritoriality in scholarship. In: Margolies DS, Özsu U, Pal M, Tzouvala N (eds) The extraterritoriality of law. History, theory, politics. Routledge, pp 13–29

Herr T (2020) Four myths about the cloud: The geopolitics of cloud computing. https://www.strategicstudyindia.com/2020/09/four-myths-about-cloud-geopolitics-of.html

Hildebrandt M (2013) Extraterritorial jurisdiction to enforce in cyberspace? Bodin, Schmitt, Grotius in cyberspace. Univ Toronto Law J 63(2):196–224

Hildebrandt M (2023) Boundary work between computational 'law' and 'law as-we-know-it'. In: Curtin D, Catanzariti M (eds) Data at the boundaries of EU law. Oxford University Press, pp 30–65
Hoeren T (2019) Datenbesitz statt Dateneigentum? MMR, p 1
Hörnle J (2021) Internet jurisdiction: law and practice. Oxford University Press
Humphreys S (2018) Data. The given. In: Hohmann J, Joyce D (eds) International Law's object. pp 191–202
Huo Z, Yip M (2021) Extraterritoriality of Chinese law: myths, realities and the future. Chin J Comp Law 9(3):328–358
Jellinek G (1921) Allgemeine Rechtslehre. Springer Nature
Johnson DR, Post D (1996) Law and borders: the rise of law in cyberspace. Stanf Law Rev 48(5):1367–1402
Kalmo H, Skinner Q (2010) Sovereignty in fragments. The past, present and future of a contested concept. Cambridge University Press
Kanalan I (2018) Extraterritorial state obligations beyond the concept of jurisdiction. Ger Law J 19(1):44
Kapczynski A (2020) The law of informational capitalism. Yale Law J 129(5):1460–1515
Kelsen H (1934) *Reine Rechtslehre. Einleitung in die rechtswissenschafttliche Problematik*, Leizpig-Wien 1934, trad.it. *Lineamenti di dottrina pura del diritto*, Torino 1952, p 52
Kelsen H (1989, or.ed. Das Problem der Souveränität und die Theorie des Völkerrechts: Beitrag zu einer reinen Rechtslehre, Mohr Siebek, 1920), Il problema della sovranità e la teoria del diritto internazionale. Contributo per una teoria pura del diritto. Giuffrè
Klabbers J (2019) Palombella L (eds). The Challenge of inter-legality. Oxford University Press
Koskenniemi M (1989) From apology to utopia. The structure of international legal argument. Cambridge University Press, pp 241–242
Kosseff J (2019) The twenty six words that created the internet. Cornell University Press
Krisch N (2022) Jurisdiction unbound: (extra)territorial regulation as global governance. EJIL 33(2):481–514
Kumar S (2021) The digital frontier: infrastructures of control on the global web. Indiana University Press
Kuner C (2019) The internet and the global reach of EU law. In: Cramona M, Scott J (eds) EU law beyond EU Borders: the extraterritorial reach of EU law. Oxford University Press, pp 112–145
Kuner C, Cate F, Lynskey O, Millard C, Ni Loideain N, Svantesson D (2018) An unstoppable force and an immoveable object? EU data protection law and national security. Int Data Priv Law 8(1):1–3
Lambach D, Opperman K (2022) Narratives of digital sovereignty in German political discourse. Governance 36(3)
Land M (2013) Towards an international law of the internet. Harv Law J 54(2):393
Lessig L (1999) Code and other laws of cyberspace. Basic Books
Lessig L (2002) Privacy as property. Soc Res 69:247–270
Lindahl H (2018) Authority and the globalization of inclusion and exclusion. Oxford University Press, p 14
Litman J (2000) Information privacy/information property. Stanford Law Rev 52(5):1286
Lomborg S, Ytre-Arne B (2021) Advancing digital disconnection research: introduction to the special issue. Convergence 27(6):1529–1535
Luhmann, N. (2004) Law as a social system. Oxford University Press
Maier C (2019) Dentro i confini. Territorio e potere dal 1500 a oggi. Einaudi
Margiotta C (2005) L'ultimo diritto. Profili storici e teorici della secessione. Il Mulino
Mari L (2011) Ordinamento, localizzazione, uniformità: quale nomos, dopo Schmitt, per l'Europa?, in Teoria del diritto e dello Stato, 1-2/2011, 76 ss
Maroni M (2022) The right to access the Internet: a critical analysis of the constitutionalisation of the Internet. Unigrafia
Massa Pinto I (2023) Territorio e potere. In Enciclopedia del Diritto. I tematici, pp 1211–1232
Marotta S (2008) L'individuo senza stato. Globalizzazione e sfera pubblica. Editoriale Scientifica

Metzger A (2017) Data as counter-performance. What rights and duties do parties have? https://www.jipitec.eu/issues/jipitec-8-1-2017/4528/jipitec_8_1_2017_metzger_data%20as%20counter-performance.pdf

Mezzadra S, Cuppini N, Frappotti M Pirone M (eds) (2024) Capitalism in the platform age. Emerging assemblages of labour and welfare in urban spaces. Springer

Mezzadra S, Neilson B (2013) Border as method or, the multiplication of labor. Duke University Press

Michaels R (2006) Two paradigms of jurisdiction. Mich J Int Law 27:1003

Michaels R (2017) Jurisdiction, foundations. In: Basedow J et al (eds) Elgar encyclopedia of private international law. Edward Elgar

Michetti M (2021) Organizzazione del potere e territorio. Legittimità dello Stato e livelli di governo. Giappichelli

Milanovic M (2015) Human rights treaties and foreign surveillance: privacy in the digital age. Harv Int Law J 56:81

Miller D (2012) Territorial rights: concept and justification. Polit Stud 60:252

Mitsilegas V, Moreno Lax V, Vavoula N (2020) Securitising asylym flows deflec tion. Criminalization and challenges for human rights. Brill Nijhoff

Moreno Lax V (2020) The architecture of functional jurisdiction: unpacking contactless control—on public powers, S.S. And others v. Italy, and the "operational model". Ger Law J 21:385–416

Moreno Lax V, Costello C (2014) The extraterritorial application of the charter: from territoriality to facticity, the effectiveness model. In: Peers S et al (eds) Commentary on the EU charter of fundamental rights. Oxford University Press, pp 1657–1683

Mullighan SP (2018 Cross-border data sharing under the cloud act. Congressional Research Service, https://sgp.fas.org/crs/misc/R45173.pdf

Musiani F (2013) Network architecture as internet governance. Internet Policy Review 2(4):2013. https://doi.org/10.14763/2013.4.208

Naef T (2023) Data protection without data protectionism. The Right to protection of personal data and data transfers in EU Law and international trade Law. Springer

Nicolini M (2022) Legal geography. Comparative law and the production of space. Springer

Nitsch C (2012) Diritto e forza nella comunità degli stati. Studi su Hans Kelsen e la teoria del diritto internazionale. Satura Editrice

Nobili Schiera G (2015) A proposito di una traduzione di un'opera recente di Otto Brunner. Scienza e politica XXVII:221–237

Núñez JE (2020) Territorial disputes and state sovereignty: international law and politics. Routledge

Obendiek, A. S. (2023), Data governance: value orders and jurisdictional conflicts. Oxford University Press

Ollino A (2022) The 'capacity-impact' model of jurisdiction and its implications for states' positive human rights obligations. QIL, Zoom-in 82:81–100

Osula AM (2018) Accessing extraterritorially located data: options for states. Nato Cooperative Cyber Defence Center of Excellence. https://ccdcoe.org/uploads/2018/10/Accessing-extraterritorially-located-data-options-for-States_Anna-Maria_Osula.pdf

Päl M (2021) Jurisdictional accumulation: an early modern history of law, empires and capital. Oxford University Press

Palombella L (2021) Interlegality: on interconnections and 'external sources. Ital Law J 7:2

Pannarale L (2012) Il diritto che guarda. Rischi della decisione giuridica, Franco Angeli

Pariotti E (2004) La giustizia oltre lo Stato: forme e problemi. Giappichelli

Pennisi C (1990) La costruzione sociologica del fenomeno giuridico. Giuffrè

Pennisi C (1997) Istituzioni e cultura giuridica. I procedimenti come strutture di comunicazione, Giappichelli

Pennisi C (2024) Il diritto come rappresentazione del sistema giuridico. Spunti di sociologia del diritto. Maggioli

Peuker E (2020) Verfassungswandel durch Digitalisierung. Digitale Souveränität als verfassungsrechtliches Leitbild. Mohr Siebek

Pino G (2003) Il diritto all'identità personale. Interpretazione costituzionale e creatività giurisprudenziale. Il Mulino

Pinto EM (2023) Territorio e potere, Enciclopedia del diritto. Giuffrè, pp 1211–1232
Pistor K (2017) From territorial to monetary sovereignty. J Theoretical Inq L 18(2):491–517
Pistor K (2019) The Code of Capital. How the law creates wealth and inequality. Princeton University Press
Pohle J, Thiel T (2020) Digital sovereignty. Internet Policy Review 9(4):47
Pollicino O (2023) Di cosa parliamo quando parliamo di costituzionalismo digitale? Quaderni Costituzionali 3:569–594
Poullet Y (1990) Data protection between property and liberties. A civil law approach. In: Kaspersen HWK, Oskamp A (eds) Amongst friends in computers and law. A collection of essays in remembrance of guy Vandenberghe. Kluwer Law International, p 161
Poullet Y (2007) Transborder data flows and extraterritoriality: the European position. J Int Commer Law Technol 2, 3
Pupolizio I (2019) Pubblico e privato. Teoria e storia di una grande dicotomia. Giappichelli
Preterossi G (1996) Carl Schmitt e la tradizione modernac. Laterza
Preterossi G (2022) Teologia politica e diritto. Laterza
Prins C (2006) Property and privacy: European perspectives and the commodification of our identity. Information Law Series 16:223–257
Punzi A (2003) L'ordine giuridico delle macchine: la Mettrie, Helvétius, d'Holbach: l'uomo-macchina verso l'intelligenza collettiva. Giappichelli
Purtova NN (2009a) Property in personal data: a European perspective on instrumentalist theory of propertization. In: de Filippi P, Gomes de Andrade NN, Fernandez-Barrera M (eds) Law and technology: looking into the future - selected essays. European Press Academic, pp 225–243
Purtova N (2009b) Property in personal data: learning from the American discourse. Comput L Sec 25:507–521
Putnam TL (2016) Court without borders. Law, politics, and US extraterritoriality. Cambridge University Press
Raible L (2021) Extraterritoriality between a rock and a hard place. QIL - Questions of International Law 82:7
Reed C, Murray A (2018) Rethinking the jurisprudence of cyberspace. Edward Elgar
Reisman D (2017) Where is your data, really? The technical case against data localization. 22 May 2017. https://www.lawfareblog.com/where-your-data-really-technical-case-against-data-localization
Renda A (2014) The digital infrastructure as the next "EU grand project". IAI., January 2014. https://www.iai.it/sites/default/files/ImaginingEurope_03.pdf, p 24
Riccobono F (2017) Antikelsenismo italiano. Giappichelli
Rigo E (2007) Europa di Confine. Trasformazioni della cittadinanza nell'Unione allargata. Meltemi
Roberts H, Cowls J, Casolari F, Morley J, Taddeo M, Floridi L (2021) Safeguarding European values with digital sovereignty: an analysis of statements and policies. Internet Policy Review 10(3). https://doi.org/10.14763/2021.3.1575
Rodotà S (1995) Tecnologie e diritti. Il Mulino
Rodotà S (2004, or. ed. 1997) Tecnopolitica. La democrazia e le nuove tecnologie della comunicazione. Laterza
Rodotà S (2012) Il diritto di avere diritti. Laterza
Rodotà S (2018, or. ed. 1973), ed. Alpa G, Elaboratori elettronici e controllo swociale, Jovene
Rojszczak M (2021) Extraterritorial bulk surveillance after the German BND act judgment. Eur Const Law Rev 17:53–77
Romano, S. (2018, or.ed. 1918) L'ordinamento giuridico. Quodlibet
Ruschemeier A (2023) AI as a challenge for legal regulation—the scope of application of the artificial intelligence act proposal. ERA Forum 23:361–376
Ruschi F (2012) Questioni di spazio. La terra, il mare, il diritto secondo Carl Schmitt. Giappichelli
Ruschi F (2019) Spazio. La questione del territorio statale. In: Andronico A, Greco T, Macioce F (eds) Dimensioni del diritto. Giappichelli, pp 345–368
Ryngaert, C. (2015a), Jurisdiction in international law. Oxford University Press
Ryngaert C (2015b) Unilateral jurisdiction and global values. Eleven
Ryngaert C (2020) Selfless intervention: the exercise of jurisdiction in the common interest. Oxford University Press

Ryngaert C, Taylor MSC (2020) The GDPR as global data protection regulation? Am J Int Law 114:5–9

Ryngaert C, Zoetekouw M (2014) The end of territory? The re-emergence of community as a principle of jurisdictional order in the internet era. In: Kohl U (ed) The net and the nation state: multidisciplinary perspectives on the internet governance. Cambridge University Press, pp 185–201

Saluzzo S (2019) The principle of territoriality in EU data protection law. In: Natoli T, Riccardi A (eds) Borders, legal spaces and territories in contemporary international law. Within and beyond. Springer, pp 121–141

Samonte M (2019) Google vs CNIL: the territorial scope of the right to be forgotten under EU law. European Papers 4(3):839–851. European Forum, https://www.europeanpapers.eu/en/europeanforum/google-v-cnil-territorial-scope-of-right-to-be-forgotten-under-eu-law

Sartor G, Viola De Azevedo Cuhna M (2014) Il caso Google e i rapporti regolatori USA/EU. Diritto dell'Informazione e dell'Informatica:657–680

Sartor G (2015) Il diritto nell'informatica giuridica. Rivista di filosofia del diritto, Special Issue, pp 71–92

Sartor G, Lagioia F (2020) The impact of general data protection regulation on artificial intelligence. Study European parliamentary research services, STOA

Sartor G (2022) L'intelligenza artificiale e il diritto. Giappichelli

Samuelson P (2000) Privacy as intellectual property? Stanford Law Rev 52:1125–1173

Sassen S (2006) Territory, authority, rights: from medieval to global assemblages. Princeton University Press

Scaccia G (2017) Il territorio fra sovranità statale e globalizzazione dello spazio economico, 3, rivistaaic.it

Scalone A (2017) Schmitt's theory of Grossraum: a post-Statal perspective? Scienza & Politica XXIV(56):179–205

Scheinin M (2013) Just another word?: jurisdiction in the roadmaps of state responsibilities and human rights. In: Langford M, Vandenhole W, Scheinin M, Van Genugten W (eds) Global justice, state duties: the extraterritorial scope of economic, social, and cultural rights in international law. Cambridge University Press, pp 212–232

Schiavello A (2023a) Conoscere il diritto. Mucchi

Schiavello A (2023b) Europa, diritti, democrazia in tempi difficili. Diritto & questioni pubbliche 2:211–219

Schiera P (2004) Lo Stato moderno. Origini e degenerazioni. Clueb

Schmitt C (or. ed. 1927) Concetto del politico. In: Caracciolo A (ed) Carl Schmitt Posizioni e concetti in lotta con Weimar-Ginevra-Versailles, 2007. Giuffrè

Schmitt C (1991, or. ed. Der nomos der erde im Völkerrecht des Jus Publicum Europaeum 1950), Il nomos della terra nel diritto internazionale dello «ius publicum europaeum». Il Mulino

Schmitt C (1972a, b, c) Le categorie del 'politico'. Il Mulino

Schmitt C (2005) Teoria del partigiano. Integrazione al concetto del politico. Adelphi

Schmitt MN (2017) Tallin manual 2.0 on the international law applicable to cyber warfare. Cambridge University Press

Schwartz PM (2003) Property, privacy, and personal data. Harv Law Rev 117:2056–2058

Scott J (2014a) Extraterritoriality and territorial extension in EU law. Am J Comp Law 62:87–126

Scott J (2014b) The new EU "extraterritoriality". Common Mark Law Rev 51:1343–1380

Scwhartz PM, Peifer KN (2017) Transatlantic data privacy law. Geo L J 106:115

Spaventa E (2016) The interpretation of Article 51 of the EU Charter of Fundamental Rights: the dilemma of stricter or broader application of the Charter to national measures, European Parliament, Directorate General for Internal Policies. https://www.europarl.europa.eu/RegData/etudes/STUD/2016/556930/IPOL_STU%282016%29556930_EN.pdf

Spinoza B (2007) Etica. Gentili G, Radetti G, Duranti G (eds). Bompiani

Spinoza B (2021, or. ed. 1677) Trattato teologico-politico (Amsterdam, 1677), Dini A (ed). Bompiani

Stepanov I (2020) Introducing a property right over data in the EU: the data producer's right—an evaluation. Int Rev Law Comput Technol 34(1):65–86

Svantesson DJ (2015a) A jurisprudential justification for extraterritoriality in (private) international law. Santa Clara J Int Law 13(2):518–571
Svantesson DJ (2015b) A new jurisprudential framework for jurisdiction. AJIL Unbound 109:69–74
Svantesson, DJ (2017), Solving the internet jurisdictional Puzzle. Oxford University Press
Szigeti PD (2016) The illusion of territorial jurisdiction. Texas Int Law J 52(3):369
Szigeti PD (2019) In the middle of nowhere: the futile quest to distinguish territoriality from extraterritoriality. In: Margolies DS, Özsu U, Päl M, Tzouvala N (eds) The extraterritoriality of law. History, theory, politics. Routledge, pp 30–48
Teubner G (2014) Law and social theory: three problems. Asian J Law Soc:234–254
Teubner G (2018) Digital personhood? The status of autonomous software agents in private law, Ancilla Iuris, https://www.anci.ch
Tilmann A (2020) Justice beyond borders—extraterritorial obligations from Thucydides to Grotius (March 30, 2020), Rechtsphilosophie - Zeitschrift für die Grundlagen des Rechts (RphZ), Forthcoming, Available at SSRN https://ssrn.com/abstract=3564495 or https://doi.org/10.2139/ssrn.3564495
Todescan F (1979) Diritto e realtà. Storia e teoria della "fictio iuris". Cedam
Tracol X (2021) The two judgments of the European court of justice in the four cases of privacy international, La quadrature du net and others, French data network and others and ordre des Barreaux francophones et germanophone and others: the grand chamber is trying hard to square the circle of data retention. Comp Law Sec Rev 41. https://www.sciencedirect.com/journal/computer-law-and-security-review, accessed 25 Jan 2022
Tucker A, De Bellis DP, Puydt PE (2017) Panarchy: political theories of non-territorial states. Routledge
Tzanou M (2021) Schrems I and Schrems II: assessing the case for the extraterritoriality of EU fundamental rights. In: Fabbrini F, Celeste E, Quinn J Data protection beyond borders: transatlantic perspectives on extraterritoriality and sovereignty, Hart, pp 99–116
Velasco C, Hörnle J, Osula AM (2016) Global views on internet jurisdiction and trans-border access. In: Gutwirth S, Leenes R, De Hert P (eds) Data protection on the move: current developments in ICT and privacy/data protection. Springer, pp 465–476
Viola F (1990) Il diritto come pratica sociale. Jaca Book
Wahl T (2020) CJEU: data retention allowed in exceptional cases. eucrim 3:184
Weber M (1990) Economia e società. Edizioni di Comunità
Weinzierl J (2021) Territoriality beyond the state: the EU's territorial claims and the search for their legitimacy. German Law J 22:650–672
Wenderhost C (2017) On elephants in the room and paper tigers: how to reconcile data protection and data economy. In: Lohsse S, Schulze R, Staudenmayer D (eds) Trading data in the digital economy: legal concepts and tools. Nomos, pp 327–356
Whitman JQ (2004) The two Western cultures of privacy: dignity versus liberty. Yale Law J 113:1151
Woods AK (2016) Against data exceptionalism. Stanford Law Rev 68:729
Woods AK (2018) Litigating Data Sovereignty. Yale Law J 128:328
Wu T (1997) Cyberspace sovereignty? The internet and the international system. Harv J Law Technol 10(3):648
Yildiz E (2019) Extraterritoriality reconsidered. Functional boundaries as repositories of jurisdiction. In: Margolies DS, Özsu U, Päl M, Tzouvala N (eds) The extraterritoriality of law. History, theory, politics. Routledge, p 215
Zaccaria G (2022) Postdiritto. Nuove fonti, nuove categorie. Il Mulino
Zech H (2015) Information as property. J Intellect Prop Inf Technol Electr Commer Law 6(3):192
Zeno Zencovich V (2021) Free-flow of data. Is international trade law the appropriate answer. In: Fabbrini F, Celeste E, Quinn J (eds) Data protection beyond Borders. Transatlantic perspectives on extraterritoriality and sovereignty. Hart, pp 173–188

Zeno-Zencovich V (2016) Intorno alla decisione nel caso Schrems: la sovranità digitale e il governo internazionale delle reti di telecomunicazione. Il diritto dell'informazione e dell'informatica 31:683–696

Zolea S (2020) Esplorazione spaziale e nuove forme di appartenenza: spunti comparativi. Cardozo Electron Law Bulettin 26:1

Zolo D (2007) Kelsen: la pace internazionale attraverso il diritto internazionale, Jura Gentium. Rivista di filosofia del diritto internazionale e di politica globale, https://www.juragentium.org/topics/thil/it/kelsen.htm

Zuboff S (2019) The age of surveillance capitalism: the fight for a human future at the new frontier of power. Public Affairs

MIX
Papier aus verantwortungsvollen Quellen
Paper from responsible sources
FSC® C105338
www.fsc.org

If you have any concerns about our products,
you can contact us on
ProductSafety@springernature.com

In case Publisher is established outside the EU,
the EU authorized representative is:
Springer Nature Customer Service Center GmbH
Europaplatz 3, 69115 Heidelberg, Germany

Printed by Libri Plureos GmbH
in Hamburg, Germany